Beyond Détente

Beyond Détente

SOVIET

FOREIGN POLICY

AND

U.S. OPTIONS

John Feffer

A Report Prepared for the
American Friends Service Committee

Hill and Wang New York

The Noonday Press

327.73047
F 32 b

Hill and Wang and the Noonday Press are
divisions of Farrar, Straus and Giroux

Printed simultaneously in Canada by Harper & Collins, Toronto

Printed in the United States of America

First edition, 1990

Designed by Irving Perkins Associates, Inc.

Library of Congress Cataloging-in-Publication Data
Feffer, John.
Beyond détente: Soviet foreign policy and U.S. options/John
Feffer.—1st ed.
p.   cm.
Includes bibliographical references.
1. United States—Foreign relations—Soviet Union.   2. Soviet
Union—Foreign relations—United States.   3. United States—Foreign
relations—1989-   4. United States—Foreign relations—1981-1989.
5. Soviet Union—Foreign relations—1985-   I. Title.
E183.8.S65F44   1990   327.73047—dc20   89-26989 CIP

Contents

Contents

Acknowledgments

MOLLY FEFFER taught me firsthand about East–West relations, and I must dedicate my efforts in preparing this report to her.

Of the sizable number of people who have contributed to this project, I would first like to thank Phillip Berryman. Phil followed each draft and revision of this manuscript, unmixing metaphors, sharpening insights, and generally straightening the sloppiness of both style and content. When this book is unclear or imprecise, it is most probably because I foolishly ignored Phil's advice.

I would also like to thank my colleagues at the American Friends Service Committee (AFSC), particularly Eva Gold, Linda Love, Myra Marino, and Michael Simmons, all of whom are responsible for bringing this manuscript to print. I benefited a great deal from their suggestions, as well as from the comments of other AFSC readers, including Bruce Birchard, Denis Doyon, Dick Erstad, Jerry Herman, Corinne Johnson, Mikel Johnson, Joe Volk, Chris Wing, and Warren Witte. Other especially helpful commenters included Thompson Bradley, Frank Brodhead, Gail Daeneker, Mary Downes, Matthew Evangelista, Joanne Landy, Everett Mendelsohn, Rajan

Acknowledgments

Menon, Zena Sochor, and John Sullivan. Finally, Arthur Wang provided some very valuable final editing. Any failings in this manuscript cannot be attributed to the advice of any of these excellent readers, who, in the midst of their own work, nonetheless found the time to correct mine.

I would also like to thank the Herbert W. Scoville Foundation for sponsoring research and writing that, in a circuitous fashion, have found their way into this work. I would like to thank the Mary Owen Barden Foundation for its support to AFSC for this book. Thanks also to my former colleagues at *Nuclear Times* magazine for their encouragement.

My family was remarkable. My brother Andrew deserves special mention for housing me for the time it took to produce a first draft. Finally, I would like to thank my friends for supporting me with food, shelter, and unflagging confidence (when my own was at half-mast). I owe them all, at the very least, a home-cooked meal in return.

Preface

ON THURSDAY NIGHT, November 9, 1989, East Berliners walked freely across the border and gathered with West Berliners to test and celebrate their new freedom to travel. North Americans watched their TVs in wonderment at the playing out of what until that moment had been an unthinkable event. But this apparently impossible event followed a series of equally dramatic and unthinkable events across Eastern Europe and in the Soviet Union. For Westerners it all added up to one hopeful and perhaps desperate question: is the Cold War going to be over and does this mean we have gone beyond détente? The answer to that question lies not only with the East but also with how the West interprets and responds. Will the West take courage and hope, trying to make the most of this new opportunity to walk out of the Cold War world and into a future of East–West peace and mutual security? Or will the West strive to take advantage of these changes for the purpose of "winning" the Cold War and dominating the world scene? These and other prospects are the topic of this book.

Beyond Détente is a result of a project of the American Friends

Service Committee's peace education research unit, NARMIC. It is yet another expression of our long effort to increase Soviet–American understanding and to break down the hostility that has been so long encouraged by the politically ambitious in both our lands. The fast pace of change, however, presents many new opportunities to overcome that hostility, as well as unknowns and challenges. We take encouragement and hope from the bold initiatives already implemented, and we pray that new and fundamental changes will work for the construction of mutual understanding, of enduring structures for peace, justice, and freedom.

Beyond Détente is an effort to understand those changes to date and to gather what we can know about them: the background, the rationale, the tactics, and the scope of change, the relationship between current foreign and domestic policies, and the prospects for the future.

The American Friends Service Committee has tried, in season and out and through every vicissitude, to relate constructively to the Soviet Union, ever since 1917 when they were both born. Our first major effort was in feeding the starving in the great Russian famine of the early 1920s. We urged diplomatic recognition long before Franklin Roosevelt granted it in 1933. We welcomed improved U.S.– Soviet relations during the Second World War, even as we continued to deplore publicly the repression of religion and the denial of human rights by the Soviet government. We protested the abrupt cancellation of lend-lease to the war-ravaged Soviet Union at the war's end.

As the wartime alliance quickly deteriorated into hostility and the bitterness of the Cold War, the American Friends Service Committee issued three publications between 1949 and 1955. *The United States and the Soviet Union* appeared in 1949 and urged the cultivation of trade relations, the reunification of Germany, and the strengthening of the United Nations. *Steps to Peace*, in 1951, argued the barrenness of military approaches to the problems of Europe and Asia, renewed pleas for the support of the United Nations, and urged large-scale programs of international aid and major efforts to achieve disarmament and the international control of arms. *Speak Truth to Power*, in 1955, explored the relevance of nonviolence in the postwar world and the impact of a nuclear arms race on the search for security.

In all that we undertook, we sought to break down the enemy

images that each side projected onto the other. We rejected the "devil theory" of history, which had Satan unpacking his suitcase first in this nation and then in the other as alliances shifted and changed. It is easy but false to accept theories that make devils of those we fear. Belligerents too easily attribute a monopoly of evil to the opponent, and doing so calls people to a strenuous exercise of their fear. And the practice of fear brought both East and West to the edge of the nuclear abyss, where we still stand.

We felt called to another way, a practice of hope. We felt that if we were for peace in general, then we had to pursue it in the particular. In the age of the Cold War, the pursuit of peace in the particular took us into controversial but productive and worthwhile areas of work.

We pioneered in exchanges of scientists, physicians, and scholars; brought leading U.S. business leaders into off-the-record meetings with Soviet leaders to promote trade; and undertook year after year a whole panoply of seminars and conferences involving Americans and Soviets. All of our share of the Nobel Peace Prize (awarded jointly to the American Friends Service Committee and its British counterpart in 1947) was given to Soviet children in the form of a gift of strep-tomycin. Seminars on the myths and realities of "the Soviet threat" have been more recently undertaken. In the 1980s, we redoubled our efforts to arrange new meetings between the United States and the U.S.S.R. and also turned our attention to Central Europe, with our ongoing series of exchanges with the United States and West and East Germany. A skeptical North American audience heard our reports of new thinking in the Soviet Union and of emerging conditions for a breakdown of the Cold War.

Now, as another step in these efforts, the American Friends Service Committee is pleased to release *Beyond Détente* as a contribution to dialogue among Americans and toward hastening the day when the two superpowers will turn from angry hostility to joint efforts to lift the quality of life of their own people and of the wider community of the world's people. This report on East–West relations comes at a unique moment, when we seem to be on the edge of what will probably be a new era. East and West may be started on a path into the future which has never before been traveled and which, in the past, was too often rejected. It is a path that could lead to East–West cooperation, to an end to nuclear threat, and to a redirection of scarce resources from war and to human needs. We believe this is a critical time to re-examine our understandings and get our bearings. And that's why we undertook to prepare this report.

John Feffer's work is heavily documented. It is not aimed primarily at the scholar, however, but rather at the nonprofessional. It is concise and readable and offers what we believe the American people urgently need: a basis for understanding and assessing what is happening in the Soviet Union and why. Events are moving so fast that one might suppose a book like this would almost immediately become dated, but because John Feffer focuses on root causes and on the structure and tactics of the reform movement, the reader is provided with an essential framework that assures continued relevance as further changes occur.

Stephen G. Cary
Chairperson, Board of Directors
American Friends Service Committee
Philadelphia, Pennsylvania
November 1989

Introduction

IN MARCH 1985, a new group of politicians came to power in the Soviet Union under the general leadership of Mikhail Gorbachev. Few observers of the Soviet scene knew what to expect from this change in government.[1] The *New York Times* editorial greeting the Gorbachev succession reveals this initial caution:

> The Soviet Union remains an amalgam of secretive bureaucracies, its policies shaped by a collective of old men. . . . Continuity, caution and consensus are the hallmarks of a system revolutionary in doctrine but deeply conservative in practice. Whatever his ambitions, Mr. Gorbachev is unlikely soon to make waves.[2]

Contrary to the *Times*'s prediction, Mr. Gorbachev indeed moved quite rapidly. On taking office, Gorbachev launched a dozen reforms aimed at virtually every aspect of Soviet society. Within two years, Soviet citizens had witnessed an anti-alcohol campaign, an anti-corruption campaign, the introduction of modest free-enterprise measures into the economy, a deliberate campaign against Stalinism, and the release of prominent dissidents, such as physicist Andrei Sakharov.

Nor did Gorbachev simply address domestic problems. In foreign policy, Gorbachev has dramatically recast Soviet positions on arms control, trade, and regional relations. From 1985 to 1989—a period of time equivalent to a single U.S. presidential term—Gorbachev has called into question and indeed overturned the prevailing Western view that the Soviet Union is incapable of change.

But Gorbachev is not the only one making waves in the U.S.S.R. Rather than the handiwork of a single charismatic individual, the present Soviet reform movement unites a range of politicians and intellectuals, including Politburo members, academicians, and artists.[3] Nor are the proposals of this group of reformers brand new: many ideas have been drawn from past Soviet leadership. The uniqueness of Gorbachev and his supporters resides in their ability to synthesize the various reformist impulses from the past into a single program combining domestic *and* international initiatives.

This latest Soviet reform program anticipates much more than cosmetic change. The reformers recognize that the U.S.S.R. suffers from a host of internal problems—from political mismanagement and rampant corruption to economic inefficiency and ethnic rivalries—that cannot be solved by mere tinkering. Given these domestic problems and the dictates of a changing international climate, reform in the U.S.S.R. is inevitable. What shape this reform will ultimately take, who will carry it out, and when—these questions are by no means easily answered. The Gorbachev supporters offer one program, but it is both fraught with contradictions and vigorously opposed in certain sectors of Soviet society. Nevertheless, four years into his administration, Gorbachev continues to challenge sacred traditions on his home turf and, with one well-timed diplomatic overture after another, continues to strengthen his already considerable international reputation.

Because of its scope, the present Soviet reform demands careful attention; the challenges that Gorbachev presents to the international community, meanwhile, merit serious response.

In the first two chapters, this book focuses on Soviet foreign policy and its roots in domestic reform. While the domestic changes in the U.S.S.R. profoundly affect the Soviet population, other countries feel the impact of these changes primarily through the medium of Soviet foreign relations. The sheer global importance of Soviet proposals— whether troop withdrawals from Afghanistan or unilateral disarmament measures—is obvious. Changes in Soviet foreign policy, coupled with sincere diplomatic responses from other countries, may precipitate the most important restructuring of international politics since World War II.

Yet, response in the United States to Gorbachev's reforms so far has been slow, hindered by traditional antagonisms, historic misperceptions, and genuine confusion. Some U.S. policy makers have advised caution; some have questioned the significance of the reforms.[4] Attempting to locate a middle ground, the Bush administration has adopted a tepid "status quo plus" stance.[5] In spite of ambivalence and skepticism, an improvement in East–West relations has indeed occurred—best exemplified by the Intermediate Nuclear Force treaty (INF), signed by the United States and the Soviet Union in 1987. On a deeper level, the lessening of tensions has begun to reshape mutual perceptions. Key Soviet policy makers, for instance, no longer regard the United States as the chief threat to Communism.[6] U.S. citizens, meanwhile, recently rated the Soviet threat only eighth in a list of ten contemporary problems facing the United States.[7]

Is this improvement in relations temporary or permanent? Are the two countries simply pausing for a détente or have they truly ended the long-standing Cold War? The third and fourth chapters of this book will attempt to define the present U.S.–Soviet relationship and will offer certain alternatives for U.S. foreign policy that could, in concert with Soviet initiatives, help change the course of international relations.

Although drawing upon contemporary research, *Beyond Détente* is not intended to be a scholarly study. It is intended, rather, for the general reader, and thus has been kept to a manageable length. Brevity, however, has its drawbacks. An accessible and yet compact treatment of such an enormous subject obviously cannot replace works of twice the length and half the scope (some of these more specialized books are listed in Appendix 6).

Finally, given the flux of Soviet reforms, the variability of the U.S. situation, and the fragility of prediction, this book will not provide definitive answers. It will only suggest certain interpretations and point toward possible alternative policies. It can only be hoped that the unfolding development of Soviet policies will bear out the tentative conclusions of this work.

John Feffer
Philadelphia
November 1989

November 1989 was a very good month for international relations, but not a particularly opportune time to finish the final revisions on a manuscript addressing East–West issues. Change in Eastern Europe was reaching fever pitch as governments changed hands within weeks of one another. First, the Berlin Wall surprised everyone by literally crumbling overnight, mirroring the deterioration in the East German ruling structures. Then the Czech government collapsed under the weight of huge protests and a new interim government composed of several prominent opposition leaders took its place. Mass protests in Bulgaria forced the government there to promise free elections. In December, a bloody revolution toppled Nicolae Ceausescu's repressive regime in Rumania. (The events are chronicled in the appendix, but because of publishing deadlines have not been integrated into the text.)

The Soviet Union did not remain disengaged from the political convulsions occurring across its Western border. Rather than preventing change, however, as it had done in generations past, the U.S.S.R. gave either tacit approval or direct support for the political transformations. Forty-five years ago, Eastern Europe was the focal point of the Cold War. Today, because of the shift in Soviet foreign policy and the efforts of Eastern European grassroots movements, the region provides the best evidence for believing that the Cold War era has ended.

Post–Cold War sentiment has been gaining popularity lately, even among those who were instrumental in fashioning the anti-Communist consensus in the first place. Judged only in terms of recent events in Eastern Europe, unmitigated optimism would in fact be warranted. Nevertheless, as this book argues, the Soviet Union is still perceived as a dangerous superpower and Cold War

myths latent in the formulation of U.S. foreign policy still operate. More critically, perhaps, the pattern of international relations forged during the Cold War era—preserving a balance of power between two alliance systems—is still in place. The Third World has yet to benefit directly from this new age.

Although U.S.–Soviet relations have indeed improved and political pluralism in varying degrees has finally come to Eastern Europe, the U.S. government still behaves according to outdated models. On December 20, the U.S. invaded Panama and demonstrated that U.S. foreign policy has yet to depart from its historic emphasis on unilateral intervention. The invasion of Panama furthermore showed that the Pentagon is still alive and well, substituting the threat of drugs and Third World dictators for the Cold War threat of the Soviet Union.

Meanwhile, the Gorbachev reforms instituted within the U.S.S.R. have by no means run their course. In the Baltic republics, for instance, independence movements have continued to challenge Soviet power. In December 1989, the Lithuanian parliament voted in a multiparty system and accelerated secession demands. Ethnic conflicts intensified in Azerbaijan and Armenia. As the 1990s begin, domestic challenges to Gorbachev and Kremlin control have not dissipated; conflicts being waged inside the U.S.S.R. have not subsided. As radical reformers continue to press for greater change, they must now more than ever point to the concrete results of *perestroika*. Should they not be able to produce those results, the future of Soviet reform, though inevitable in the long term, becomes unpredictable in the short run. Yet that success depends a great deal on the course of international relations. Without a restructuring of Western foreign policy, Soviet reform may falter.

The success of *perestroika* and the end of the Cold War: the 1990s may witness the realization of both these goals. Now more than ever, it is necessary to understand the changes transforming the Soviet Union and international relations—we may never have a better opportunity.

J.F.
January 1990

Beyond Détente

1

The Domestic Roots of Soviet Foreign Policy

Our foreign policy is today to a greater extent than ever before determined by domestic policy, by our interest in concentrating our efforts on constructive activities aimed at improving our country. And that is why we need lasting peace, predictability and constructiveness in international relations.

— MIKHAIL GORBACHEV, *before the 27th Party Congress*[1]

THE CONNECTIONS BETWEEN a nation's foreign and domestic policies are sometimes self-evident. No one would disagree, for instance, that centralized economic planning influences the structure of foreign trade or that a country's internal politics in part determine the course of its diplomacy. While these links may be self-evident, however, they are by no means simple. The present Soviet reform movement, for example, encompasses an enormous number of domestic changes; determining the meaning of these changes, much less their impact on the conduct of Soviet foreign policy, is not easy.

One thing is certain, however: Gorbachev and his colleagues are not the first Soviet politicians to link foreign policy reforms deliberately to domestic concerns.[2] In 1918, for instance, Lenin concluded a peace treaty with the Germans in order to turn attention to the pressing domestic needs of the fledgling Soviet Union. In the early 1920s, Lenin secured contracts with Western capitalists in order to attract needed investment capital. Recognizing the unlikelihood of imminent world revolution, Lenin viewed these accommodations with the West as an opportunity for his government to fulfill revolutionary promises to its citizens.

3

Even in the 1980s, as Gorbachev and his colleagues maneuvered for power within the Soviet political system, the interplay between domestic promises and foreign policy objectives remained fundamental. While the U.S.S.R. was unquestionably a military superpower, the Soviet public still endured chronic food shortages, insufficient urban housing, and a government that was often insensitive and corrupt. Nearly seven decades after the 1917 Revolution, the comrade-on-the-street could complain: "What are we doing in Afghanistan and Cambodia, when here at home we have no meat?"[3]

Following the Leninist pattern, the solution to the guns-versus-butter dilemma would appear simple: Make peace with Soviet adversaries abroad and redirect resources to Soviet citizens at home. But Soviet leaders, like those of most governments, trade guns for butter only when they perceive a reduced threat to national security—in Gorbachev's words, a condition of "lasting peace" and "predictability." To tackle the myriad internal problems, Soviet reformers sought stability by proposing a series of foreign policy initiatives to improve relations with the United States, Europe, the Third World, and the United Nations.

These initiatives are not, however, proposed with the sole intent of improving the Soviet domestic situation. Rather, Soviet reformers approach foreign policy *in the same manner* as they approach domestic problems. They employ, in other words, a similar template. Just as the reformers want to "rationalize" the Soviet economic process by eliminating waste and corruption, they expect to "rationalize" U.S.-Soviet relations, replacing a prohibitively expensive arms race with a more mutually beneficial trade relationship. Although always in part determined by internal factors, Soviet foreign policy reforms also stand by themselves. The Soviet leadership supports arms reduction, for instance, not only to save money but also because it has come to appreciate the limits of military force.

An examination of the domestic roots of the Soviet "new thinking" offers one fruitful approach to the critical question "Why are the Soviets suddenly making so many foreign policy overtures?" Without substantial understanding of this complex domestic program, Soviet foreign policy initiatives appear to be strangely unattached to any purposes and therefore cause for potential suspicion. Gorbachev's foreign policy begins to make sense when viewed either as a response to domestic imperatives or as one element of a more encompassing world view.

What is this domestic reform package? The modernization of the Soviet Union that the Soviet reformers want so dearly depends upon two conditions: consolidation of support within the Soviet political system and the structural rehabilitation of the Soviet economy.[4] Exploring these wide-ranging political and economic reforms will help us understand how changes within the Soviet Union influence changes in external policy. A concluding section outlines the domestic challenges to the reform effort.

Gorbachev's Program

Gorbachev and his supporters face a dilemma: Should they fine-tune existing political and economic mechanisms or pursue the more dramatic path of establishing entirely new structures? In practice, this is not an either-or choice, for even the most thoroughgoing of revolutions cannot wipe the slate clean. The Bolshevik Revolution of 1917, for instance, could not extinguish religious beliefs and practices or entirely remove "bourgeois" managers from industry.

Instead of explicitly choosing one path over the other, present-day reformers have pursued both simultaneously. Even while modifying the centrally planned economy, they are introducing limited private enterprise and new wage and price policies—practices associated more with free-market capitalism than with centrally planned Communism. While initiating moderate political reforms such as secret balloting, Gorbachev and supporters have championed multicandidate elections and have further indicated that they would like in the near future to dissociate the Communist party from the daily workings of Soviet government.

This two-track program is simultaneously a product of failed radicalism and a deliberate strategy born of pragmatism. Defenders of the status quo, acutely aware that the gravity of Soviet problems demands some response, are by definition not interested in radical change—this influential group demands (and must be placated with) slower-paced reforms. On the other hand, many Soviet policy makers and citizens find moderation unacceptable given the sheer inability of the existing system to solve contemporary problems. The reformers must balance the concerns of these two groups even when compromise seems impossible. How, for instance, can a centrally planned economy be strengthened by the shuffling of industrial ministries while at the same time being undermined by free-market mechanisms? How can party members effectively supervise the separation of the party from government activity?

These tensions not surprisingly can be found *within* the program of reform. Gorbachev supporters have both encouraged and discouraged economic cooperatives; promoted allies such as Vadim Medvedev and demoted Boris Yeltsin, the cheerleader for radical reform; and begun an anti-alcohol campaign and brought it to an early end. The success of the reform movement hinges on its ability to reconcile these apparent paradoxes within the Gorbachev agenda and indeed throughout all Soviet political life.

POLITICAL STRATEGY

Present Soviet reform process has introduced a number of Russian words into the English vocabulary: *glasnost, perestroika, demokratizatsia*. In a Soviet context, these terms often overlap. Most frequently, however, *glasnost* (openness) refers to greater freedom of political and cultural expression; *perestroika* (restructuring) applies more generally to the overhaul of the economic system; *democratizatsia* (democratization) encourages greater participation from workers in the workplace and from citizens in the electorate. For the reformers, *glasnost* and democratization are political strategies designed to win support for a larger, predominantly economic, agenda —*perestroika*.

Though these Russian words were new to Western ears, their meanings derive from Soviet history. In order to understand the relationship between these terms, a brief look at the Soviet political past is useful.

In February 1917, after the first Russian revolution, a Provisional Government reflecting several political persuasions replaced Tsar

Nicholas II. Numerically small but distinctly militant since its founding in the earlier part of the century, the Bolshevik party under Lenin's leadership refused to cooperate with this new Russian government. Instead, in October 1917, the revolutionaries conspired with elements of several other political parties to seize power in a second revolution and create a new government.[5]

At first, the Bolsheviks fostered decentralized decision making at the level of local soviets (or councils) elected by workers and peasants, putting into practice Lenin's famous revolutionary slogan "All Power to the Soviets."[6] But after favoring non-Bolshevik candidates in the 1918 elections, these locally elected soviets lost real decision-making power to top Bolshevik party organs such as the Central Committee and Politburo.[7] Government and party, in other words, became indistinguishable.[8] According to the Bolsheviks, the subsequent pressures of civil war, foreign intervention, and economic crisis made the transition to a one-party state a pragmatic method of safeguarding the revolution from adversaries at home and abroad.[9]

The concentration of authority in one institution—the Communist party[10]—did not foreclose the possibility of complex politicking and passionate debate in the early Soviet government. Arguments over the economic future and even the political organization of the country divided the Bolsheviks into various factions.[11] This early political diversity is critical for modern Soviet reformers who look for suitable historical precedents that predate the uniformity of political opinion imposed by Stalinism.[12] In their more radical proposals, Gorbachev and his colleagues reach back to those scant months before party domination; recalling Lenin's "All Power to the Soviets," they suggest a Soviet government distinct from the Communist party. In other words, today's reformers are seeking to legitimize their proposals with alternatives—earlier versions of *glasnost, perestroika*, and *demokratizatsia*—culled from the first decade of Soviet history, before Stalin transformed the roles of government, party, and leader.

Upon consolidating power in 1929, Stalin compressed a one-*party* state into a one-*man* state, and consequently the political diversity of the 1920s became an early casualty of his tenure. Stalin behaved as no Bolshevik politician had previously or has since: ruthlessly eliminating political opposition; murdering intellectuals, officials, and officers through party and army purges; and concentrating power in his own hands, trusting an ever dwindling group of Politburo advisers.

When Stalin died, in 1953, political divisions resurfaced: what had become a personal dictatorship again expanded into a party dictatorship. The party—or rather, one segment of the party—took advantage of Stalin's demise to wreak revenge on those who had carried out Stalin's policies. Party officials who had been close to Stalin, because of their complicity in past crimes, favored reticence bordering on amnesia. Nikita Khrushchev, on the other hand, built his position in the party by challenging Stalinism head-on. At the Twentieth and Twenty-second Party Congresses, in 1956 and 1961, Khrushchev gave extensive speeches on the errors of Stalinism, denunciations that were as much tactical as moral. By criticizing Stalin, Khrushchev undermined the power of those still in government who had served during the Stalinist purges. With these politicians reeling from the charges, Khrushchev could consolidate his own leadership and deflect challenges from Stalinists and neo-Stalinists within the Politburo and the Central Committee.

Khrushchev confined virtually all his criticism to Stalin's purge of *party* members, ignoring the other deaths associated with Stalinism: peasants, dissidents, soldiers. As historian Mark Field observes, Khrushchev considered Stalin's major crime the replacing of "the cult of the party" with the "cult of the personality."[13] As spelled out in his Party Congress speeches, Khrushchev believed that Stalin had usurped the party's rightful position as the vessel of the revolution.

It is ironic that Khrushchev, like Stalin, did not succeed in balancing party power and personal ambition. Khrushchev's attempt to divide the party into agricultural and industrial wings and increase party membership, combined with the promotion of his own cult of personality, contributed to his eventual downfall.[14] Khrushchev's encouragement of greater political participation through local soviets only served to condemn him further in the eyes of the party. An arrogant politician, Khrushchev had irritated too many important people and upset too many traditional structures; thus he was eased out of office in 1964.

His successor, Leonid Brezhnev, balanced the dictates of party and personality more to the satisfaction of his colleagues. After the paranoia of the Stalin years and the volatility of the Khrushchev period, the Brezhnev era meant job security for party and government figures, bringing with it an increase in corruption and inefficiency that such bureaucratic immobility often produces.

Under Brezhnev, the *nomenklatura*—or privileged group of officials—attained supremacy. Traditionally, these Soviet bureaucrats receive better housing, better food, better vacations, better medical care: in short, a better standard of living.[15] Such obvious inequities in a society committed in principle to abolishing class differences have caused great resentment among the population. But party officials during the Brezhnev era were well insulated from the reproach of their comrades. Mollified by professional perks, the *nomenklatura* even tolerated the self-glorification in which Brezhnev so frequently indulged.[16] Brezhnev's cult of personality was effectively counterbalanced by the cult of *nomenklatura*.

The succession struggle occasioned by Brezhnev's death in 1982 (but anticipated several years previously) yielded two ailing leaders, one a reformer, the other a Brezhnev stand-in. The reformer, Yuri Andropov, began several campaigns that influenced Gorbachev, including one that struck at the very heart of the Brezhnev enterprise: an anticorruption drive. Concerned about this threat to a carefully built patronage system, the Brezhnev camp united to bring one of their own—Konstantin Chernenko—into office upon Andropov's death in 1984.

Playing a caretaker role, Chernenko pointedly ignored Andropov's hesitant reforms. But a new generation of political leaders—of neither Chernenko's nor Brezhnev's vintage—waited in the wings for their opportunity. It came unexpectedly when Chernenko died, in March 1985, and Mikhail Gorbachev and his allies came to power.

Gorbachev's rise to power differed in many respects from previous Soviet successions. Only fifty-four upon taking office, Gorbachev was substantially younger than his septuagenarian predecessors. He was also relatively inexperienced and had graduated from a post notorious for being a Central Committee dead end—agriculture secretary.[17] Moreover, Gorbachev was extremely articulate, capable of public speaking without a prepared text, charismatic, fluent in the diplomatic manners of the West—a marked departure from the leaden styles of Brezhnev and Chernenko and the cold reserve of Andropov.

In other ways, however, Gorbachev closely resembles past Soviet leaders. He achieved power by aligning himself with influential patrons, just as others had previously used the network.[18] During his tenure in agricultural affairs, both in the Stavropol region and in Moscow, Gorbachev was not in the forefront of innovation. Though he might have formulated various plans in his head, he did not reveal the scope of his reform program until shortly before reaching office.[19]

The timing of Chernenko's unexpected death was especially fortuitous for Gorbachev. With three important Brezhnevites out of town, Gorbachev's backers barely triumphed over the Brezhnev camp's preferred candidates.[20] As Soviet émigré Zhores Medvedev has observed somewhat hyperbolically, "If Chernenko had lived for another month, Gorbachev would probably not have stood a chance of becoming General Secretary."[21] Whether through connections or by chance, Gorbachev clearly did not make it to the top by his own bootstraps.

Both products and critics of the system, Gorbachev and his allies have found themselves in a delicate situation: While using traditional methods of establishing authority, at the same time they criticized those very methods. It is therefore not difficult to understand why they have adopted a two-track program of traditional and radical reform: they have no other practical choice. Assuming the best intentions of the reformers, the traditional reforms will pave the way for more democratic institutions that will in turn ensure the longevity of the entire Gorbachev enterprise.

Traditional Reform

One time-honored method of reorienting the Soviet political system is the reorganization "from the top down" of government and party positions at all levels. Such housecleaning installs allies who support not only the administration's policies but its very political existence. In remaking the Soviet political system, Stalin established the precedent. Supervising party appointments from 1919 on, he quietly built a power base by installing supporters throughout the party. Though his ambition was initially checked in the Politburo by Leon Trotsky and then Nikolai Bukharin, Stalin's private patronage system provided sufficient leverage by 1929 to neutralize these opponents.[22] Once in power, Stalin continually repopulated party and government positions, in part to prevent any adversary from following his steps to power.

In order to weaken previous power bases, Stalin's successors followed a similar pattern of reorganization. Khrushchev used political appointees to attack Stalinist officeholders; Brezhnev reorganized the political system to the advantage of his own supporters; Andropov, in his short tenure, attempted to sweep these same Brezhnevites out of the system; Gorbachev continued where Andropov had left off.

After a year in office, Gorbachev and supporters had succeeded dramatically with their gambit, taking an important step in ensuring their own political survival. By March 1986, one fifth of all officials in primary party organizations had lost their posts, including 24 first secretaries in the Russian Republic and 23 of 78 in non-Russian republics. Of the 23 heads of the Central Committee Secretariat departments, 14 had been replaced;[23] 39 of 101 members of the government's Council of Ministers were new.[24]

In one particularly representative move, after a young West German piloted his plane through the Soviet air defense system in 1987 to land in Red Square, the reformers turned an embarrassing breach of security into a stunning political opportunity.[25] Immediately following this bizarre stunt, the government dismissed Defense Minister Sergei Sokolov (an opponent of military reform) and replaced him with a Gorbachev protégé, Dmitri Yazov, who jumped over fifty of his seniors into the top position. Rather than waiting for the slow democratic process to raise Yazov to the Politburo, the reformers quickly used the dramatic event and executive authority.

In October 1988, Gorbachev engineered a party shake-up that brought party moderates and *perestroika* enthusiasts to equal proportions in the Politburo. One year later, in September 1989, Gorbachev finally established a clear majority of reform supporters in the Politburo by ousting from the top two leading conservatives, Ukrainian party head Vladimir Shcherbitsky and KGB boss Viktor Chebrikov. In less than five years, Gorbachev had consolidated his position and ensured that his program would remain on Politburo agendas for at least a generation.

The use of historical criticism to discredit past administrations and present opponents is another traditional Soviet political technique. Much as Khrushchev used anti-Stalinism and Brezhnev used anti-Khrushchevism, the Andropov and Gorbachev administrations have gained political mileage by calling into question Brezhnev's record. Declaring that era one of stagnation and errors in foreign policy, the Gorbachev reformers have sought to discredit opponents tied to the past administration, simultaneously establishing a clear contrast with their own policies. This strategy has the added benefit of placing the entirety of the blame for present problems on the shoulders of previous leaders.

To legitimize their program further, the reformers have even enlisted the deceased for support, rehabilitating the reputations of discredited Bolsheviks. To date, these political rehabilitations have centered on figures such as Grigorii Zinoviev, Lev Kamenev, and Nikolai Bukharin, who in the 1920s proposed alternative political, economic, and social paths for the Soviet Union to follow.[26] It is critical for Gorbachev and his allies to recapture these lost alternatives. In the absence of an unimpeachable Bolshevik past, the reform program could be vulnerable to accusations that it deviates from the path of socialism. To counter such criticism, the reformers must repair the holes that Stalinists and neo-Stalinists have rent in the fabric of Soviet history.

These techniques—from governmental restructuring to the use of history as a weapon—place the reformers firmly in the Soviet political tradition. Yet, Gorbachev and supporters *are* testing the boundaries of acceptable political behavior. Many of their proposed changes go beyond the limits of previous reform.

With their reforms, Khrushchev and Brezhnev separated party from leader, thereby repudiating Stalin's monarchism. If the Gorbachev administration can inject procedural democracy into the Soviet political system, the U.S.S.R. may witness the further separation of party from state, a rejection not only of Stalinism but of certain critical aspects of Leninism as well.

Unprecedented Reform

To understand how a group of Soviet leaders comes to propose dramatic political change, we must look first at the leaders themselves.

The Gorbachev administration includes a new generation of leaders who did not take part in or even live through the 1917 Revolution. These leaders had neither to side for or against Stalin in the 1920s nor to prove their allegiance to Stalin in the subsequent decades. Since they rose through party ranks for the most part *after* the era of party purges and mass executions, they are not burdened with any Stalinist skeletons in their past. Nor is the Second World War a critical defining point. The present reformers have lived the better part of their lives in a time of relative peace and prosperity. Contrast these leaders with Brezhnev's generation, who lived through the fear and deprivations of both Stalinist paranoia and World War II.

Gorbachev and his allies also have an ambivalent relationship with the military. Every previous Soviet leader has maintained strong ties with this politically important and economically powerful institution. Yet, at the funeral of Chernenko, Kremlin observers noted that Gorbachev did not place military leaders in their customary positions of importance at his left hand. Nor does Gorbachev share the fascination that Brezhnev had for military honors. Military analyst Dale Herspring writes, "Somehow the idea of Gorbachev's appearing in public in a marshal's uniform replete with several pounds of medals would appear totally out of character."[27]

One reason for this ambivalence lies in the educational and professional backgrounds of the Gorbachev reformers—largely in economics, history, and education.[28] Gorbachev himself was trained in law. By contrast, many Khrushchev- and Brezhnev-era politicians were engineers, who traditionally viewed the world through the prism of heavy industry. Engineers-turned-politicians were influenced by one of heavy industry's major beneficiaries: the military.

The Soviet reformers have imposed a "cult of modesty" not only upon the military but also upon themselves.[29] Less than a year after taking office, Gorbachev warned party officials not to exhibit "fawning" behavior.[30] The following possibly apocryphal anecdote neatly illustrates the point. Gorbachev rings up *Pravda*'s editor-in-chief, Viktor Afanasyev, and asks him if he has the works of Lenin in his office. "Of course," comes the response. "Then be good enough to quote him in future," Gorbachev admonishes, "and not me."[31]

A new generation brings new ideas. The first indication of possibly dramatic political reform came with *demokratizatsia*, originally an effort to involve more workers in the political life of the workplace through multicandidate elections for plant managers. Eventually, democratization began to spread into the realm of party and government life.

Although democratization has figured in the rhetoric of reform since Gorbachev took office (and has often appeared in rhetoric of previous leaders), two years passed before the rhetoric could be translated into practice. In January 1987, Gorbachev outlined a plan that would permit more than one candidate to stand for party elections conducted by secret ballot. Secret balloting and multicandidate elections first appeared in western Siberia the following month. By September 1988, the Soviet press reported that half of all party positions were contested and that one third of the leaders elected were new (compared with one fifth the previous year).[32] For a country that has routinely held elections with only one candidate, the possibility of opening up the process represents an important departure.

Since democratization began, new independent political clubs have been formed to bring issue-oriented discussions to a larger audience. These new independent clubs differ from the traditional party education classes teaching the doctrine of Marxism-Leninism in that they feature a wider range of political perspectives. One such association declared as its purpose "to renovate social practice in the spirit of the ideals of socialism, democracy, humanism, and progress." An account of this new organization relates that:

anyone can join provided they accept the "three nyets": "no" to violence and the propaganda of violence; "no" to ideas of national or racial exclusiveness and hostility to other nationalities; "no" to claims to a monopoly on truth.[33]

In 1988, at a government-sanctioned meeting of all such clubs professing a socialist orientation, representatives endorsed views that several years earlier might have been grounds for jail sentences: free trade unions, freedom of religion, the lifting of travel and emigration restrictions, and an end to *nomenklatura* privileges.[34] From this diverse group of clubs eventually emerged the Popular Front, composed primarily of democratic socialists, with four members of the Communist party on the Coordinating Council. 35 By permitting and even encouraging such diversity of views, the Gorbachev administration has won valuable allies from the ranks of the intelligentsia, an important group of artists and intellectuals that Khrushchev neglected to cultivate. 36

With reform initiated from the top, reformers have a greater chance of controlling the pace. But Khrushchev, unlike Gorbachev, relied too heavily on this technique and failed to institutionalize his reforms. Through democratization, Gorbachev and his supporters hope that the widespread support that Khrushchev lacked will come their way by way of the ballot box and the independent clubs. Responding to a suggestion at a party meeting to revive the Stalinist technique of widespread party purges, Gorbachev replied:

> I think that if the Central Committee again starts to purge bureaucrats, we won't get anywhere. We have tried to do many things from the top; it does not help. Today we try, through the reform, through the media, to put all of society into motion. And then the bureaucrat will not know where to go. 37

Current moves toward democratization involve thousands of elections, dozens of new bylaws, and the creation of often overt challenges to one-party rule. The Gorbachev administration is not simply seeking political support through this upheaval of the system. Democratization, it hopes, will also revitalize Soviet society through the new ideas and initiatives developed by Soviet citizens. 38 Without innovation, the economy would continue to falter; without new economic and intellectual proposals, the Soviet Union would continue to be outpaced by other countries. That the campaign, by its very design, tends to bring into public office supporters of democratization and therefore politicians more favorably inclined to the full Gorbachev program of reforms endows the changes with a quality of political farsightedness as well.

Not content to settle for democratization alone, the Soviet reformers are seeking another reform long considered impossible by Western observers—removing the Communist party from the daily workings of government. 39 At a dramatic party conference in June

1988, the Gorbachev camp proposed just such a strategy. Although conservative party forces wrested substantial concessions, the reformers nevertheless began the process.[40] This despite a common perception in the West that any reforms aimed at weakening the party would be a fatal step for the reformers.[41]

Attacking party power is risky. The Communist party in the U.S.S.R. counts as members roughly 10 percent of the adult population, including a large proportion of the nation's college graduates.[42] With its functionaries monitoring many facets of Soviet life, from the military to the bureaucratic, the party wields enormous influence and, like entrenched organizations everywhere, invariably strives to preserve the status quo. Any reformer of the Soviet system must at some point come to terms with the party. And, obviously, any reformer who targets the party for reform must expect considerable resistance.

At the 1988 party conference, the Gorbachev camp placed measures aimed at dissociating the party from the government on an agenda of reform that both recalled previous proposals (secret balloting, multicandidate elections, civic political organizations) and introduced some new ones (limited terms of political office, protection of individual rights from government surveillance). Concerning the party, the critical piece of policy outlined the creation of a "Congress of People's Deputies," a government body that would have as members 1,500 regional deputies and 750 appointed officials drawn from party committees, trade unions, and other organizations. This congress would select a legislature, the Supreme Soviet, and a president.[43] Echoing the historic Bolshevik rallying cry "All Power to the Soviets," the changes would make local soviets more powerful and, in theory, capable of replacing local party representatives. However, conservative party forces won a major concession at the 1988 party conference: local party bosses would automatically head these soviets. In other words, the separation of party from government was far from completed.[44]

Elections to the Congress of People's Deputies took place in March 1989. Nearly 3,000 candidates ran for the 1,500 open seats, and some of the results were startling. Boris Yeltsin, the maverick removed from the Politburo the previous year for his outspoken radicalism, gained 89 percent of the vote from his Moscow district. Nationalists throughout the Baltic states of Lithuania, Latvia, and Estonia gained seats. Key Communist party officials lost, such as nonvoting Polit-buro member Yuri Solovyev.

In May, when the congress opened, an estimated *200 million* Soviet citizens watched via television as congress deputies exercised their rights of *glasnost*, insisting that Gorbachev submit to questions from the floor before choosing him as president, sharply contesting proposed initiatives, grilling potential ministers, and subsequently blocking eight nominees. Radical reformers among the deputies formed a bloc—now known as the Inter-Regional Group—and pro-posed initiatives, including one designed to make the Supreme So-viet completely independent by forcing members to resign their party affiliations. The initiative failed, proving that the separation of party and government has yet to take place. Nevertheless, this new government—the Congress of People's Deputies and the recon-stituted Supreme Soviet and Council of Ministers—is far from a docile party creation.

What effect does this governmental restructuring really have? Gorbachev and his allies—and perhaps more important, party con-servatives in governmental positions—are now more accountable to the public and subject to recall through the ballot box (a fact well demonstrated during the March 1989 elections, when a large num-ber of important party officials were defeated). Though party officials still control the soviets and occupy many government seats, the president—in this case, Gorbachev—cannot be removed by the party structures. Freed from the fear of party retaliation for attacks on its privileges, Gorbachev can theoretically push his reforms more effectively through the legislature. On the other hand, a president freed from party oversight could potentially assume unchecked power. Given the hasty, almost improvisational character of these political reforms, the full implications of the new Soviet government structure may only be understood several years after it has begun to function.

As the end point of his political reforms, Khrushchev envisioned a "withering away" of state functions, according to the tenets of Com-munism,[45] and the gradual transfer of administration to local so-viets.[46] The present reformers do not have such a utopian vision. Democratization enfranchises political allies within the intelligentsia, allows attacks on entrenched party interests, and seeks to invigorate political life at the level of the ordinary citizen and worker. It is difficult to speculate at this early point in its campaign how many concessions the Gorbachev camp will have to make to conservative interests and, in the end, whom the resultant political hybrid will serve. Whether democratization continues to apply to changes within a one-party system (involving multicandidate elections or limited tenures of office) or expands into a multiparty parliamentary system remains to be seen. As the changes lean toward the latter, however, they obviously begin to challenge the Leninist model of a one-party state.

Focusing on the dramatic challenges of political *perestroika*, the Western press frequently compares the Gorbachev reforms with Khrushchev's and speculates that Gorbachev may likewise be ousted. Despite support from many sectors of Soviet society, Gorbachev may in the future lose his position as a result of internal political shifts or external crisis. But the current reforms are not the product of a single person. Should the individual be removed, the reforms would continue, in one form or another. In the past, many reforms have continued even after the reformers have left office. Khrushchev's initial agricultural and industrial programs, for instance, were a necessary corrective to the excesses of Stalin. The Brezhnev administration would not have dared to revive pre-Khrushchev economic mistakes, regardless of its aversion for Khrushchev's other reforms. The Gorbachev policies likewise address critical Soviet problems. Consequently, even those critics opposed to the method of innovation generally agree with its thrust. But the possibility of a conservative backlash should not be dismissed casually.

The success of the overall Gorbachev political program depends on how well the reformers balance "top-down reform" with "reform from below." By consolidating support at the top in traditional ways and building future support among the populace through *glasnost* and democratization, the Soviet reformers hope to accomplish the rest of their program. Given the limitations imposed by the political system and perhaps the constraints of their own aspirations, the reformers are combining both types of reform. But can democracy be imposed on a political system when the very tenets of democracy demand participation from below?[47] Soviet intellectuals, for instance, worry as much about a benevolent dictatorship under Gorbachev as they do about a return to Stalinism.[48] Faced with conservative reaction in the party and demands for greater democracy from the intelligentsia, Gorbachev may not be able to fashion such a dictatorship, even if he wanted to. The question remains: What kind of political system will Gorbachev and his supporters be able to fashion?

In order to maintain political authority—through the support of allies and adversaries alike throughout the party and government— these reformers must inevitably produce results. A concrete measure of success will be seen in an improved economy. The longevity of the Gorbachev administration, then, hinges to a large degree on the question of rubles.

ECONOMIC AGENDA

Gorbachev and his colleagues view economic reform as the crucial point at which their international initiatives and political reforms converge. According to their strategy, political restructuring enfranchises sufficient domestic allies and a new foreign policy will produce sufficient capital (through savings in military spending and entrée into multilateral lending circles) to accomplish a dramatic overhaul of one of the world's three largest economies. Why is the Gorbachev administration taking such domestic and international risks when muddling through—as the Brezhnev administration did—would seem the safer course? The reformers recognize that the Soviet economy is now caught midway between realizing great potential and succumbing to grave crisis. Only dramatic change can achieve the former and avoid the latter.

On the positive side of the balance sheet, the Soviet Union's Gross National Product (GNP) is either second or third largest in the world, after the United States and Japan. The U.S.S.R. produces twice as much steel as the United States, and it manufactures more machine tools and processes more lumber than any other country.[49] It pumps the world's largest amount of petroleum and natural gas, mines the world's second-largest amounts of gold and coal, and has large reserves of crucial resources, such as manganese, cobalt, chrome, and uranium.[50] It leads the world in the production of tractors, reinforced concrete, woolens, sugar beets, potatoes, milk, and eggs.[51] These natural riches and productive capacity have prompted the Central Intelligence Agency (CIA) to suggest that the Soviet Union is the world's most self-reliant country.[52] Khrushchev once boasted that by 1980, the Soviet Union would have the highest standard of living in the world.[53] Though Khrushchev's prediction never came true, Soviet GNP did indeed quadruple in the three decades after the Second World War.[54]

By the 1980s, however, the economy was experiencing a significant downturn in growth and productivity. Workers produced less, malingered more, and commented that "the government pretends to pay us and we pretend to work." Industrial production had declined, and a string of disastrous harvests had cut agricultural yields. Soviet consumers consequently faced longer lines and fewer goods. The economic problems in the Soviet Union formed a vicious circle: workers would not work harder to earn more money unless that money could buy more consumer goods, but more consumer goods could not be produced until more workers worked harder.

In an increasingly competitive international economic market, the Soviet Union traded from its considerable stock of resources but could provide virtually no services and very few finished products that the West desired. According to one optimistic estimate, only 20 percent of Soviet manufactured goods was of acceptable quality and suitable for export to the West.[55] The resultant trade dependency on raw materials tied the Soviet economy to fluctuating world commodity prices.[56] Isolated from the international economic system by an inconvertible currency, the U.S.S.R. could remain protected from some of the vicissitudes of international finance, but it could not reap the benefits of increased trade, access to investment capital, and greater availability of multilaterally financed loans.

Though proud of its record of having leapfrogged into the modern economic age in mere decades, by the 1980s the U.S.S.R. was not keeping pace with the outside world. In order to render its economy internationally competitive, the U.S.S.R. realized that it had to modernize its outmoded industrial sector and boost its agricultural production. Here again, Gorbachev and supporters sought inspiration from Soviet history.

* * *

The October Revolution ushered in a new group of leaders in the Soviet Union, but not a unified economic program. In the early days, the Bolsheviks engaged in considerable debate over the economic path to Communism: heavy industrialization or light; nationalized land or land in private hands; worker-owned enterprises or state-owned; the use of capitalist managerial techniques or the wholesale rejection of these techniques.

Before a debate on economic policy could properly emerge, a civil war intervened, pitting the Bolshevik Red Army against the anti-Bolshevik White Army. To provide needed resources for the government and to undercut the political opposition economically, Lenin introduced what later became known as "War Communism": a program of large-scale nationalization of industry, disenfranchisement of the middle class, elimination of legal private enterprise, appropriation of produce, and restrictions on workers' rights.

In 1921, after threats to the Soviet government had been contained, Lenin veered sharply in his economic planning, introducing the New Economic Policy (NEP). On the heels of famine and economic disintegration brought on by the civil war, NEP allowed free enterprise and legalized ownership of private property for the first time since 1917. Much of the previously illegal commerce (black market) became instantly legitimate, and NEPmen, as the new entrepreneurs came to be known, brought Western goods and salesmanship to the revived Soviet consumer market.[57]

NEP stressed the need for certain accommodations with capitalism. Earlier, Lenin had recruited "bourgeois" managers to help run the first Soviet industries. Under NEP, Western-style managerial techniques, particularly Taylorism, grew more widespread in Soviet industry. Taylorism was a system of dividing work into ever more specialized and routine tasks in an effort to wring greater efficiency from workers. When Lenin enthusiastically embraced this technique in 1918 and promoted it later under NEP, the alternative of worker-controlled factories gradually evaporated.[58]

But NEP did not solve the riddle perplexing economists during the 1920s: How could the Soviet Union become industrialized and yet preserve its agricultural strength? Ironically, in 1928, ten years

21

after a proletarian, or industrial workers', revolution, 80 percent of Soviet citizens were still peasants, and neither capital nor skilled manpower was available to create the industrial nation that the Bolsheviks had envisioned.[59] One political faction, led by Leon Trotsky, favored heavy industrialization at the expense of the agricultural sector; another faction, led by party theorist Nikolai Bukharin, urged industrialization but at a cautious pace that did not disrupt the fragile relationship between the working class and the peasants (the historic link between hammer and sickle).

Both of these factions lost *politically* to Stalin, who exiled Trotsky but appropriated in a rather unsophisticated manner much of his program. In 1928, ostensibly because of several poor harvests, Stalin canceled NEP, over the objections of Bukharin and others, guiding the Soviet economy through another series of convulsions. Stalin introduced rapid collectivization for the agricultural sector and the five-year plans that became the backbone of the state-controlled and -planned economy. Capital siphoned from the agricultural sector during the seizure of land and produce from peasants—known euphemistically as "primitive socialist accumulation"—eventually made the massive industrial advances of the 1930s possible.

Stalin's solution to the economic riddle of the 1920s unquestionably brought the Soviet Union into modernity. But the costs were high. During collectivization, millions died of famine or state violence and millions more were imprisoned in political purges. Stalin transformed a flexible political structure, a thriving culture, and a diverse economy into a rigid entity, anchored by a large centralized bureaucracy in Moscow.[60]

Khrushchev's inheritance from Stalin was a heavy one indeed. Admitting that agricultural production under Stalin had diminished to pre-Revolution levels, Khrushchev eased restrictions on private plots and pioneered numerous innovations. The farming experiment in the "Virgin Lands" of Central Asia, for instance, brought tremendous early success, boosting harvests from 80 million to 136 million tons between 1953 and 1958.[61] In the industrial sphere, Khrushchev experimented with a form of "self-financing," putting factory profits back into workers' bonuses, housing, and improvements in machinery.

Many of Khrushchev's later agricultural ventures failed, however, and Brezhnev had to restore stability (and considerable capital) to the agricultural sector. Industrial production in the 1960s and early '70s responded to the Brezhnev program of improved investment and labor incentives, registering increases comparable to those of the 1950s. Sensitive to public demands, Brezhnev also began to swing production toward consumer needs, continuing a trend started under Khrushchev. In 1960, for instance, 8 percent of the population owned television sets, 4 percent owned washing machines, and 4 percent owned refrigerators. By 1985, efforts particularly of the Brezhnev administration had brought TVs to 99 percent of the population, washing machines to 70 percent, and refrigerators to 92 percent.[62] But as in the Khrushchev era, economic success came early for Brezhnev and did not endure. Political corruption, inaccurate economic forecasting and reporting, and a general malaise in the workplace eventually eroded economic performance.

After Brezhnev died in 1982, Andropov attempted an economic revitalization campaign, but his early death put an end to this reform. Chernenko did not take the baton. The dismal state of the Soviet economy in the early 1980s even led economist Marshall Goldman to revise his previously positive evaluation into "I have turned around and am now a pessimist."[63]

On the eve of the Gorbachev succession, the Soviet government had still not solved several long-standing economic problems. Because of three legacies of Stalin—an emphasis on heavy industry, collectivized agriculture, and inflexible central planning—the Soviet economy lagged behind other major industrial economies. Heavy industry could not produce profitable high-tech electronic goods; collectivized agriculture was not producing sufficient food; inflexible central planning produced excessive bureaucracy and waste.

In 1985, Gorbachev and colleagues were in a bind similar to that encountered in 1928 in the final years of the NEP: Where could the U.S.S.R. find the capital necessary to bring its economy up to international standards? Stalin and the heavy industrializers brought the U.S.S.R. into the twentieth century on the back of the agricultural sector. In order to propel the U.S.S.R. into the twenty-first century, the present reformers are looking to international finance. While fostering international contacts, the Gorbachev camp is meanwhile exploring several options, looking at modernization on the one hand and free-market mechanisms on the other.

The following three sections examine concrete examples of "socialist" economic reform. Three different strategies—East Germany's improved centralized planning, Hungary's experiments with market mechanisms, and France's response to trends in the international economy—have provided Soviet reformers with possible models. However, rather than choosing one example over another, the Gorbachev administration seems to be borrowing elements from each.

Modernization

With the eighth-largest economy in the world, East Germany is cited as proof of what can be done within the limits of Communism's centralized planning.[64] By many indicators, East Germany compares favorably with West Germany: they have similar GNPs as well as rates of growth, infant mortality, and life expectancy.[65] East Germany ranks fifteenth in the world in total trade volume and highest in per capita trade in Eastern Europe.[66] Given the destruction of World War II and the number of resources that the Soviet Union removed (informal reparations) between 1945 and 1953, the country's economic performance is remarkable. Of course, East Germany benefits a great deal from its relationship with West Germany, receiving cash subsidies and gaining back-door access to many of the trading privileges of the European Common Market. And support has come from the U.S.S.R. as well. Since 1971, the flow of resources has reversed, and East Germany has particularly taken advantage of Soviet energy subsidies.

Instead of decentralizing its economy and relying more on plant managers to determine prices and wages, East Germany has since the early 1970s gone in the opposite direction, toward *kombinate*, or large administrative units that supervise industrial production. Such *kombinate* improve upon many of the virtues of centralized planning: easier resource allocation, exceptional organizational stability, and economies of scale (the more of a given commodity produced, the cheaper the manufacture of each unit of that commodity).[67] Many of the usual defects of central planning are evident in East Germany: poor planning, waste of labor and raw materials, technological stagnation.[68] These latter factors contribute to the shortages of consumer goods and bureaucratic inefficiency common to most centrally planned economies.

The Gorbachev administration has occasionally moved in the direction of the East German example of modernizing central planning. In 1985, for example, Gorbachev transformed five ministries and one committee into one supercommittee in order to streamline governmental management of agriculture.[69] (In a reverse, however, this superministry, Gosagroprom, was dismantled under the 1989 agricultural reforms.) In another attempt to improve central planning, the reformers have rearranged ministries to be more sympathetic to joint arrangements with foreign companies.

Without abandoning the principles of centralized planning, the Soviets could greatly improve industrial efficiency. For instance, although the U.S.S.R. leads the world in lumber production, it utilizes only 30 percent of trees cut down, compared with 95 percent for the United States, Canada, or Sweden.[70] In critically important steel making, the Soviets only make 4 percent of their steel by the most efficient method, continuous casting; the figure for Japan is 86 percent.[71] Were the Soviet Union simply to bring its production techniques up to par with those of other industrial powers, it would enjoy significant productivity increases. But the problem of improving machinery applies not only to steel casting or utilizing lumber: the need for machine retooling is industry-wide. Gorbachev has pushed for an 80 percent increase in machinery investment. According to his plan, by 1990 two thirds of all production will be handled by new machines.[72] In addition, the Soviet government since 1986 has renewed its perennial attempts to improve quality control (but apparently with few concrete gains to date).[73]

To improve labor productivity, the Gorbachev administration is pursuing several tacks, still within the framework of central planning. Almost immediately upon taking office, Gorbachev targeted an endemic Soviet (and earlier, Russian) problem: alcoholism. In the 1970s, two Soviet economists suggested that alcoholism accounts for a 10 percent drop in the productivity of Soviet workers.[74] The strict anti-alcohol program imposed during Gorbachev's first year—limiting supply, raising prices, restricting the hours of retail sales—led to widespread grumbling and Gorbachev's first unflattering nicknames.[75] Unfortunately for the U.S.S.R., a full 12 percent of state revenues derives from liquor sales and taxes.[76] The 35 percent drop in alcohol revenues after six months of the campaign reportedly cost the Soviet government *seven billion dollars.*[77] Like many Soviet austerity measures, the anti-alcohol campaign did not bring about immediate economic gain. For all these reasons, the campaign has been recently downplayed.

Another labor-related problem facing the reformers is declining population in key geographic areas. From 1970 to 1980, the labor force increased 24 million. In the 1980s, however, the Soviet government projects only a 6 million increase.[78] As Soviet émigré economist Vladimir Kontorovich observes, however, "almost all of the growth of the labor force comprises people of Muslim origin, who have on average lower skills than the rest of the population and are reluctant to migrate to labor-short regions."[79]

The solution to the demographic problem seems simple: a massive job training program that would train new workers and retrain displaced workers. So far, such a program has not emerged. The Soviet government may be dragging its feet because of a traditional reluctance to spend large amounts of money in the Central Asian republics for upgrading skills that would, given the unwillingness of the population to relocate, require transferring key industries to the area (traditional Slavic antipathy toward non-Slavs, especially Central Asian Moslems, no doubt contributes to the problem). To solve the problem, Kontorovich has a controversial prescription: "redundant white-collar workers are a potential new source of factory workers in the Gorbachev regime."[80] *Perestroika* would then amount to "downward mobility," an equation that might generate a good deal of social unrest. More likely candidates for filling the labor need are soldiers released from duty in Mongolia and Eastern Europe under both current and proposed troop demobilization. This maneuver would also serve the purpose of defusing any potential challenge to the government launched by disgruntled and unemployed veterans.

The above proposals have focused on refinements in managerial techniques, machinery, and labor relations but not on substantial changes in the economic system. The effect of such changes would be to streamline managerial techniques and bring backward technology more in line with current international standards: in short, to rationalize a centralized economy that has grown both inefficient and disarticulated.[81]

But are the Soviet reformers content simply with the East German model? At the opening of a Central Committee meeting in June 1987, Gorbachev surveyed the first two years of economic changes and summed up the progress: "There are changes, but they are insignificant and not radical."[82] According to economist Anders Aslund, significance and radicalness have nothing to do with the move away from streamlining à la East Germany: "GDR measures simply do not appear applicable."[83]

Market Socialism?

Since the 1970s, Hungary has represented the most market-oriented socialist country in Eastern Europe. The New Economic Mechanism (NEM) introduced in 1968 was the centerpiece of a reform package around which then General Secretary Janos Kadar built his "liberal" reputation.[84] In establishing certain market mechanisms, NEM mirrored Lenin's NEP of the 1920s, though each was a response to different economic conditions. Under NEM, for instance, plant managers set commodity prices according to the market rather than by government policy. NEM tied wages to profits, established a bond market financed by the national bank, and encouraged joint ventures with foreign companies. During the 1970s, Hungary's economic indicators rose dramatically and, as U.S. journalists endlessly pointed out, the shelves of Budapest supermarkets were considerably better stocked than their Moscow counterparts.

Yet, in the 1980s, Hungary's growth has been severely curtailed. Reliance on foreign capital has led to a $17.7 billion hard-currency debt, the highest per capita in the socialist world.[85] Hungary has fallen prey to an all too common contemporary bind: the monetary reforms instituted have both allowed the country to compete internationally and subjected it to the exigencies of the international economic system. As long as foreign countries buy Hungarian goods produced in newly retooled factories, the securing of international loans appears a brilliant strategy. When the loans simply fuel domestic consumption and Hungarian exports drop, the loans must still be paid—in hard currency—and a debt crisis ensues.

Despite this mixed economic performance, Hungary apparently

serves as an economic model for Soviet reformers. In a July 1988 meeting with the new Hungarian Communist party chief, Karoly Grosz, Gorbachev reportedly said, "It is probably the Hungarian endeavors and the Hungarian perceptions that are the closest now to those of the Soviet Union."[86]

Whether the reformers are looking more to Hungary's NEM or into their own past and Lenin's NEP is difficult to determine. In either case, Gorbachev has been careful to note that the unusual economic ideas he presents have impeccable socialist pedigrees. So too do most reform economists. "There is the usual unity," writes one such Soviet economist. "Everyone is for restructuring, everyone quotes Lenin, and everyone cites party decisions to prove their point."[87] These superficial resemblances perform a critical function: if Lenin, for instance, allowed private enterprise to flourish in the Soviet Union in the 1920s, then certainly such an experiment in the 1980s squares with Marxist doctrine.

A first step toward the increased use of markets in the Soviet Union entails an attack on centralized planning. Although the reformers introduced some measures to improve central planning, they have also sought to change the system dramatically. In 1986, Gorbachev asked,

> Can an economy which runs into trillions of rubles be run from Moscow? This is absurd, comrades. By the way, this—the fact that we have tried to manage everything from Moscow until quite recently—constitutes our common or main mistake.[88]

The bureaucracy that directs the Soviet economy had by the 1980s grown to monstrous proportions. According to economist Marshall Goldman, the state's top economic organ (Gosplan) handles 7 million documents and makes 83 million calculations annually. The price committee sets 200,000 prices each year;[89] a typical enterprise director receives 3,000 orders per year and is expected to prepare 11,000 reports annually.[90] At the 1988 party conference, frustration with this bureaucracy drove one delegate to complain:

> Enough. I can't stand this proliferation of paperwork. At the 27th party congress it was said that if each delegate, when he

gets home, doesn't tear up five or six forms, he went for nothing. I understand one thing. It's useless to fight the forms, you've got to kill the people producing them.[91]

Even if such comments overstate the point, the director of an industrial plant or a collective farm has long labored within a bloated and inefficient managerial structure. By turning much of the economic decision making over to these plant managers—giving them authority to bypass the government in order to secure contracts with other Soviet plants and suppliers, as well as international investors and markets—the reformers expect to ease the burdens both on the government and on the governed.

A key feature of this decentralization is *self-financing*, a proposal taken from the Khrushchev years. Under self-financing, a director has authority to split profits with the government, retaining half for workers' bonuses and machine retooling. This plan is designed to improve worker productivity and enhance the efficiency of the industrial process. By 1988, over 60 percent of industrial and agricultural production was governed according to principles of self-financing.[92]

Self-management, meanwhile, involves a more profound change: not only does an enterprise retain its profits, but it also sets prices, decides production quotas, and establishes individual contracts for supply of materials and delivery of finished goods. Although there have been several experiments with this type of self-management, it functions more in radical theory than in actual practice.

For either of these forms of decentralization to work, of course, the Soviets must produce a new breed of managers who have the expertise to handle restructured domestic industries and large-scale joint ventures with foreign countries. The U.S.S.R. is now sending its managers abroad for training. But it is not simply job retraining, it is managerial ideology as well. According to one Soviet magazine:

> Not a few Soviet executives are still unable to get used to the idea that the model of centrally directed socialism has virtually exhausted itself and that joint enterprises, stockholders' property, and the market mechanism do not signify a return of capitalist methods sullying the once impeccable planned economy, but a return of common sense and the use of the economic levers effective since the dawn of time.[93]

With decentralization under way, Gorbachev waited only a year and a half before sponsoring legislation legalizing certain forms of private enterprise. In some respects, the move was as much strategic as ideological. For years, Soviet citizens had engaged in unofficial private enterprise through a black market similar to one that functioned during War Communism. Not only did the latter-day underground economy recycle sneakers and jeans scavenged from tourists; plumbers, electricians, even doctors offered their services after hours for special rates. By legalizing a portion of this economic activity, the Soviet government could simultaneously tax what had previously been unreported income and undermine the black market.

But such private enterprise measures, as mentioned earlier, also represent a change in principle. Taking their cue from the West, the reformers have begun to embrace the notion that innovation stems largely from individual initiative and personal incentive, rather than in social or collective enterprise.[94] The cutting edge of the Soviet economy, therefore, has become the Soviet entrepreneur who develops a new service that Soviet citizens want or the ambitious moonlighter who sells a product that satisfies a demand in the marketplace.

The most common form of private enterprise is in fact a compromise between state sector work and private ownership: the cooperative sector. Since the Law on Cooperatives was adopted in May 1988, cooperatives have provided a group of citizens the opportunity to run small-scale self-financed and self-managed enterprises. Cooperative restaurants and cooperatively run hospitals, for instance, are popular in the U.S.S.R. today. As of January 1989, there were 77,548 cooperatives, employing 1.6 million workers, with a significant number located in the Baltic republics.[95] While encouraging these ventures, on the one hand, the government has also been careful to control their spread. A December 1988 bill, for instance, restricted cooperatives in what they could do and how much profit they could make.[96]

The new market orientation does not apply simply to risk-taking entrepreneurs or moonlighting workaholics. The Soviet leadership also passed legislation tying wages closer to output and making prices a function of demand. A more recent bankruptcy act shuts down unprofitable Soviet business and could eliminate thousands of jobs.

Market mechanisms are therefore spreading *throughout* Soviet society.

Gorbachev has composed a similarly dramatic set of reforms for agriculture. Recognizing that the population will not wholeheartedly support *perestroika* without seeing results appear on store shelves, the Gorbachev administration eased restrictions on private plots in 1987 in an effort to boost production. The agricultural situation in the U.S.S.R. needed the reform. The farming sector receives enormous subsidies ($32 billion), and yet one third of the food intended for internal consumption never gets to the consumers.[97] According to 1982 data, private farming in one Central Asian republic accounted for 46 percent of its meat production, 40 percent of vegetable production, and 40 percent of milk production, all on less than 1 percent of cultivated land area. Figures for other republics, while perhaps less dramatic, nonetheless underscore the failure of state farms to provide crucial foodstuffs.[98]

When the conservative Yegor Ligachev became Central Committee secretary for agriculture in 1988, U.S. analysts speculated that this occasional opponent of Gorbachev might hinder farm reform. In October 1988, however, Gorbachev announced a move away from collectivization and toward the kind of reform that China had undertaken several years previously. In a televised speech to farmers, Gorbachev proposed measures that would allow families or groups to rent land from state or collective farms.[99] In March 1989, Gorbachev went even further, dismantling the agricultural superministry, allowing private farmers to lease land for life, calling for a system of cooperative banks to provide funds for farmers, and even proposing a stock market to provide additional financing. Before these changes could boost production, however, the U.S.S.R. admitted in the next month to taking a temporary shortcut by importing consumer goods to meet public pressure.[100]

Agricultural reform is not the only method of improving the availability of consumer goods. Another radical strategy is closely connected to Soviet foreign policy: namely, steering industries away from military production and toward fulfilling domestic needs. In March 1988, Gorbachev directed defense industries to re-equip 260 plants to manufacture equipment for producing food and consumer goods.[101] Between 1988 and 1995, he said, defense industrial ministries were to "provide 17.5 billion rubles of machinery—out of a total of 37 billion rubles—for the food-processing sector—almost as much as the total value of machinery installed in food processing for 1980–1987."[102] The guns-into-butter transformation has already begun, at a more rapid pace than successfully concluded arms control treaties might otherwise justify.

In the high-tech arena, meanwhile, the reformers realize that effective competition with other industrialized countries hinges upon extending the Soviet Union's role in the computer world. Presently, the U.S.S.R. relies on mainframe computers to direct much of its centralized planning. In order to extend computerization throughout the country, however, the Soviets are slowly turning to smaller computers. By the end of 1987, the U.S.S.R. could claim only 200,000 microcomputers (compared with over 25 million in the United States).[103] U.S. intelligence agencies estimate a four- to ten-year U.S. lead in microcomputers and considerably longer leads in other key technologies.[104]

To enable smaller computers to knit together various sources, the U.S.S.R. is embarking on a major expansion of its telecommunications. The Soviet population now averages 10 phones per 100 people, the lowest per capita distribution of telephones of any industrialized nation. For 1987, the government pushed through a 17 percent increase in telecommunications expenditures; by the year 2000, Soviet officials hope to boost the per capita phone distribution to 30 per 100.[105]

To play catch-up in the computer and telecommunications realms, the U.S.S.R. must undergo perhaps the most profound decentralization it has ever attempted: an information revolution. The more the Soviet government trusts its citizens with an unrestricted flow of information, the more its citizenry can participate in the economy, in domestic political debate, and, eventually, in foreign policy.

Within four years, the Gorbachev administration has attacked numerous sacred cows—collectivization, central planning, the government's information monopoly—and has absorbed, one by one, the radical suggestions of the past. In the June 1987 issue of the leading Soviet journal *Novy Mir*, economist Nikolai Shmelev proposed the abolition of state subsidies and price setting, the acceptance of unemployment as natural, and the devaluation of the ruble to world market rates.[106] By 1989, the Soviet government had begun to accept unemployment as necessary (if not natural), had seriously called into question the government pricing and subsidies system, and was edging closer to floating the ruble in the world currency market.[107] Despite opposition from various sectors, the Gorbachev administration seems to be taking NEM and NEP one step further, and the radical economists have consequently become even more daring.[108]

Initial assessments of the Gorbachev economic program have been mixed. For the period 1985–1986, the CIA measured increases in GNP (4.2 percent), industrial output (3.6 percent), and agricultural output (7.3 percent).[109] But in 1989, U.S. analysts pointed to a Soviet government budget deficit of 100 billion rubles, a 2 percent decline in agricultural production and a mere 2 to 2.5 percent improvement in industrial output.[110] Determining the success of any economic program is very difficult with such short-range indicators. Some sectors of the Soviet economy have responded positively to reallocation of resources, and others have improved output through streamlining and modernization.

But an economic system, like a living organism, needs time to recover after the sustained trauma of progressive deterioration followed by radical surgery. The Soviet government does not expect its economic program to produce results until the middle to late 1990s. That expectation may be overly optimistic. Will the reformers be given the time necessary to prove the worth of their proposals? The government has openly criticized many political and economic aspects of the U.S.S.R.; the population expects effective alternatives. In other words, the hopes raised among the population by *glasnost* may not be fulfilled by an economic program that in the short term leads to major unemployment, social unrest, and no noticeable improvement in the standard of living. The reformers must therefore win the confidence of the public in order to put through austerity measures that may, despite their unpopularity, produce economic success in the long term.

Within their domestic context, the economic changes in the Soviet Union, whether fine-tuning central planning or offering a more dramatic vision of market socialism, represent according to the government a search for growth and greater efficiency within socialist parameters. But a set of external factors—generated by the international economic system—will also shape the reform program. The result may be anything but socialist.

Internationalism

East Germany represented socialism through improved centralized planning. Hungary offered a market approach to socialism. The example of France, meanwhile, reveals some of the problems that all countries, capitalist or socialist, face when reckoning with the international economic system.

In 1980, after Socialist François Mitterand became president, many expected not surprisingly that the country would move in a socialist direction. By 1983, several of the economic policies of this administration were hard to term socialist. The Mitterand government had undertaken a supply-side restructuring of the economy (encouraging investment rather than consumption) that reflected in some important respects the Thatcherite and Reaganite "revolution." The perennial socialist call for full employment had been replaced by policies targeting inflation as the gravest threat facing the country. To bring down the rate of inflation, the French government accepted increased unemployment rates; to encourage the corporate climate, it advocated greater privatization of government business; to save money, it cut government programs (except the military). [111]

France was not the exception to the rule. As economic analyst Joyce Kolko points out:

> It is now evident that it does not matter whether government economic policymakers call themselves free-market, Keynesian, or socialist. They all consistently pursue the same capitalist economics when in positions of power. . . . In the mid-1980s all of the governments in the [Organization of Economic Cooperation and Development] were ready to "bite the bullet," to accept ever higher levels of unemployment in order to restructure their economies to compete better in the new international division of labor and for investment capital. [112]

Centrally planned economies that traditionally rejected such capitalist reasoning now seem eager to adopt it. In China, where the government has introduced free-market mechanisms at a rate far outstripping that of the Soviet Union and its socialist trading partners, the Chinese people are also being asked to bite the bullet. While many rural Chinese are enriching themselves from the rapid privatization of agriculture, urban residents, who make up 20 percent of the population, are struggling under inflation approaching an annual rate of nearly 50 percent. [113]

The Soviet Union has decided that it will tolerate these economic drawbacks in exchange for having access to more foreign capital. [114] Since Gorbachev came to power, the Soviet Union has repeatedly expressed interest in joining international economic organizations. Not only has the U.S.S.R. petitioned to be accepted in regional organizations such as the Asian Development Bank, it has also approached such major capitalist organizations as the International Monetary Fund (IMF) and the General Agreement on Tariffs and Trade (GATT). [115] Of course, the privilege of membership includes such responsibilities as sizable contributions to the IMF and such risks as possible debt problems resulting from international borrowing.

Tempted by visions of high-tech imports and favorable terms of trade, however, Soviet officials will accept both the responsibilities and the risks. They apparently are willing to expose *perestroika* to international capitalist restructuring, bringing inflation and unemployment to a country that previously scorned them as the evils of capitalism. On the up side, the U.S.S.R. has already reported modest success in its tentative experiments with international finance: "The Soviet bank is said to be particularly adept at trading, making huge profits with timely sales of the dollar and mark." [116] In 1988, the U.S.S.R. for the first time entered a bond into the European bond market.

In order to stimulate the war-torn economy in 1921, Lenin turned to the international business community. Today's reformers hope too that by attracting a greater flow of capital into the U.S.S.R., foreign investments and trade will break the gridlock in the economy. Joint ventures with foreign businesses have been encouraged several ways. In addition to the restructuring of ministries, the Soviet government in 1987 introduced a law allowing repatriation of profits and in October 1988 announced it would permit foreign firms to own a controlling share in plants established on Soviet soil. A consortium of major U.S. companies—including Ford, Nabisco, and Kodak—will shortly be bringing, among other things, computer disks and chocolate chip cookies to the Soviet Union. But by the beginning of 1989, only 191 joint ventures had been registered, with total assets of under a billion rubles—a disappointment to many Soviet economists who had hoped for greater capital investment.[117]

The Soviet Union may want to join international agencies to take advantage of East–East relations as much as East–West relations. By 1985, Japan had become the world's leading capital exporter and the U.S. the leading debtor nation.[118] Through participation in international economic organizations, the Soviets can better monitor and take advantage of this shift of capital from the Atlantic to the Pacific rim, perhaps even fashioning an economic alliance with Japan and China. As a substantially Asian country, the U.S.S.R. can, by participating in Asian trading consortiums, rise in the tail winds of regional economic success.

The Soviet Union has also expressed concern over the debt paralyzing numerous countries in the Third World. But discussions on Third World debt (as well as the debt of industrialized nations) are held within the IMF and the World Bank and among finance ministers of capitalist countries. To influence these discussions—and to be able to structure debt refinancing on terms favorable to its export strategy—the U.S.S.R. must join the international economic community.[119] At present, the IMF imposes upon debt-ridden countries austerity programs that stress exports and limit imports. If the U.S.S.R. pushes for an international solution that eases the pressure on the affected countries to be more export-oriented, it could eventually have access to numerous additional markets for the goods produced in its newly modernized factories.[120] (Of course, the Soviets have a debt of their own: for 1986, $38.2 billion, the servicing of which ate up 23 percent of hard-currency export earnings.[121])

Before that distant day when the international debt problem is resolved, the U.S.S.R. would like to increase the quantity and improve the quality of its trade with industrialized capitalist countries, which today accounts for only 31 percent of total Soviet trade.[122] One major obstacle in gaining access, for instance, to the large U.S. market is U.S. trade policy. The U.S.S.R. is not among the more than 150 nations that currently enjoy most-favored-nation status (MFN) with the United States. In the 1970s, Congress passed two pieces of legislation—the Jackson-Vanik and Stevenson amendments—tying MFN status to emigration rates for Soviet Jews. Without the benefit of MFN, which would eliminate trade barriers to Soviet goods, the U.S.S.R. cannot draw closer economically to the United States.

But the U.S.S.R. must also develop a different kind of product to export. Eighty percent of its trade with the West consists of energy sales.[123] Until recently, the U.S.S.R. has traded heavily in raw materials—lumber, coal, natural gas, oil—to bring in needed hard currency. And as the finance minister of any Third World country knows, falling commodity prices and the invention of synthetic materials endanger export strategies so reliant on raw materials.

The more the Soviet economy comes in line with international finance, the more the task of restructuring will be taken out of Soviet hands. Although the U.S.S.R. will not have to submit anytime soon to IMF-sponsored austerity programs, critical economic decisions on terms of trade, currency rates, and certain market mechanisms will be handled by international financiers—an ironic twist for a country that repudiated such forces at its very inception in 1917.[124]

In joining the capitalist card game, Gorbachev perhaps believes he retains an ace in the hole—the tremendous human and physical resources of the U.S.S.R. Whether he and his supporters ultimately play their cards right or not, this drive toward the internationalization of the Soviet economy has significant impact on the conduct of its foreign policy.

Rival Programs

Just as support for the Gorbachev camp is not uniform or easily characterized, those who oppose its programs defy neat categorization. Some Soviet citizens and officials oppose democratization but wholeheartedly support economic restructuring. Some support both, but consider *glasnost* to be socially disruptive. Some oppose all challenges to the status quo.

The following comments address several positions critical of the Gorbachev program, from the vantage point of conservatives, republican nationalists, and independent socialists. These forces today influence, and might in the future unseat, the Gorbachev reformers. Any evaluation of the potential success of the Soviet reform movement—and the future, therefore, of Soviet foreign policy— must take these groups into account.

CONSERVATIVE CRITICS

A deeply conservative strain runs through Soviet society. Many Soviet citizens worry that newfangled policies might lead to increased crime, drugs, materialism, selfishness, economic inequality, and instability—all ills once associated with the spread of capitalism. This deep-seated ambivalence to change has taken several different forms.

In March 1988, the traditionally conservative government and party paper of the Russian Republic, *Sovetskaya Rossiya*, published a clear attack on the Gorbachev administration. Nina Andreyeva, a Leningrad chemistry teacher, wrote a letter complaining of a "leftist-liberal" sentiment permeating Soviet society that consisted of

> the denigration of Stalin, the affection for Western values, modernism in the arts, the rise of independent political groups, indifference to the "political treason" of Soviet citizens who want to emigrate, and a declining respect for party discipline. [125]

Andreyeva expressed classic conservative positions that have appeared, give or take some subtleties, in every Soviet administration from Lenin to the present. The official government newspaper *Pravda* waited three weeks to respond, finally issuing an editorial denouncing the letter (which *Sovetskaya Rossiya* eventually retracted). It would be too facile to dismiss this letter as an aberration. [126] Not only do these views have supporters in high positions but they also strike a chord in the Soviet citizenry. Of the letters *Pravda* received in response to its editorial, 25 percent supported Andreyeva's arguments. [127]

It is not simply the occasional party official or disgruntled citizen who warms to Andreyeva's critique. Some influential intellectuals have aligned themselves with this band of conservatives and garner considerable popular support. Books by conservative authors Valentin Pikul and Vasily Belov have, for instance, sold over 2.5 million copies each.[128] Another popular writer, Yuri Bondarev, has proposed, for instance, changing Volgagrad's name back to Stalingrad. In the overblown style of Russian jingoism, Bondarev argues his point: "Our cities—historic cities connected to the biographies of our ancestors, our histories, our sufferings, heroism and in general the history of our people—should have those names which they have always had, which they have carried since olden days." (In a footnote to its interview with Bondarev, the reform-minded *Ogonek* neatly deflated Bondarev by pointing out that Volgagrad was named Tsaritsyn from the sixteenth century to 1925.)[129]

The tradition of Russian chauvinism, from which many of these conservatives derive inspiration, extends back to the nineteenth century.[130] These attitudes more recently have also surfaced in the writings of Alexander Solzhenitsyn and in the intellectual movement of the late 1960s known as Young Guardism. The movement is by no means monolithic: there are Stalinists, Russian Orthodox fundamentalists, status quo bureaucrats, monarchists, and anti-Semitic xenophobes.

The group that exemplifies this latter tendency is Pamyat, originally formed to preserve historical landmarks and monuments. Pamyat, or "memory," inveighs against an imagined consortium of international Zionists and freemasons that has allegedly infiltrated Soviet bureaucracy.[131] Pamyat argues that workers should not be inspired by additional salary, but rather by a patriotic fervor not dissimilar to that associated with Stalin's policies.[132] In times of economic hardship, the values promoted by Pamyat have had extraordinary influence. During the stagnant 1970s, journalist Christian Schmidt-Hauer points out, Stalin himself received accolades:

Just as if Stalin's victims had never existed, a naïve belief sprang up that the great dictator would have solved all economic problems. And the deeper Brezhnev's regime sank into lethargy and corrupt self-interest, the more Soviet citizens, chatting in queues, in beer parlours and at bus stops, praised the dead Generalissimo. Stalin had reduced prices every year, they said, and made sure of proper discipline.[133]

Union of Soviet Socialist Republics (U.S.S.R.)

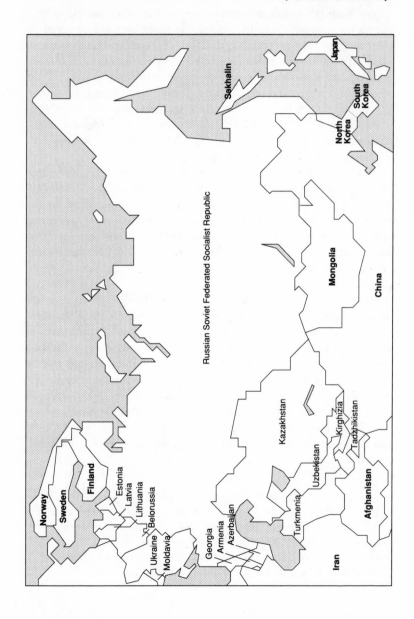

Should *perestroika* prove as incapable as Brezhnev reforms of literally delivering the goods, the ultraconservative messages of Pamyat and its intellectual allies might gain greater acceptance. Should these views eventually influence policy, the effect would be a move away from Western influences. The effect on foreign policy— whether isolationism in the form of Fortress Russia or expansionism patterned after the tsars—could be devastating. [134]

REPUBLIC NATIONALISM

Another source of nationalist challenge comes from the Soviet republics. Traditionally, the many non-Russian ethnic groups in the Soviet Union have, with some exceptions, been kept from Kremlin power. [135] Given the difficulties of wiggling into the national power structure, many republic politicians chose instead to build local patronage systems. A good number achieved remarkable success. In Kazakhstan, for instance, during the greatest successes of the local machine in the 1960s and 1970s, "republic elites were able . . . to pack universities with professors and students of the indigenous nationality and to take control of an ever greater number of levers of economic and political power." [136] Immensely wealthy cotton barons ruled like feudal lords in the Central Asian republics. Until being ousted in September 1989, Ukrainian party boss Vladimir Shcherbitsky successfully resisted many of the liberalizing reforms of the Gorbachev camp.

But the republics have not simply been hotbeds of conservativism and reaction. During his tenure as first party secretary in Georgia from 1972 to 1985, Eduard Shevardnadze was a pioneer of economic reform, and Georgia became an early laboratory for experiments that would eventually be tested nationally under Gorbachev. [137] Among the Baltic republics, meanwhile, Estonia frequently has drawn more inspiration from neighboring capitalist Finland than from Moscow.

Because of these differences in the republics' attitudes toward reform, successive administrations in Moscow have pursued sharply different policies. Brezhnev, for instance, tolerated and even encouraged republican satraps, ignoring the corruption and crime in exchange for political support. Gorbachev has taken a different tack toward elites in the conservative republics, making a special effort to undermine Brezhnev's former allies. When their leaders have been challenged, several national groups have fought back, and long-simmering separatist sentiments have boiled over. In Kazakhstan in 1986, for instance, local citizens rioted to protest the removal of their leader, Dinmukhamed Kunaev, a corrupt Brezhnevite who nonetheless was a Kazakh.

On the other hand, the Gorbachev strategy toward the more reform-minded republics has, especially in the case of the Baltic republics, tested the limits of compromise politics. The independent political organizations in these republics—the Popular Fronts of Estonia and Latvia and Lithuania's Sajudis—ran candidates in the March 1989 elections for the Congress of Peoples' Deputies and won most of their allotted seats. Their platforms: independent political structures, economic systems, even the right to conduct autonomous foreign policy. It did not take long before key elements of these platforms were implemented. In July 1989, after much haggling, the Soviet legislature approved measures guaranteeing virtual political and economic autonomy for Estonia and Lithuania.[138] Latvia, meanwhile, has called for a "special status" that would allow it the same autonomy as its Baltic neighbors during a "transition to complete independent statehood."[139]

The nationalities picture is complicated by the many different ethnic groups residing side by side in the same regions. The U.S.S.R. contains over a hundred nationalities, scattered across fifteen republics and a greater number of "autonomous regions." Recent events in the Soviet Union have shown that confrontation does not occur simply between Moscow and the various republics but *within* particular regions. In Nagorno-Karabakh, a predominantly Armenian community located within Azerbaijan, the Armenians and Azerbaijanis have clashed since 1988, with the Armenians calling for the territory to be taken away from Azerbaijan and tied to Armenia. In Georgia, the Abkhazians (who, by the way, constitute only 17 percent of Abkhazia) recently called for their own autonomous region, provoking Georgians to counterprotest and the Soviet special forces in turn to suppress Georgian nationalism (killing over twenty protesters in April 1989 with clubs and poison gas even as Georgian police tried to protect the demonstrators).[140] In June 1989, a conflict broke out in

Uzbekistan between Uzbeks and Meskhetes, ending with over a hundred dead and 16,000 Meskhetes evacuated from the area. In Estonia, ethnic Russians have called on Moscow to help preserve their rights as Estonia pushes closer to independence.[141] These intrarepublic conflicts may spring from diverse causes. The Uzbeks and Meskhetes have been feuding for years; the Nagorno-Karabakh feud is compounded by religious differences (Christian Armenians; Moslem Azerbaijanis); the Georgian-Abkhazian issue may have been fueled by ultraconservatives to further their political aims.[142]

But these intrarepublic conflicts share with other nationality struggles a concern for protecting ethnic rights—whether as ethnic minorities in the Soviet Union as a whole, as ethnic majorities in their own republic (or regions, as in Nagorno-Karabakh), or as ethnic minorities in particular areas. This protection includes safeguarding the local language and history and ensuring access to university and government positions. The less assimilated the republic, the more radical, naturally, the demands (the Baltic states frequently call for secession, the Ukrainians generally articulate less radical demands). When republican nationalists do not demand independence from the Soviet Union, the Gorbachev administration can compromise. Secession from the Soviet Union, however, is at present considered too great a constitutional challenge to federal power, one that might give rise to civil war.[143]

In dealing with the national question, the Gorbachev administration is pursuing the most delicate of strategies: cultivating a buffer group of intellectuals and supporters within the republics who simultaneously support *perestroika* over the objections of entrenched interests and reject secession over the objections of separatists.[144] (In the Baltic republics, regional Communist party officials occupy this position, publicly supporting independence efforts but trying to temper the demands of the mass movements.) Whether Gorbachev can successfully realize this strategy—keeping the reform-minded republics within the Soviet federation and yet ridding all republics of conservative political and economic elements—will depend on the capacity of *perestroika* to invigorate the economy. If *perestroika* does not provide more consumer goods and fulfill social promises, citizens in the republics will not willingly turn away from the proven advan-

43

tages of the patronage systems. Similarly, the increasingly independent republics will want to remain within the federation only if such a tie continues to be economically and politically beneficial.[145]

INDEPENDENT SOCIALISTS

Opposition to present reforms is not confined to conservatives or to republic nationalists. Even in their more moderate forms, the economic changes proposed by the Gorbachev administration come very close to repudiating the historic Soviet promises: subsidized food, housing, and health care; full employment; rough equality of wages. For these reasons, many Soviet workers and other citizens are balking at a perceived dismantling of the Soviet welfare state. Such critics are not necessarily conservatives fearful of losing their privileges or fending off the infiltration of Western values. Many ordinary Soviet citizens worry that *perestroika* will add up to nothing more than a lost job, higher prices for bread, and a rising class of *nouveau riches*. As the independent Soviet socialist Boris Kagarlitsky observes:

> The essence of the matter is that, under the guise of "reform," workers are being forced to pay for the economic miscalculations of the bureaucracy, bad management, structural imbalances and the pre-crisis situation of the economy. It is perfectly clear that such proposals cannot find mass support. In data obtained from surveys more than 70 per cent of the population are opposed to them.[146]

Kagarlitsky and other democratic socialists in the Soviet Union, such as Roy Medvedev and the members of many independent political clubs, oppose a mere fine-tuning of the top-heavy bureaucratic economic management.[147] But they do not advocate in its stead an acquiescence to the market as the solution to all problems of centralized planning. Rather, reformers on the left favor greater democracy for workers: more worker participation in the management of factories. This demand also reflects a desire for greater democracy throughout society. Kagarlitsky writes:

> It is important to change economic priorities in such a way that people really become the major goal. Decision-making must be

decentralized and democratic procedures must be created which are incompatible with both bureaucratic and technocratic approaches to administration. . . . It is not a question of choosing between plan and market (in any modern society there are both). The genuine choice today is between a developing civil society and bureaucracy. [148]

The new left realizes that the Soviet state *could* combat the seamier elements of capitalism and thus prevent greater social inequality, but remains unconvinced whether it *will*.

How realistic are these concerns?

Although the Soviet Union has, until recently, claimed that full employment had been achieved, that claim belies hidden unemployment, especially in the Central Asian republics, where the rate of new jobs has not kept pace with rising rates of population. In January 1986, the Soviet government launched a public discussion of joblessness, on the heels of the introduction of extended pay for unemployed workers unable to find new jobs. [149] One year later, the Soviet press acknowledged that in the Central Asian republic of Uzbekistan, one million citizens were jobless. [150] The present economic reform will only add to these numbers, not only in Uzbekistan but throughout the country. In industrial ministries alone, decentralization will eliminate 700,000 jobs. [151] Nor can these workers necessarily expect jobs in other sectors. Moscow expects that its mechanization program alone will throw 13 to 19 million workers out of jobs. [152] Such workers can expect as little as two months' notice and two months' unemployment pay. After that, they must find jobs, mostly with the ineffectual help of the state. [153]

The Gorbachev administration has taken great pains to assure the population that any job dislocation that takes place during *perestroika* will be temporary; all workers are to be relocated in comparable jobs. Since the bankruptcy laws have yet to be widely applied and the new mechanization has not really started, it is difficult to judge the reformers' claims. In light of the example of French socialism, these claims seem somewhat disingenuous, especially for an economy unaccustomed to such dislocations.

Other important government guarantees have been subsidized food, rent, and health care. While apartments are often difficult to obtain, especially in Moscow and other large cities, and health care may not meet Western European standards, the costs of these services have nonetheless remained reasonable. Food prices, however, remain a bone of contention. In the past, government announcements decreeing price increases for staples such as bread and cheese often have been met with calamitous reaction. In 1962, a radio announcement in the Ukrainian city of Novocherkassk of "temporary" rises in milk, meat, eggs, and other food products led to mass riots and a confrontation with the Soviet military that left dozens of protesters dead.[154] The price rises were quickly rescinded. In 1987, the government announced a rise in food prices to provide money for better social services.[155] The increase, being moderate, produced only grumbles and hoarding, but no riots.[156]

The most serious sign of discontent with living conditions came in July 1989, when over 300,000 coal miners in Siberia and the Ukraine went on strike. Praising the workers "for taking matters into their own hands," Gorbachev moved quickly with concessions—1,500 tons of soap, 1,000 refrigerators. Somewhat satisfied, workers returned to the mines, ending the crisis in little over two weeks.[157] Before returning to work, the miners achieved a key political demand when Gorbachev agreed to allow each republic to decide on the dates for local elections. Taking Gorbachev at his word on democratization, the workers wanted earlier elections in order to get their own candidates in office before the strike became a forgotten issue.

In defense of *perestroika*, but from a position sympathetic to the democratic socialists, Abel Aganbegyan, a chief economic adviser and Gorbachev supporter, maintains that the social contract will be strengthened by the reforms, not weakened. Housing will be improved and rents kept low; agricultural output will be raised to improve the food supply; more government money will be directed toward public health and education (medical staffs and teachers have already been given 30 percent increases in salary).[158] Perhaps most critically, Aganbegyan appears to share the concerns of the Soviet left on the issue of management reform:

The distinctive feature of this reform is industrial democracy moving towards self-management in enterprises. The increased

46

role of the workers in enterprises will involve them in determining the enterprise plan, the allocation of resources and the election of managers. [159]

One conclusion to be drawn from this debate on the future of Soviet economic reform is that there is no single way to adapt socialism. Soviet economic thinking comprises two major strains: greater worker democracy and greater accommodation with market forces and international finance. Although the government may, for reasons of principle and populism, preach the rhetoric of the former, a pragmatic desire to compete in the international economic world may dictate adaptation to the latter. [160] Because industrial democracy involves a micro-level change and aligning the Soviet economy with the international economy is a macro-level process, these concerns are often expressed in the same breath, and potential contradictions are not confronted (e.g., trends in the world economy may not favor greater worker control of enterprises).

The French government, despite its socialist affiliation, imposed austerity programs that international capitalists applauded. The Mitterand government argued that it *had no alternative given the French financial position.* Soviet reforms, some argue, will benefit only a small sector of the population—Soviet professionals—and not the greater bulk of the population. [161] This trend too may not be as much a repudiation of principle as an acceptance of international economic realities.

To the average Soviet citizen, this dilemma of *perestroika* has a very concrete dimension: the simultaneous desire for market benefits on the one hand and continued socialist guarantees on the other. Whether the Soviet government can satisfy these two demands—or even if it ultimately intends to do so—remains to be seen.

Independent socialists serve as an important reminder that socialism is not dead in the U.S.S.R. Although the government may endorse market principles and curry favor with international capitalists, the Soviet government and many of its domestic critics still consider themselves socialists. The U.S.S.R. still identifies with other socialist countries in formulating a "socialist" foreign policy. As Soviet policy makers come to adapt their definition of socialism, however, this "socialist" foreign policy will also change.

In Soviet history, domestic and foreign policy reforms have gone hand in hand. Lenin's dramatic economic turnabout with NEP accompanied a substantial warming in relations with the United States and other Western powers. The death of Stalin and the easing of internal controls in the 1950s paralleled a withdrawal of Soviet forces from Finland and Austria and the cultivation of several arms control treaties with the United States.

Periods of tight internal controls within the Soviet Union have for the most part meant more aggressive foreign policies. Stalin's police state mirrored his policy of keeping a tight rein on Eastern Europe. Brezhnev's suppression of human rights at home dovetailed with Moscow's suppression of human rights in Czechoslovakia in 1968.

The connections between internal and external Soviet policies are by no means easily drawn, since so many factors affect the formulation of each. Nevertheless, certain conclusions can be drawn. A policy of greater social and political freedom in the Soviet Union generally leads to a foreign policy more apt to encourage similar freedoms in the societies of Soviet allies. A policy of greater economic openness in the Soviet Union generally leads to the fostering of closer trade relations, especially with the West. Such liberal political and economic policies also permit greater foreign influences on Soviet society, thereby raising the expectations of Soviet citizens.

The Gorbachev reformers seem acutely aware of these interrelations between the realms of domestic and foreign policy. In September 1988, a key Gorbachev supporter in the Politburo, Alexander Yakovlev, turned his attention to foreign affairs. According to Georgi Arbatov, of the Institute for the Study of the U.S.A. and Canada, "somebody needs to integrate foreign and domestic policy, and Yakovlev is the bridge, the man who knows it all."[162]

Yakovlev's job: to ensure that a more open foreign policy improves the chances of the domestic program's success. But even with "lasting peace" and "predictability," can the Soviet economy, given its chronic problems, be reformed? It has always been popular in the West to predict imminent Soviet economic collapse. It would be wise to remember, however, a 1950 report to President Truman that described the Japanese economy as in a "disadvantageous position . . . arising out of obsolete plant and equipment and aggravated by inefficient and wasteful use of manpower."[163] With international help (primarily from the United States), Japan performed its economic miracle. The Gorbachev administration's success also depends to a significant degree on foreign support for its policies, in the form of improved trade relations and new military relationships—in short, détente.

The Soviet Union has traversed a great distance since 1917: from an isolated revolution surrounded by hostile powers to a nation more than ever reliant on friendly relations—with those very same powers.

2

The New Thinking in Soviet Foreign Policy

THE 1977 Soviet Constitution (Article 28) lists the aims of Soviet foreign policy as

> ensuring international conditions favorable for building communism in the U.S.S.R., safeguarding the state interests of the Soviet Union, consolidating the positions of world socialism, supporting the struggle of peoples for national liberation and social progress, preventing wars of aggression, achieving universal and complete disarmament, and consistently implementing the principle of the peaceful co-existence of states with different social systems.

Other governments, however, have characterized Soviet policy very differently. The U.S. government has rarely considered the Soviet Union sincere about its disarmament goals, many Afghanis no doubt wondered after their country was invaded in 1979 whether the Soviet had indeed repudiated aggression, and Peruvian guerrillas fighting against a Soviet-supplied Peruvian government would certainly take issue with the idea that the Soviets support national liberation struggles.

Since the drafting of the last Constitution, in 1977, the U.S.S.R. has not significantly changed its rhetoric. The Gorbachev administration still talks of preventing war, furthering social progress, and achieving disarmament. The real impact of Gorbachev's "new thinking" in foreign policy lies not in rhetoric so much as in *action*. Since 1985, the U.S.S.R. has accepted on-site verification of arms control treaties. Not only have Soviet military forces withdrawn from Afghanistan, but the U.S.S.R. has admitted that its invasion was a serious error. Gorbachev has announced unilateral military force reductions in Europe. The question concerning Soviet foreign policy is no longer whether these changes are simply rhetorical or truly significant. Rather, the question becomes: What do these unquestionably significant changes mean?

Gorbachev's domestic program, as we have seen, has been, in part, a determining factor behind Soviet foreign policy initiatives. This chapter will examine these initiatives against the background of the history of Soviet foreign relations.

Like most empires, Russia under the tsars was preoccupied with expansion and consolidation. During the half millennium from 1300 to 1800, the Russian empire grew from a set of loosely connected principalities to encompass the Caucasus to the south, Finland to the north, Lithuania and Poland to the west, and Siberia to the east. By the nineteenth century, the empire had grown vast and unwieldy. Military defeat in the Crimean War in the middle of the century suggested that although Russia continued to annex territory, its imperial power could not match that of the European empires. When tiny Japan defeated the Russian navy in 1905, it was apparent that the Russian empire would not last long.

When the Bolsheviks replaced the tsars in 1917, they brought with them a unique world view, a Communist program that not only could unify the country but also could spread beyond the borders of the Soviet Union. Although in many respects anti-Western (anticapitalist, antibourgeois, antiliberal), this Bolshevik Communism was nonetheless internationalist in that it sought to promote bonds between working classes of different countries.

For the Bolsheviks, the Russian Revolution was but a first step, severing the "weakest link" in the chain of imperialism—the decrepit Russian empire. Russian workers and peasants looked to the Revolution as a potential answer to their domestic problems of hunger and inequality. But Bolshevik theoreticians such as Leon Trotsky took into consideration more than the Russian predicament. Trotsky argued that the Bolsheviks should create a "permanent revolution" that could seize Europe and then spread to other continents.

Hard realities rendered such internationalism impractical. The first difficult foreign policy question facing the new Soviet Union concerned Germany and World War I. Russia under Tsar Nicholas II had allied itself with France, Britain, and the United States against the Austro-Hungarian empire and Germany. Some Bolsheviks maintained that the Soviet Army should continue to fight German imperialism not as an ally of other imperialist powers but in an effort to propel the German working class toward revolution. Yet, to draw exhausted and disillusioned Soviet soldiers to the side of the Revolution, Lenin had promised an end to Russian participation in World War I. He was reluctant to go back on his word, especially since army support would be crucial for quelling the domestic counterrevolution the Bolsheviks anticipated. While support for the revolution was strong in major cities and certain regions, large portions of the former Russian empire—the Ukraine, Central Asia, Siberia—resisted fiercely. The expected civil war broke out in 1918, uniting the various opponents of Bolshevik power in an unsteady coalition known as the White Army. The Bolsheviks desperately needed a consolidated Red Army. Accommodation with Germany, though humiliating, was seen as necessary to save the Revolution.

Germany was not the only power hostile to the new Soviet government. Very few countries greeted the Bolshevik Revolution with anything more positive than guarded suspicion. Nationalization of many Western concerns and the refusal to pay foreign debts to the West incurred under tsarism clearly did nothing to enhance the Soviet reputation in Western eyes. After the U.S.S.R. and Germany concluded their peace treaty, Russia's former allies decided to continue the war against Germany on Russian soil and simultaneously destabilize the new revolutionary Soviet government. In 1918, the Allies, including the United States, landed military forces in the North and East at Archangel and Vladivostok and eventually joined forces with the White Army in several skirmishes against the Bolsheviks. British troops advanced from the south. Many countries supplied arms to the anti-Bolshevik factions. In the end, no coalition ever mustered enough unity to defeat the encircled Soviet state.

By 1921, with the foreign intruders repulsed and the major pockets of internal resistance suppressed, the liberal economic policies of Lenin (NEP) mellowed Western antagonism. In the 1920s, for instance, 40 percent of U.S. industrial exports went to the Soviet Union.[1] The concerns of Soviet foreign policy began to resemble those of other countries—namely, trade and balance of power. Some Soviet leaders even favored abandoning, if only temporarily, the Bolshevik dream of a single Communist world in order to concentrate instead on resolving problems within Soviet society. "Permanent revolution" gradually lost favor as "building socialism in one country" became a more acceptable platform.

Circumstances encouraged such realism: revolution had not spread across the world in the aftermath of World War I. Despite one Bolshevik's prediction that all Europe would be Communist by 1919, Europe in fact had begun to swing in another direction, with Italy and Hungary turning to fascism shortly after the war.[2] Shortly thereafter in China, Chiang Kai-shek brutally suppressed his Communist allies, postponing a Communist revolution in that country for more than two decades. As fascism gained power in Germany in 1933 and in Spain in 1939, the Soviet Union played the foreign policy game cautiously. In 1939, Stalin demonstrated that strategy had taken complete precedence over ideology when he orchestrated a nonaggression pact with the Nazis (whom he had denounced less than a year before as the worst enemy of Communism). Irony succeeded irony. After the German invasion of the U.S.S.R. in 1941, the Soviet government found itself in an alliance with the very powers that had invaded its country two decades earlier—the United States, Great Britain, and France.

Despite incomparable losses in World War II (including 20 million Soviet lives), the U.S.S.R. managed to increase its territory, expanding into the Baltic republics, Bessarabia, parts of Poland and Finland,

Tuva (on the border with Mongolia), the Kurile Islands, and part of the island of Sakhalin in Soviet Asia. East Germany also fell into the Soviet camp, part of the fruits of sharing in the victory against Nazism. Elections of varying degrees of legitimacy brought Communist governments to Czechoslovakia, Poland, and Hungary. Having learned from the German onslaught of 1941 that weak neighbors make a poor defense, Stalin after the war took steps to protect the Soviet Union from former allies turned enemies—military and political—to establish a "friendly" perimeter.

In 1953, upon the death of Stalin, a new collective leadership, from which Khrushchev eventually emerged as first among equals, engineered a shift in foreign policy. The U.S.S.R. withdrew from Austria, abandoned military and naval bases in Finland, and participated in negotiations to end the Korean and Indo-Chinese wars. The Warsaw Pact Treaty, signed on the same day as the Austrian Peace Treaty, served notice that although the Soviet Union was tempering Stalin's foreign policy, the socialist countries in Eastern Europe would be militarily unified. The crushing of the 1956 Hungarian uprising also indicated that the U.S.S.R. would go to great lengths to keep its perimeter as "friendly" as possible.

Khrushchev exhibited a certain brashness in foreign policy. Later called "adventurism" by his political opponents, Khrushchev's style precipitated crises in Berlin, leading to the building of the Berlin Wall to separate East from West, and in Cuba, over the placement of nuclear missiles. Despite this intermittent brinkmanship, Khrushchev's most important contribution to the language and practice of Soviet foreign policy was his conception of "peaceful coexistence," a refinement of earlier accommodationist policy: the Soviet Union would live alongside capitalism, remain wary of it, but refrain from provoking it into conflict.

Although Khrushchev's successor, Leonid Brezhnev, held to the doctrine of peaceful coexistence, this rhetorical adherence did not preclude breaking the peace to preserve Soviet national security. The Red Army's 1968 invasion of Czechoslovakia initiated what later came to be known as the Brezhnev doctrine: the U.S.S.R. would intervene in the affairs of neighboring Communist countries to defend embattled governments (a policy foreshadowed by the 1956 Soviet invasion of Hungary). The invasion of Afghanistan in 1979 was a more recent expression of this policy. Outside the defensive perimeter, the Brezhnev administration interpreted peaceful coexistence as détente with the West over European issues but selective confrontation in the Third World, for instance in Ethiopia and Angola. When détente faltered in the mid-1970s, the Soviet government continued to add to its nuclear stockpile and conventional armaments deployed in Europe and relied for the most part on supplying arms to the Third World to gain influence there.

On the eve of Gorbachev's succession, Soviet foreign policy had little focus; policy makers had no consistent policy on maintaining influence in Eastern Europe or gaining influence in the Third World. The U.S.S.R. had accepted a costly status quo in the Cold War with the United States and was unclear about how to defuse East–West tensions without compromising strategic imperatives. The muddle in external affairs reflected and to a degree accentuated the muddle in domestic politics and in the economy: a stagnant economy was the domestic equivalent of a stagnant world view.

As they attempted to rationalize domestic inefficiencies, the Gorbachev reformers took a fresh look at Soviet policy toward the rest of the world. The characteristics of this "rationalized" foreign policy in East–West relations, Eastern Europe, regional relations outside Europe, and multilateralism are instructive. Soviet policy makers have put forward proposals targeting each of these aspects of international relations. As we shall see, however, a certain logic binds the disparate elements together.

East-West Relations

ARMS CONTROL

After the INF treaty mandated the removal of its SS-20s, the U.S.S.R. has pursued a third "zero option" by calling for the elimination of SNF, has looked to START negotiations to reduce ICBMs (including SLBMs and GLCMs), has sought to go beyond the MBFR and CDE talks by implementing "reasonable sufficiency" and "non-provocative defense" in conjunction with the CFE talks, and has tried to deep-six SDI by enforcing a "strict" interpretation of the ABM treaty.

At first glance, it would seem that only a code breaker could make sense of this string of initials and jargon. But hidden behind these abbreviated terms is evidence of the most profound change in Soviet foreign policy under Gorbachev: a radical new attitude toward controlling the arms race. The following account of the genesis of this new attitude provides the clues for deciphering the coded language of arms control.

The contours of Soviet "new thinking" on arms control and disarmament can perhaps best be seen in the negotiations that eventually produced the Intermediate Nuclear Force Treaty (INF), which led to the elimination of intermediate-range nuclear missiles from Europe and Asia. Ratified by the U.S. Congress in 1987, the treaty has been touted by hard-liners in the West as a victory for the "bargain from strength" school of dealing with the Soviets. The complex developments leading to the INF treaty, however, tell a different story.

In 1977, the Soviet Union began replacing its intermediate-range nuclear missiles facing Europe, removing SS-5s and substituting SS-20s. Although mobile (therefore less vulnerable) and more accurate than its predecessor, the SS-20 missile did not provide any greater range (3,700 km in both cases).[3] Capable of striking only within the European "theater," the SS-20 was a nuclear weapon with a limited range. It was also not a weapon that substantially improved Soviet capacity to destroy the region.[4]

In 1979, NATO began using the SS-20 deployments to justify the placement of U.S. intermediate-range weapons, the Pershing II and Cruise missiles, in Western Europe. Though declared "theater" weapons by the U.S. government, Pershing II and Cruise missiles were actually strategic in nature: they were capable of striking the Soviet Union itself, not simply Soviet allies within the European theater. As such, the new U.S. Euromissiles represented a significant advance over the existing Euromissiles, the Pershing I, in range and in accuracy and were categorically different from the SS-20s. With improved accuracy and the ability to reach Soviet territory within minutes, the Euromissiles pushed the U.S.S.R. closer to a launch-on-warning posture, in which even false indications of incoming missiles would initiate a Soviet nuclear response.

Although the United States claimed the deployments were necessary to balance the nuclear equation, plans to develop the Pershing II missile and substitute it for Pershing I in Europe actually originated in 1971, six years before the Soviets deployed SS-20s.[5] Independent of Soviet plans, the United States had decided to upgrade its Euromissiles to provide its allies with a concrete reassurance that the Atlantic alliance between North America and Western Europe still held (a move welcomed by many European leaders). Only later did the Soviet Union's SS-20s serve to make a potentially unpopular modernization of the nuclear arsenal more palatable to the U.S. Congress as well as to the citizens of the United States and Europe.

Negotiations to reduce, eliminate, or otherwise affect the deployment of the INF missiles began in 1979. The failure of these negotiations to reduce Soviet SS-20s or prevent deployment of U.S. Pershing II and Cruise missiles stems from the deteriorating arms control relationship between the United States and the Soviet Union. Since the détente of the early 1970s had come to an end, both sides had adopted inflexible postures on arms control. In the 1980s, the Soviet arms control agenda included the following demands: reductions in U.S. forward-based systems (in this case, nuclear-armed aircraft), inclusion of French and British nuclear weapons in negotiations, and, since 1983, forestalling the Strategic Defense Initiative (SDI) or "Star Wars" (space-based ballistic missile defenses). The United States, meanwhile, demanded extensive on-site verification of treaties, elimination of Soviet intermediate-range nuclear weapons based in Asia, and deep cuts in long-range weapons through the Strategic Arms Reduction Talks (START)—in part to neutralize the area of greatest Soviet nuclear strength, in part to make the SDI system more feasible.[6] In the late 1970s and into the 1980s, any of these demands could have produced "bargaining chips"—weapons systems that function as pivotal concessions in negotiating reductions in the systems of one's adversaries. But no effective agreements emerged and no bargaining chips were sincerely offered—reflecting a steady worsening in the climate of U.S.–Soviet relations.

In 1981, the Reagan administration unveiled the "zero option," offering to forgo the Pershing II and Cruise deployments if the Soviet Union eliminated its SS-20s. It was a proposal that, because of uncompromising stipulations, the United States knew the Soviets would not accept. The Brezhnev administration believed it needed the SS-20s to balance the European nuclear equation, offset U.S. superiorities in forward-based systems and sea-based missiles, and counter British and French nuclear weapons. The U.S.S.R. also insisted on a maximalist position, rejecting *any* U.S. INF deployments.[7] Each side believed it was acting in its own best security interests; neither side saw any compelling reason to compromise.

This impasse made an arms control treaty to stop the INF deployments of both sides very unlikely. The U.S.S.R. offered several concessions but would not budge from its maximalist position.[8] The United States began deploying Euromissiles in late 1983. SS-20s remained untouched.

The forces that eventually cut this arms control knot largely came from outside the negotiating process. Two enormous grassroots movements—the European campaign against U.S. INF missiles and the Nuclear Freeze campaign in the United States—elevated the anti–nuclear weapons viewpoint to the platforms of several influential political parties in NATO countries.[9] In 1985, a new Soviet leadership added another wrinkle to the situation: unprecedented flexibility on arms control issues. A series of Soviet initiatives began to challenge NATO governments already well aware of the mass appeal of antinuclear sentiment on both sides of the Atlantic.

Within one month of taking office, Gorbachev gave his first major East–West policy speech and with it the announcement of a moratorium on deployment of Soviet intermediate-range missiles in Europe.[10] Three months later, in July 1985, he announced a unilateral moratorium on the testing of nuclear warheads that he promised would become permanent if the United States made a similar pledge. The United States did not take up the Soviet challenge.

In October 1985, Gorbachev unleashed another flurry of proposals: reduction of strategic nuclear weapons by 50 percent, prohibition of the testing and deployment of space weapons, and a willingness to reduce land-based missiles aimed at Europe. Built into the first two proposals was a challenge to the Reagan administration and its stated desire to pare down strategic weapons through START: if the United States wanted treaties on strategic weapons, then the Strategic Defense Initiative (SDI) would have to be a bargaining chip.

In addition to fearing an arms race in space, the U.S.S.R. worried that "Star Wars" would allow the United States to launch a first strike with impunity. At the 1985 Geneva summit, the first time the leaders of the two superpowers had met since 1979, the Soviets voiced these concerns and discovered that SDI was not in fact a bargaining chip. Reagan truly believed in SDI for ideological and strategic reasons (though others in the administration approved of using it as a bargaining chip to extract major Soviet concessions). Agreements on nuclear weapons in Europe would not proceed until this SDI obstacle was cleared.

Within a month of the fruitless Geneva summit, Gorbachev made another offer: a freeze on all Soviet and U.S. medium-range missiles in Europe, followed by reductions on both sides. Scarcely another month passed before the next proposal was on the table: a comprehensive disarmament plan dubbed in the West "Disarmament 2000." Under this elaborate long-term plan, intermediate-range missiles would be eliminated over the course of five to seven years, nuclear and conventional disarmament would proceed in a mutual and verifiable fashion until completed in the year 2000, and the financial resources freed would, in part, be directed toward international economic development. Furthermore, in an important policy reversal, the Soviet government declared that it would consider British and French nuclear arsenals separate from U.S. missiles.

Despite lack of interest from the United States, Soviet proposals continued, including a summit to discuss solely the nuclear test ban question (the unilateral moratorium was still in progress) and concessions if the United States agreed to forgo space-based defenses for fifteen to twenty years. In an important change in principle, the U.S.S.R. also permitted a private U.S. organization, the Natural Resources Defense Council, to verify the testing moratorium on-site at Semipalatinsk.

In one stroke, the October 1986 Reykjavik summit changed the climate of arms control. Gorbachev and Reagan came close to an agreement eliminating all intermediate-range missiles in Europe and limiting warheads outside Europe to one hundred on each side. Such a staggering proposal—the virtual elimination of all intercontinental land- and submarine-based missiles—would have been an enormous step toward disarmament. In a repeat of Geneva, however, SDI had come between the superpowers and this goal; Reagan simply refused to put any brakes on his cherished "Star Wars" program.

Taken collectively, Soviet concessions were having a demonstrable effect on the hearts and minds of Europeans. According to polls conducted by the United States Information Agency in 1987, Europeans overwhelmingly considered Gorbachev, not Reagan, the more forthcoming in arms control negotiations. In Germany, where a conservative government staunchly supported NATO, the gap was widest: 72 percent of Germans polled looked to Gorbachev as peacemaker, only 9 percent to Reagan. Pressure for NATO to respond to Gorbachev was increasing.

The breakthrough finally came in late February 1987, only two days after the U.S.S.R. resumed nuclear tests. Gorbachev announced a plan that resembled President Reagan's "zero option" of six years previous: the elimination of all medium-range missiles in Europe within five years without concomitant agreements on either strategic weapons, forward-based systems, French and British nuclear arsenals, or SDI. The Gorbachev administration had virtually scrapped the entire Soviet arms control agenda of the previous decade in pursuit of an agreement. The maximalist position of the Brezhnev administration was no more.

Even this rewriting of Soviet policy was not sufficient for the Reagan administration. Immediately on the heels of these Soviet concessions, the United States demanded another: extensive on-site verification measures. When the U.S.S.R. agreed to this form of treaty verification—a measure it had opposed for years—the Reagan administration and NATO were truly perplexed. Unexpected Soviet compliance with virtually every U.S. demand confronted U.S. policy makers with a serious problem. On the one hand, the Soviets offered an arithmetically attractive deal with the proposed INF treaty— destroying roughly four warheads for every one U.S. warhead. On the other hand, a U.S. withdrawal of nuclear weapons from Europe would violate a Reagan administration promise of a "nuclear umbrella" over its NATO allies.

It was only when the new zero option became more comprehensive that an agreement could be reached. Reagan eventually accepted the double zero option (eliminating shorter-range INF), and the U.S.S.R. subsequently agreed to a global double zero option (giving up all its medium-range missiles in Asia). After resolving a side issue on Pershing 1A missiles, which the United States and West Germany at first refused to include in the treaty, the two superpowers finally agreed in principle to the INF treaty in September 1987.

The history of the negotiations behind the INF treaty does not simply reveal Soviet "new thinking" on arms control. It demonstrates as well that the INF treaty was the end product more of remarkable Soviet flexibility than of U.S. hard-line policies. The Soviets agreed to unlink INF negotiations from SDI, agreed to a modified zero option, threw into the deal its Asian missiles, compromised over on-site verification, and agreed, in the end, to destroy far more warheads than would the United States.

Why the sudden Soviet about-face on arms control? Again, this sea change in foreign policy reflects in part domestic economic concerns—in this case the economic implications of military spending. While foreign trade is expected to bring in needed hard currency and foodstuffs, it is really from guns that the reformers expect to make butter. Since the 1960s, the Soviet Union has allocated a significant percentage of its Gross National Product to the military (15 to 17 percent by CIA estimates).[11] Imagine, the reformers urge their colleagues, all the rubles that could profitably be redirected. In light of the economic difficulties outlined in the previous chapter, such a proposal must hold considerable appeal for Soviet policy makers desperate to locate funds for industrial modernization and increased consumer goods.

Cutting back on military production also fits the reformers' desire to wean the Soviet economy away from its reliance on heavy industry.[12] Historically, the two concerns have gone hand in hand: the armament industry was a chief beneficiary of rapid industrialization during the 1930s. World War II and the Cold War permitted the defense ministries to receive as many resources as they annually requested, resources that were then sent to industries run as inefficiently as their U.S. counterparts.[13] For national security reasons, the Soviet government has tolerated this drain on the economy and has hesitated to disrupt the mutually supportive relationship of hammer and missile. In contrast, the Gorbachev camp is actively seeking to sever the link, challenging both the military establishment and heavy industry. For the reformers, then, the future entails turning swords not into sickles but rather into canned tomatoes and home computers.

For this transformation to be successful, the Soviet Union must push the arms control debate far beyond the INF treaty. After all, this treaty did not save the U.S.S.R. any money: verification and dismantling costs have actually increased expenses. And only 4 percent of the superpowers' nuclear arsenals were affected. But the INF treaty did send a signal to the Soviet military that it should not expect enormous government subsidies to continue. For the signal to translate into an official practice, the Gorbachev administration requires additional treaties covering the remaining nuclear weapons in Europe, the strategic weapons that are the mainstays of the nuclear arsenals, the prohibitively expensive SDI option, and most important, the conventional weapons that absorb close to 80 percent of the military expenditures of both sides.

In terms of the nuclear weapons still in Europe—the short-range nuclear force, or SNF—the United States and Britain have rejected negotiations and supported a modernization campaign to improve the quality and quantity of these battlefield nuclear weapons. [14] The West German government's position, as it emerged during 1989, was to delay modernization and begin immediate talks with an eager Soviet Union on reducing and potentially eliminating these weapons (the third and final zero option).

With NATO threatened by this internal division, Gorbachev offered another unilateral measure in May 1989 to demonstrate continued Soviet interest in the third zero option: a cut of 500 weapons—a 5 percent reduction—from short-range nuclear forces in Europe. In a hard-fought compromise at the June NATO summit, the United States agreed to put off modernization until 1992 and support talks on the weapons. But Bush was careful to add that the aim of the negotiations would be "partial" reductions: "Partial means partial," he emphasized. "There will be no third zero." [15]

The Soviets have also expressed interest in reducing their most important nuclear weapon: the land-based intercontinental ballistic missile (ICBM). In June 1989, START negotiations resumed, and both sides indicated that a 50 percent reduction over seven years in long-range missiles would be possible, although the treaty would not cover submarine-launched Cruise missiles.

The Soviets have traditionally been concerned with negotiating "Star Wars" out of the heavens. "Star Wars" has been mentioned several times in the preceding discussion: as a "bargaining chip" that was never played, as a major element of U.S. nuclear strategy, as a chief worry of Soviet policy makers. SDI is not one but three different *types* of system: a population defense, a protector of key military sites, and an offensive weapon. Reagan originally spoke of the system in the first sense: as a grand protective bubble over U.S. territory, a constellation of lasers and remote-control debris that would knock out all incoming nuclear weapons. As military planners began to estimate the staggering costs of such a system and scientists began to predict that even under a best-case scenario it would be only 95 percent effective (thus allowing in a sufficient number of nukes to destroy the United States), SDI became more useful in its second sense, as protection for missile silos and other military installations.

In both senses, however, SDI could act as (and could certainly be perceived as) an offensive weapon. If U.S. military strategists deemed either the U.S. population or U.S. nuclear capability sufficiently protected, the United States might consider a first strike on the Soviet Union a viable option.[16] Rather than making the world safe from nuclear weapons, SDI turns out to be a tremendously destabilizing system, providing neither side with enhanced security.

The strongest supporters of SDI were, one decade earlier, vigorous opponents of the ABM treaty.[17] Antiballistic missile systems (ABMs) were also supposed to defend cities and military sites from incoming missiles—but from a terrestrial, not celestial, location. Realizing that such a defensive weapon would only encourage more military spending, the U.S.S.R. and the United States eventually agreed to limit the number of ABM sites to one per country. The Soviet Union has argued that SDI violates this treaty, if not in word then certainly in intent. The Reagan administration "broadly" interpreted the ABM treaty to condone space-based defense systems and proceeded to pour billions of dollars into SDI's research and development. The Soviets have until recently preferred not to reduce their stock of long-range weapons unless SDI is shelved (the fewer long-range weapons the Soviets could throw at SDI, the more effective and therefore threatening the system would become).[18] In September 1989, however, Foreign Minister Shevardnadze announced that interpretation of the ABM treaty—and consequently the SDI system—should not stand in the way of a strategic nuclear weapons agreement. The dispute over SDI and the ABM treaty has not been resolved, simply postponed.

SDI, though expensive, is not the chief fear of Soviet accountants. After all, conventional weapons—tanks, artillery, aircraft—and the troops that use them consume most of the military budgets of the superpowers. Without agreements on these nonnuclear weapons, arms control will not free substantial funds for re-allocation in the Soviet economy. Without cuts in conventional weaponry, the Gorbachev plan to trim the military by 14 percent and weapons production by 19 percent—and eventually slash the defense budget by a third—will simply not materialize.[19] But such agreements have not been forthcoming. The Mutual and Balanced Force Reduction talks (MBFR) dragged on for fifteen years, producing few results—not even a set of mutually satisfactory definitions. While the related conference on Confidence- and Security-Building Measures and Disarmament in Europe (CDE) has produced several agreements, including the monitoring of military exercises and the prior notification of large troop movements, no concrete steps have been taken to reduce conventional armaments. In these negotiations, NATO has continually insisted on large asymmetrical reductions in Soviet tanks, while Warsaw Pact negotiators have traditionally countered that NATO possesses a large advantage in air and sea power.

Here, too, Soviet initiatives have been instrumental in breaking the deadlock. A key element in recent Soviet thinking on conventional arms is the recasting of Warsaw Pact doctrine to switch the emphasis from offense to defense.[20] The Soviet Union has declared the avoidance of war to be the most important aspect of its military posture and has therefore begun systematically to structure preemptive or first-strike options out of its forces. Military analyst John Steinbrunner explains:

> The calculus implicit in these principles accepts some risk about the potential outcome of a hypothetical war in order to increase insurance that it will not be initiated. It assumes that there is no

inexorable reason for war between the Warsaw Treaty Organization (WTO) and NATO and that Soviet national security can
safely rest on the assumption that major war will be indefinitely
avoided.[21]

Another Gorbachev term for this new military doctrine is "reasonable sufficiency": the Soviet military will maintain only the requisite
force to prevent the outbreak of war. As a basis for streamlining the
military, this principle dovetails with the rationalizing of the Soviet
economy. The Gorbachev administration treats the military as it
would an inefficiently run enterprise: military operations too must
suffer the effects of the cost-benefit analysis of "new thinking." Since
the military old guard is reluctant to suffer these cuts, they are being
retired or relegated to less important assignments. Military officers
such as Defense Minister Dmitri Yazov have consequently risen in
the political hierarchy in proportion to their support for "reasonable
sufficiency."[22]

This change in doctrine has also been translated into specific and
concrete proposals. An important first effect of the shift was a new
Soviet willingness to make asymmetrical cuts in conventional
weapons, thus eliminating what had previously been a point of contention between the arms control negotiators. The first stage in this
process was the submission of "official, responsible data" on the
forces of both superpowers. Should imbalances appear, the Soviets
said, asymmetrical cuts should follow—on both sides.[23]

In his December 1988 speech to the United Nations, Gorbachev
dramatically built upon this concession. He pledged a reduction over
two years of 500,000 troops (withdrawing a total of 50,000 from
Hungary, Czechoslovakia, and East Germany), 10,000 tanks (including half of the Warsaw Pact tanks stationed in Eastern Europe), 8,500
artillery systems, and 800 combat aircraft.[24] With these remarkable
unilateral proposals, Gorbachev challenged NATO in an effort to
break the deadlock in arms control negotiations over conventional
weapons (much as Soviet concessions on nuclear weapons accelerated the INF negotiations).

These unilateral proposals are now becoming unilateral actions,
and though they by no means eliminate Soviet offensive weapons
from Europe, they nonetheless indicate a desire to see the major

hardware of the two military alliances dismantled. Though dramatic, these concessions were only the beginning.

In the spring of 1989, the U.S.S.R. presented its proposal at the Conventional Forces in Europe (CFE) talks, the successor to both the MBFR and CDE negotiations. Following its promise to make asymmetrical cuts, the Soviets offered to reduce 40,000 tanks, 47,000 artillery pieces, and 42,000 armored vehicles.[25] In agreeing to reduce the levels of both sides, the Soviets have agreed, for example, to eliminate between fifteen and eighteen tanks for every one tank the United States eliminates. According to one Pentagon official, the Soviets "have come forward with some numbers that basically are a severe limitation on themselves and nobody else."[26] For their part, the United States and NATO agreed to include aircraft and personnel limits, a concession previously avoided. Not only have the Soviets acknowledged their own superiority in certain categories of conventional weapons in Europe, they are proposing to remove these superiorities in what would amount to unilateral disarmament.

Obviously, the U.S.S.R. is not withdrawing all its forces facing Western Europe. Substantial Soviet conventional forces will remain even if the first round of CFE talks produces a treaty. And many of the most numerically significant Soviet reductions will be little more than spring cleaning (most of the tanks to be eliminated, for instance, are pre-1965 models).

The planned disarmament is nevertheless important. The most expensive element of the military—nonnuclear weapons—will finally be subject to arms control. The doctrine of reasonable sufficiency will be demonstrated in a verifiable manner. Further, if the first round of CFE achieves reductions to equal levels, successive negotiations will mandate additional symmetrical cuts. The most tangible sign of the Cold War—troops and tanks stationed in Europe forty years after the end of World War II—will gradually become less important. As it loses its capacity to threaten, the military hardware of the two alliances will no longer irrevocably divide Eastern from Western Europe. On this last point, the Soviet Union is pursuing a far-reaching policy, of which arms control is but one element.

WESTERN EUROPE

One traditional interpretation of Soviet policy toward Western Europe is the "wedge-driving" theory: the Soviet Union appeals to the Western European countries as fellow family members in their common home—Europe—in order to disrupt the Atlantic alliance. While the new Soviet leadership has certainly taken advantage of divisions within NATO (especially on the question of nuclear weapons based in Europe), the wedge driving has been more an occasional technique than a deliberate foreign policy goal.

Rather than trying to weaken NATO loyalties, the U.S.S.R. has recently preferred to project itself as peacemaker in the political sphere and dealmaker in the economic sphere. With regard to Western Europe, the U.S.S.R. has tried the strategy before. In 1975, at the crest of the previous détente, the U.S.S.R. signed the Helsinki Accords, which divided European questions into three baskets: security, cooperation in the economic and scientific spheres, and human rights. Although it yielded important confidence-building measures and spurred the development of human rights movements in Eastern Europe and the U.S.S.R., the Helsinki framework reflected desired goals rather than legislating concrete actions. When the thirty-five nations met again in 1989, a change in Soviet policy was evident, as the U.S.S.R. accepted more stringent guarantees for human rights and prepared the ground for significant cuts in conventional weapons.[27] The message to Western Europe was clear: the Soviets were more cooperative than ever before.

In this latest incarnation as peacemaker, the Soviet Union need only appear more willing to compromise on arms control questions than the United States. The diplomatic advantages of this policy are important. By wooing NATO leaders such as Margaret Thatcher and Helmut Kohl, the Soviet Union can accelerate the next round of arms talks—on both short-range nuclear and conventional weapons.[28] Without critical Western European support for treaties, the CFE talks would, for instance, probably achieve no more than the previous MBFR talks.

Meanwhile, as dealmaker, the Soviet Union negotiates critical joint economic projects that bring in hard currency and high-technology imports. The trend did not begin with Gorbachev. The

Europe

1982 oil pipeline deal was a prime example of a cooperative venture between Western Europe and the Soviet Union (negotiated over the objections of the United States). More recent Soviet readiness to do business has already reaped significant rewards. In ten days in October 1988, Western European countries (and Japan) offered $9 billion in credit to the U.S.S.R., exceeding by $1 billion the entire new lending to the Soviets in the previous three years.[29] The Soviet government plans to use such lines of credit to reform the food and consumer goods industries. For their part, European leaders expect to gain further access to the huge Soviet market.

The unification of the Common Market in 1992 is of critical importance to the Soviets. As a financial entity, Europe exports three times as much as the United States or Japan. Equally important, it imports twice as much as the United States and six times as much as Japan.[30] On the one hand, a united Europe will serve as a source of commodities and high technology. On the other hand, should the U.S.S.R. develop more marketable exports, the new Europe will serve as a critical selling place. With this integrated market to the West and the successful Pacific economies to the East, the U.S.S.R. can turn its geographic position into gold. Whether as a financial center, an import-export haven, or simply a conduit for transportation and communication, the U.S.S.R. could emerge as a reinvigorated economic superpower. But it needs capital to develop these potentials (as well as to fulfill pressing domestic needs).

Since that capital has not been forthcoming from the United States, the U.S.S.R. must look elsewhere. Forty percent of new lending to the U.S.S.R. comes from Japan and 30 percent from West Germany (only 2 percent comes from the United States).[31] The majority of joint ventures are with Western European firms. Soviet managers are being sent to Western European training centers. In terms of providing pivotal economic support for the new Soviet policies, Western Europe is far out in front of its Atlantic allies. If a wedge separates the Atlantic alliance, it will be because Western Europe wants it that way, for economic reasons.

Defusing the military confrontation of alliances on European soil is a component of Soviet economic strategy. Such a decoupling, however, could only be mutual: a wedge driven in the Atlantic alliance would have to be balanced by a wedge driven in the Warsaw Pact. As such, the implications of arms control and Soviet–Western European relations bear heavily on the future of the other participants in the Soviet military alliance. If the wedge-driving theory applies anywhere, it is to the U.S.S.R.'s relations with Eastern European countries, many of which are now unusually interested in becoming part of the common home of Europe.

Eastern Europe

Poland and Hungary are now multiparty states—an unthinkable development several years ago. Furthermore, present Soviet leadership has encouraged these transformations—twenty years ago, invasion would have been more likely. The alliance system, so much a part of the Cold War confrontation, is breaking apart, with its first fault line running from Warsaw to Budapest. This ongoing process has a familiar ring. Recent events seem to indicate that the Cold War is slowly being replayed—in reverse.

Soviet foreign policy toward Europe during and after World War II served as a major impetus for U.S. Cold War policy. Allegations of Soviet expansionism in the region—funding Greek insurgents, grabbing Eastern Europe, undermining democratic governments in Western Europe—in part led to the U.S. policy of containment, the establishment of the Central Intelligence Agency and the National Security Council, and the bisection of the world into East and West. Soviet actions, in other words, precipitated U.S. hard-line responses. This version of events, however, does not quite capture the origins of the Cold War.

In a secret meeting in 1944, Churchill and Stalin sat down in Moscow to discuss the division of postwar Central Europe. In the infamous "percentage plan," Churchill conceded to Stalin the right to "take" Hungary, Bulgaria, and Rumania while "keeping" Greece in the Western camp. Influence in Yugoslavia was to be shared equally.[32] Poland had been gradually ceded to Soviet influence at the Allied conferences in Teheran, Yalta, and Potsdam.[33] Prior to the end of World War II and certainly before Churchill's formal christening of the Iron Curtain in 1946, two camps—East and West—had been established, with the consent of both sides.[34]

But these secret deals and high policy decisions remained in the background. Immediately following World War II, East and West were ostensible allies, working together on the restructuring of Europe and looking forward to a possible world order presided over by the newly created United Nations. On the surface, then, the countries of Eastern Europe sought to establish their own governments with the advice and consent of both East and West. In the first round of postwar elections, Eastern European Communist parties commanded a majority of votes only in Czechoslovakia, and in all countries political coalitions emerged. While the Soviet Union unquestionably lent support to the Communist partners in these coalitions, it nonetheless pursued an "inclusionary" line[35]—respecting the political balance of power in Eastern European governments and abiding by previous agreements on spheres of influence such as Yalta.[36] When Hungarian Communists, for instance, wanted to take power immediately after voters in the 1945 elections by a slim majority endorsed a revolutionary course, Moscow disagreed. At the time, the U.S.S.R. did not want to push the West (even though, according to the Stalin–Churchill agreement, the U.S.S.R. had the "right" to Hungary).[37]

Two key issues eventually led to the abandoning of this inclusionary line. The most obvious postwar blunder was the treatment of the "German problem." A unified, re-armed Germany was Stalin's major security concern. Yet, the Allies never agreed on specific targets for German reparations and, in the spring of 1946, halted existing payments. The de-Nazification program bogged down, U.S. intelligence began using former Nazis as informants on the Soviet Union, and West Germany was permitted to re-arm (joining NATO in 1955, only ten years after the war's end). Having seen a defeated Germany rise again after World War I to attack Russian soil, the Soviet Union was understandably irritated at this lax treatment of the "German problem."

The other Western miscue was more subtle. In February 1946, when the Allies were still theoretically allies, Stalin made a speech predicting an "inevitable" war. U.S. officials reacted immediately, calling on their chargé d'affaires in Moscow, George Kennan, to explain the speech. Kennan responded with the now famous "long telegram," which later grew into the policy of "containment." In this communication, Kennan pointed out something the U.S. government mysteriously ignored: Stalin had not been referring to an inevitable war between the U.S.S.R. and the West but an unavoidable conflict between England and the United States.[38] In the minds of U.S. policy makers, however, this interimperial war that Stalin (mistakenly) envisioned became an East–West conflict, to be triggered by Soviet expansionism that must in turn be contained.

Given these mistakes—plus a good dose of paranoia from Stalin and vigorous anti-Sovietism from Churchill—a Cold War was hard to avoid.[39] And in the growing divisiveness of this Cold War, the tenuous political coalitions of Eastern Europe quickly collapsed. Stalin turned to an "exclusionary" policy, encouraging Communist parties in 1947 to seize power throughout the region. The West followed a similarly aggressive policy. Several U.S. actions during the period— for instance, the Marshall Plan and National Security Act of 1947 —served in part to hasten the disintegration of the region's independence, by enforcing the East–West divide. Even George Kennan, the theoretical architect of containment, recognized the perverse implications of these policies. As historian John Lewis Gaddis points out:

> Kennan regarded several of [the U.S. government's] major actions between 1948 and 1950—the formation of the North Atlantic Treaty Organization, the creation of an independent West German state, the insistence on retaining American forces in postoccupation Japan, and the decision to build the hydrogen bomb—as certain to reinforce Soviet feelings of suspicion and insecurity, and, hence, to narrow opportunities for negotiations.[40]

Ironically, the very policies designed to preserve Eastern European independence served in the end to compromise it.

Through the 1950s and 1960s, the interplay between the hard-line policies of both superpowers continued to have an unfortunate effect on Eastern Europe. Refusing to let Eastern European countries determine their own political paths, the U.S.S.R. frequently intervened militarily or threatened to do so: in East Germany (1953), Hungary (1956), Poland (1956), and Czechoslovakia (1968). Meanwhile the United States just as readily reinforced the division of Europe. In 1955, NATO accepted West Germany into its ranks. The Soviets were appalled that a mere decade after losing the war, Germany was entering a military alliance. The U.S.S.R.'s response was to create its own military alliance in 1955—the Warsaw Pact. In the 1960s, the United States developed "flexible response," a military doctrine of preparing for both conventional and nuclear war in Europe. The Soviets responded by stationing troops in Czechoslovakia.[41] By 1968, this Soviet tendency to consolidate its position vis-à-vis Western Europe and the United States produced the Brezhnev doctrine, a policy statement no more respectful of the sovereignty of neighboring countries than the United States' Monroe Doctrine.

Since World War II, Soviet relations with Eastern Europe have reflected a tension between a stated desire for unity and a recognition of national differences. With some exceptions, Stalin and Brezhnev favored undifferentiated unity. A hostile world, they reasoned, necessitated a common front against the West; the imperialists would otherwise exploit divisions. Many Eastern European leaders, though avowed Communists, preferred to emphasize the particularly national character of their country's development. In Yugoslavia, Tito's independence led to the severance of his country's alliance with the U.S.S.R. Albania's Enver Hoxha also guided his country away from Soviet influence. With these examples fresh in his mind, Khrushchev modified Soviet policy to permit Communist countries to pursue their own paths to socialism, confident that such flexibility would lead to less rancor in the alliance. On two occasions, however, the policy was significantly amended: in 1956 (Hungary)[42] and 1961 (the Berlin Wall).

The Gorbachev reformers have deliberately resuscitated Khrushchev's initial policy toward Eastern Europe. The Soviet Union, according to Gorbachev, has "unconditional respect in international practice for the right of every people to choose the paths and forms of its development."[43] Does this apply to Eastern Europe, the first line of defense for the Soviet Union? Yes, says Gorbachev:

All parties are fully and irreversibly independent. We said that as long ago as the 20th Congress. True, it took time to free ourselves of the old habits. Now, however, this is an immutable reality.[44]

The Twentieth Party Congress in 1956 featured Khrushchev's defense of multiple paths to socialism. The old habits Gorbachev refers to are the errors of Brezhnevism and the Brezhnev doctrine: intervention and direct Soviet control.[45]

Gorbachev and his supporters still hope to preserve a defensive perimeter in Eastern Europe, apparently not through military force but by a prudent relaxing of controls. The national security goal remains the same—only the method has changed. The implications for Eastern European governments, however, are enormous, the opportunities for Eastern European citizens unprecedented.

Eastern Europe is not just an undifferentiated lump of countries. Marked historic and sociocultural differences separate the region's peoples—differences so marked, in fact, that several Eastern European countries simply do not get along. Hungary and Rumania, for example, have been waging a political battle for the past several decades over the status of ethnic Hungarians living in the Transylvania region of Rumania. Polish–East German tensions continue to break out over the border port of Szczecin. A play by Czech dissident Vaclav Havel opened in a Warsaw theater in 1989; former Polish premier Mieczyslaw Rakowski attended the premiere while Havel sat in a Czech jail. Regardless of a common socialist perspective, the "bloc" is not very bloc-like.

With the startling events of 1989, Eastern Europe has emerged as an even more disparate region. After roundtable negotiations between Communist parties and opposition movements, Poland and Hungary legalized multiparty systems and are taking the Gorbachev political reforms several steps further. East Germany, with thousands of émigrés streaming to the West and with a new leader as of October 1989, seems destined to follow. Czechoslovakia, meanwhile, has remained relatively immune from the changes going on around it. Rumania and Bulgaria have become more repressive, especially toward ethnic minorities. Yugoslavia, having pursued an independent path since 1948, is now struggling with inflation and increasing ethnic tensions.

Soviet leaders have clearly encouraged the camp of radical reform (Hungary, Poland), quietly spread the gospel of *perestroika* to the camp of damage controllers (East Germany, Czechoslovakia), and tried to distance themselves from the Stalinist holdovers (Rumania, Bulgaria). Will the model of radical reform serve as further inspiration for Soviet reform and pull the rest of Eastern Europe along? Or will the more conservative models continue to withstand the winds of *glasnost* and *perestroika* and act as a brake on Soviet reforms?

Poland is an excellent example of what is now possible in the new era of Soviet foreign policy. The Hungarians and Czechs, in 1956 and 1968, respectively, instituted reforms in some ways less dramatic than the Polish changes of 1989 and were promptly invaded by the Soviet Union. The Polish "revolution," by contrast, clearly had the backing of the Soviet leadership.[46] Without tacit support from the East, an illegal opposition movement could never have become a majority partner in a newly elected Polish government, all within seven months.

Never had an opposition movement in Poland had such success. In 1956, Polish workers protested for "Bread and Freedom," and seventy-four people died in the ensuing riot. In 1968, Polish students joined what seemed to be an international student protest movement only to be met by government repression. In 1970, workers in the Baltic ports went on strikes; in 1976, Poles rioted in protest over scheduled price increases on food; neither protest achieved political gain.

By 1980, many Polish workers and intellectuals had participated in several underground movements. With the rapid decline of the Polish economy, a new movement emerged, in the Gdansk shipyard in the north and the Silesian coal mines in the south: an independent trade union called Solidarity. Led by ex-electrician Lech Walesa, Solidarity grew to an almost unbelievable size: 10 million members (including a third of all Communist party members) out of a population of 36 million. Nor did Solidarity simply formulate trade union demands. It developed an economic and political platform that challenged many of the assumptions of central planning and one-party rule.

But 1981 was not a good year for change. The Soviet Union had invaded Afghanistan two years earlier, and the Brezhnev doctrine appeared to be intact (although Brezhnev himself showed signs of senility). The United States had meanwhile adopted a get-tough attitude toward the Soviets. The Cold War had been revived, and as in the immediate postwar period, independence efforts in Eastern Europe would suffer. In December 1981, General Wojciech Jaruzelski seized the reins of government, declaring martial law and banning Solidarity.[47]

Solidarity went underground: many members went to jail, many became hopelessly pessimistic about the possibility of change. In 1985, the government declared an amnesty, released political prisoners, and set about the difficult task of gaining a national consensus necessary to rebuild the shattered economy. There was hopeful news from Moscow: Gorbachev had come to power, pledging allegiance to the old Khrushchev line of different paths to socialism. The Polish government decided to test the waters. In October 1987, the government announced sweeping economic changes, including the creation of a securities market, a rise in prices, an increase in unemployment, a lessening of centralized control, and the liquidation of unprofitable businesses.[48] In an unusual move, the government also offered the Polish people an opportunity to approve this economic reform in a national referendum. In one of the most startling election results ever in a Communist country, the Polish people failed to endorse the economic package, indicating an unwillingness to bear the burdens of *perestroika* in inflation and labor give-backs.[49]

In May and August 1988, a new generation of workers struck at key factories. Stirred by this post–martial-law group of protesters, Solidarity began once again to voice its demands. The government initially stalled but finally agreed to a series of unprecedented negotiations, beginning in February 1989. Lasting six weeks, these round-table talks achieved a remarkable number of agreements in a short period of time. Solidarity was re-legalized. Quasi-free elections were set for June, with the Communist party (PZPR) and its lesser allies, the Peasant and Democratic parties, guaranteed 65 percent of the seats of the major chamber, the Sejm. Another chamber, the Senate, was reinstated, and elections to this body were to be unrestricted. On other issues, Solidarity was allowed to publish a daily and a weekly newspaper and produce election bulletins for radio and television. Though not eliminated, government censorship was diminished. A broad and somewhat ambiguous economic platform was ratified. Protection of the environment, restructuring of the legal system, and safeguarding of wages from inflation were all passed.

Solidarity, through its political arm, the Citizens' Committee, quickly organized for the elections. The results of the two rounds of June elections were unambiguous. With but one exception, Citizens' Committee candidates won every contested seat. Though Solidarity supporters occupied 99 out of 100 Senate seats and 35 percent of the Sejm, the Polish Communist party and its allies, the Democratic and Peasant parties, still held a majority.

The selection of Jaruzelski for president raised much debate, barely garnered sufficient votes, but eventually passed. In August, however, Solidarity balked at the Communist party's candidate for the critical position of prime minister: General Czeslaw Kiszczak, a figure closely associated with martial law. In a surprise move, the Communist party's traditional allies, the Democratic and Peasant parties, joined with Solidarity to propose longtime Solidarity activist Tadeusz Mazowiecki for the top government position. The Communist party, after some hesitation, went along. When Mazowiecki named his cabinet in September, eleven seats went to non-Communists, only four to the Communist party.

The implications of this apparently simply political process are enormous. For the first time, a ruling Communist party voluntarily relinquished a sizable portion of its power to its opposition. Poland now possesses the first truly coalitional government in Eastern Europe in forty years. The victory is not, of course, total. The Polish Communist party still retains control over defense and internal security; it also maintains influence over the economic system through the *nomenklatura*. Solidarity has pledged not to withdraw Poland from either CMEA (Council on Mutual Economic Assistance) or the Warsaw Pact, even though it may want to. Furthermore, Solidarity must now take responsibility for solving Poland's considerable economic problems, including $40 billion of foreign debt, spiraling inflation, food shortages, and unprofitable heavy industry.

But Poland has accomplished what the Soviet reformers have not yet managed: a multiparty state and the removal of the Communist party from government functions. Gorbachev and his reformers have consciously drawn inspiration from previous Eastern European experiments in reform. It will be interesting to see how much they borrow from Poland. As it stands, however, Poland is a testament to how far the Soviets have already gone in transforming the rhetoric of self-determination into actual practice.

Hungary is the other example of radical change in the region. When he replaced longtime Communist party leader Janos Kadar in 1988, Karoly Grosz pushed the Hungarian economy even further along Gorbachev's lines. He even had advice for the Soviet leader: "So far [Gorbachev] is only surface plowing. Now he has to cut deeper."[50] Now Hungary has weathered its own roundtable negotiations, has witnessed the rise of new legal parties, and is preparing for democratic elections in June 1990. At its Fourteenth Congress, in October 1989, the Hungarian Communist party renamed itself the Hungarian Socialist party and removed all vestiges of Stalinism from the Hungarian constitution. A sign of the times, Grosz is now the conservative, sharing a transitional four-person presidency with three noted reformers. Opposition parties are already forming shadow cabinets; the U.S.S.R. watches these events with apparent approval of the pragmatism of Hungarian Communists.[51]

With talk of democracy and capitalism sweeping their next-door neighbors, the Communist parties of Czechoslovakia and East Germany have so far resisted the sharing of power with opposition groups and large-scale implementation of free-market principles. The industrial outputs of both countries serve as one cushion. Between 1976 and 1980, both East Germany and Czechoslovakia devoted 60 to 70 percent of industrial investment to the modernization of existing plants (Poland, by comparison, used only 25 percent for that purpose).[52] The more conservative countries, according to certain indicators, have healthier economies than their reformist neighbors.[53]

East Germany's future relies in part on the actions of West Germany. East and West Germany are now like the twin children of divorced parents living in separate houses, hoping in the back of their minds that the differences that led to the separation will someday be reconciled. Since West German leader Willy Brandt expanded upon *Ostpolitik* (Eastern Policy) in the 1970s, the two Germanys have been able to move closer together despite the vicissitudes in the relations of their parents.

Under *Ostpolitik*, West Germany offers trade privileges and technology to East Germany. Cooperation is not confined to the economic sphere. In 1986, the Social Democratic party of West Germany (SPD) and the Communist party of East Germany (SED) jointly endorsed a zone free of nuclear and chemical weapons in Central Europe. Erich Honecker's September 1987 visit to West Germany was the first visit ever by an East German party chief—all sides concerned took pains to dispel any hopes or fears of a reunited Germany.

When thousands of East Germans began leaving their country for the West in the fall of 1989 (across the newly liberalized Hungarian-Austrian border), talk of reunification resurfaced. Just as failure to resolve the "German question" had contributed to initiating the Cold War, the same question—two Germanys or one—was reappearing at the potential close of the Cold War.[54] This is not surprising. Divided Germany has always been the Cold War writ small. For forty years, the two alliances have focused on armaments, not deep political disagreements such as the future of Germany. With possible arms control treaties leading to the lessening of military tensions in Central Europe, the political questions for which the tanks and nuclear weapons have substituted gain that much more prominence. One can only hope that the "German question" will be handled with greater aplomb during the waning of the Cold War than it was during its waxing.

From Poland to East Germany, the guarantors of political change have been independent political groups. Changes in Soviet foreign policy toward the region have, in most cases, simply given these groups more political space within which to operate. Some independents are enthusiastic about reforms in the Soviet Union, while others are skeptical. All demand reform in their own countries. As these groups become increasingly united across national boundaries—Polish and Hungarian activists demonstrating in Czechoslovakia, Green activists from across the region calling for a cleaner environment—they come to represent the future of Eastern Europe.[55]

If a consistent ideology unites these diverse voices, Hungarian writer George Konrad's neither-East-nor-West perspective comes the closest:

> I am neither a communist nor an anti-communist, neither a capitalist nor an anti-capitalist; if one must absolutely be for and against something, I consider a permanently open democracy to have the greatest good, and the ideological war that constantly casts the shadows of atomic war on the wall to be the greatest evil.[56]

This marriage of peace and human rights issues, combined with a strong concern for economic reform, can be found throughout Eastern Europe. In addition to Solidarity, for instance, Poland is home to the conscription resistance group Freedom and Peace (WiP), which has expanded its focus to include a wider range of political issues. In May 1987, despite government pressure, the group held a peace conference in Warsaw with 250 participants from thirteen countries: "the first unofficial East–West conference for activists ever held in Eastern Europe."[57] In 1988, the Polish government conceded to an important WiP demand by considering alternatives to military service.[58] Another Polish organization, the "Orange Alternative," offers more surrealistic protests against the government, sponsoring demonstrations in mock support of Stalin and Santa Claus.[59]

In Czechoslovakia, the decade-old human rights group Charter 77 brings together Communists, democratic socialists, liberals, and conservatives. In its 1985 "Prague Appeal," Charter 77 stressed many familiar themes:

> We do not seek to turn Europe into a third superpower but instead to overcome the superpower bloc structure by way of an alliance of free and independent nations within a democratic and self-governing all-European community living in friendship with the entire world.[60]

The Czech government has thus far resisted internal liberalization, much less pan-Europeanism.[61] After permitting thousands of Czechs to demonstrate on the twentieth anniversary of the Soviet invasion of 1968, the government proceeded to arrest and discipline key dissidents, including many Charter 77 members. It may be only a short time before these same dissidents become members of a coalition government, as have their Polish and Hungarian counterparts. The Czech Communist party is, after all, becoming isolated in its resistance to change.

In East Germany, independent political voices have come from movements within the Lutheran (Evangelische) Church. Activists published the "Berlin Appeal" in 1982, calling for denuclearization of Europe and withdrawal of foreign troops from the two Germanys. In September 1987, a church-led peace drive attracted a thousand people to the first demonstration allowed to proceed without prior government approval. Yet, East German police also have arrested several church activists, the government has forcibly ejected activists from the country, and censors routinely keep the more suggestive Soviet publications out of the country.[62] In September 1989, an independent political party, the New Forum, announced it would field candidates for the 1990 parliamentary elections. Drawing explicitly on the Polish and Hungarian reforms, the group is pressing for the end of one-party rule in the country.[63] By October, the aging Honecker was gone, replaced by Egon Krenz, who promised various liberal reforms. Massive demonstrations throughout East Germany (for instance, one by 500,000 people in East Berlin in November 1989) highlighted demands for free speech and free elections.

Hungarian activists have capitalized on a post-Chernobyl wave of environmentalism, focusing for the past several years on a hydroelectric project at Gabcikovo-Nagymaros, on the Danube north of Budapest, that they charge will endanger water supplies. The movement claims more than 10,000 supporters and produced the first *samizdat* (underground) environmental journal.[64] In June 1989, the movement could not only claim support, it could proclaim victory. The Hungarian government announced that it was suspending the dam project.

Will radical change in Eastern Europe end in a repeat of 1956 or 1968? Although Soviet intervention cannot be ruled out, it would cost the present Soviet leadership not only all its foreign and domestic reforms but probably its political position as well. Conservative Soviet politicians would take the opportunity to reassert authority in light of a perceived failure of the "new thinking." For the Gorbachev wing, then, acceptance of Eastern European independence makes political sense. Clearly Gorbachev had this in mind when he gave the Polish Communist party the green light to negotiate away its power.

Much more likely, 1955 will serve as the appropriate example. In that year, the Soviets withdrew from both Finland and Austria. Today both these countries maintain their independence and their neutrality. But 1955 was only a minor thaw in East–West relations: the bloc system remained intact. For the Cold War truly to end, the alliances must wither away as they once consolidated. First, coalition governments will appear, as the U.S.S.R. resurrects an "inclusionary" policy. Next, the "German question" will be resolved, whether in the form of reunification plus disarmament and strict neutrality or some mutually acceptable variation of change. If Germany continues to become neutral, so eventually will the rest of Europe—and the Cold War, as far as this region is concerned, will have ceased to serve any function.

The Soviet Union is unlikely to allow complete demilitarization of Eastern Europe unless NATO responds in kind on force reductions and political reconciliation. East Germany will only become free of Soviet troops when West Germany follows suit with NATO forces. Eastern Europe's future, then, is dependent upon decoupling, a process in which both superpowers must participate just as they once contributed to dividing the region forty years ago.

Regional Relations[65]

Soviet foreign policy toward the world outside Europe has tended to waver between maintaining good relations with capitalist countries and helping to create countries of "socialist orientation." In other words, Soviet policy has swung between two poles: supporting revolution in the Third World and accommodating the security interests of Western capitalist countries. Recent Western media coverage has emphasized that the Gorbachev administration is shifting Soviet policy away from revolution and toward accommodation.[66] Commentators have made the case that, for instance, in Latin America, the Soviet Union under Gorbachev is more interested in encouraging trade relations with Argentina than in supporting leftist insurgents in El Salvador. But as the history of Soviet relations with the Third World reveals, this development is not uniquely the creation of Gorbachev and his supporters.

Since World War II, the U.S.S.R. has gone through three main stages in dealing with the Third World, roughly associated with the tenures of Stalin, Khrushchev, and Brezhnev.[67] Under Stalin, the U.S.S.R. concentrated attention on Eastern Europe. Stalin, in general, was wary of revolutions in the Third World, considering them more of a threat to Soviet interests than an opportunity.[68]

> [T]he hallmarks of Stalin's foreign policy were its lack of involvement in anticolonial revolutionary movements and its efforts to mollify the more aggressive capitalist powers, either through direct negotiations with them or through "collective security" pacts with the less aggressive capitalist powers.[69]

Revolutions, Stalin understood, represented challenges as much to European colonialism as to the U.S.S.R.'s position as the center of world Communism. As first Yugoslavia, then China and other countries diverged from Soviet control and influence, Stalin's instincts proved correct.

Under Khrushchev, however, the U.S.S.R. initially abandoned Stalin's caution and took a more activist stance toward the Third World, cultivating allies in the Middle East (Egypt), Southeast Asia (Indonesia), Latin America (Cuba), and Africa (Congo). As nations began to gain independence from colonial powers, the Soviets came to view revolution as a potential medium for Marxist ideas and, ultimately, a sufficient condition for future alliance.

This optimistic attitude toward movements of national liberation did not last long. By the 1960s, Soviet policy began to move away from the Third World, as Soviet leaders acknowledged that the U.S.S.R. could not compete with the United States. The Soviet ability to project its power beyond its borders—whether by sea or by air—paled in comparison with U.S. projection of power.[70] The Soviet Union may have wanted to back Third World struggles, but it simply could not defend them directly. As a result, many Third World countries in which the Soviet Union had invested so much time and money simply fell away from Soviet influence. The most notable was perhaps the former Soviet ally Indonesia, where a 1965 U.S.-backed coup resulted in the slaughter of at least 300,000 suspected Communist sympathizers.[71] Countries of "socialist orientation" and national liberation movements no doubt took careful note of Soviet unwillingness or inability to respond.

During the Brezhnev administration, the U.S.S.R. gave rhetorical support and substantial arms to Third World countries but displayed considerably less activism (especially compared with China). During this time, the Soviet Union supported threatened Third World governments (Angola, Afghanistan, South Yemen, Cuba, Ethiopia) much more frequently than national liberation struggles. The U.S.S.R. simply reaped more consistent benefits from established governments (through trade and military alliances) than from often marginalized independence movements. In Soviet policy toward national liberation struggles, *Realpolitik* began to prevail over ideology.

The Gorbachev administration continues in the Brezhnev tradition, though perhaps accentuating this "deromanticization" of attitudes toward the Third World.[72] Unlike their predecessors, however, the Gorbachev reformers are not interested in preserving even a façade of interest. At one time, the Soviet press ran stories of heroic struggles in the Third World between "freedom fighters" (leftist insurgents) and "protofascist imperialist dictatorships" (Western-backed governments). Such stories are becoming scarce, and Soviet foreign policy analysts consequently have more leeway for criticism.[73] The Soviet public seems to approve of the trend. In a recent poll, subscribers to *Literaturnaya Gazeta,* one of the more sophisticated Soviet periodicals, ranked stories on national liberation movements and on the Third World in general *last* in popularity (after stories on other socialist countries).[74]

The Gorbachev administration, in its "new thinking" on military disengagement from Third World struggles, simply puts the best face on an obviously bad situation: the U.S.S.R. has not succeeded in winning much influence in the Third World despite years of efforts and rubles (Angola, for instance, cost $1 billion annually; war in Afghanistan, $1.7 million a day[75]). In this fourth cycle in Soviet attitudes to the Third World, the U.S.S.R. wants to avoid offending large capitalist nations but, more important, acknowledges that its attempts to gain influence in the regions through military means are counterproductive. Andrei Kozyrev, a top Soviet official, offers this startling reassessment: "Our direct and indirect involvement in regional conflicts leads to colossal losses by increasing general international tension, justifying the arms race, and hindering the establishment of mutually advantageous ties with the West."[76] A characteristic of the revised Soviet attitude toward regional relations is an emphasis on diplomatic and economic engagement rather than on military intervention or isolationism.

An important prerequisite for this new thinking is the rejection of bipolar thinking. The Kremlin's ideologist since October 1988, Vadim Medvedev, has stated clearly that the U.S.S.R. no longer considers the United States the imperialist enemy, the source of all trouble and discontent throughout the world.[77] Such a high-level rejection of Soviet Cold War thinking paves the way for the U.S.S.R.'s military disengagement from various areas of the world and potentially, in conjunction with the United States, a future bilateral commitment to nonintervention covering Latin America, Africa, Southwest Asia, and the Asia/Pacific region.

LATIN AMERICA

Historically, the Soviet Union has had little influence over either Latin American governments or indigenous movements for national liberation—in part because of the region's proximity to the United States.[78] The 1962 Cuban missile crisis remains the only instance in which the U.S.S.R. deliberately antagonized the United States in the region. This event, however, was less an attempt by Khrushchev to provide a springboard into the hemisphere than a misguided effort to neutralize a massive U.S. superiority in intercontinental weapons. Basing medium-range missiles in Cuba, Khrushchev thought, would also balance the large number of theater nuclear missiles based in Europe (and Turkey) facing the Soviet Union. He did not realize how strongly the United States would react to this action. The move would be the first and last time that the Soviet Union would explicitly threaten the United States in what it regarded as its backyard.

Despite U.S. dominance in Latin America, the U.S.S.R. has man-

Latin America and the Caribbean

aged to exert real influence over Cuba and, to a lesser extent, Nicaragua, but that influence has been by no means unmitigated.

The 1959 Cuban revolution caught the Khrushchev administration by surprise. Prior to the revolution, Fidel Castro had kept his 26th of July Movement distant from the Cuban Communist party, which was committed to mass organizing, the electoral process, and accommodation with the existing Batista regime. Upon taking power, Castro first directed overtures to the United States, which brusquely turned them aside. The Soviet Union, finally realizing what a strategic ally Cuba could be, began formalizing trade agreements with Castro in 1960, eighteen months after the revolution.[79] The Soviet decision to withdraw its nuclear missiles in 1962 damaged relations with Cuba, and that split widened further over differing assessments of chances for revolutionary change elsewhere in Latin America. The Cubans favored guerrilla insurrection; the Soviets favored the path of parliamentary change.[80]

This insistence on political paths to change severely hampered the U.S.S.R.'s ability to exert influence over various nationalist movements, including the Sandinistas in Nicaragua. In the 1970s, Nicaragua's Communist party, like the Cuban Communist party before, urged political work over armed insurrection and thus found itself marginalized from growing revolutionary activity. Capitalizing on public sentiment and with virtually no help from Moscow, the Sandinistas, not the Communists, led the overthrow of the Somoza regime in 1979. As in the Cuban situation, Nicaragua has moved closer to the U.S.S.R. in direct proportion to a deliberate U.S. strategy to isolate it.[81]

Today, Cuba and Nicaragua both receive Soviet economic aid but have very different attitudes toward the Gorbachev reforms. Although still accepting over $5 billion in Soviet subsidies annually, Castro has publicly criticized Gorbachev's market-oriented experiments.[82] The Nicaraguans, meanwhile, have received several indications that the U.S.S.R. will not singlehandedly buoy up their economy.[83] The government has generally relied more on economic help from neighboring Latin American countries as well as the Common Market and multilateral lending institutions (though the United States has tried to shut the door on these latter resources).[84]

The U.S.S.R. has provided an average of $500 million in annual military aid to Nicaragua. Yet, twice as many Soviet military advisers help the Peruvian government in its war against a Maoist national liberation movement (Sendero Luminoso) as once assisted the Nicaraguan government in its war against the U.S.-backed contras.[85] In April 1989, Gorbachev called for an end to all outside military aid to Central America. The United States immediately demanded that the Soviets first stop arming the Nicaraguan government. The U.S.S.R. responded that they had already stopped the flow of military assistance. The U.S. government has not pressed the issue further.

In dealing with national liberation movements in Latin America, the U.S.S.R. has negotiated very delicately, always cognizant of the U.S. record of intervention in the region. Having discovered the ineffectiveness of its political strategy in anticipating revolutions in Cuba and Nicaragua, the U.S.S.R. has directed the Salvadoran Communist party to join as a minority in a broad coalition (FDR–FMLN) of popular resistance. The Soviet Union has furnished precious little military support for the insurgency, despite the continual unsubstantiated accusations of the Reagan administration.

Rather than deliberately antagonize the United States, the Soviet Union has distanced itself from military struggle and concentrated on potentially lucrative trade relations with Latin American governments. This accommodating policy has sometimes placed the U.S.S.R. in uncomfortable positions. Perhaps the best example of such a dilemma was Soviet relations with Argentina from 1979 until 1983. Because of a need for grain following the 1979 U.S. grain embargo, the U.S.S.R. refrained from criticizing the Argentine government, even though the military dictatorship of General Jorge Videla directed an internal war against dissent, primarily of the left, which resulted in tens of thousands of civilians dead.[86]

Far from sponsoring revolution in its Latin American policy, the Soviet Union has recently behaved more like an entrepreneur in search of resources and large, safe markets. When Foreign Minister Eduard Shevardnadze visited Latin America in 1987, he paid special attention to Brazil and Argentina, precisely the industrializing countries that can provide technological goods, raw materials, and in turn large consumer markets for Soviet goods. In October 1988, Brazilian President José Sarney made an unprecedented trip to the Soviet Union which culminated in several agreements, including a treaty to cooperate in space. In the same month, Argentina and the U.S.S.R. renegotiated several trade agreements signaling an increase in Soviet exports to the country.[87] From 1970 to 1982, Latin American exports to the U.S.S.R. increased tenfold,[88] and the Gorbachev administration wants to improve upon that trend and thus to even out its large trade imbalances with several of the region's countries.[89]

The primacy of economics has informed Soviet policy toward Latin America for many of the same reasons that economic *perestroika* has been the chief reference point for Soviet domestic policy. This new market strategy is not peculiar to Latin America. De-emphasizing considerations of military strategy and ideological purity, the Gorbachev reformers increasingly view regional relations through a new prism of economic necessity. They have taken the cost-benefit analysis from the arms control sphere and applied it to Soviet regional relations.

AFRICA

Upon rejecting colonial rule after World War II, many African nations opted not only for governments independent of the colonial powers, but independent economic systems as well. Repudiation of colonial economic models led many emergent countries to explore socialism and Marxism. African leaders nonetheless sought to adapt Marxism to African conditions. Though grateful to the Soviet Union for material aid, African socialist leaders such as Julius Nyerere, of Tanzania, adhered to a policy of nonalignment, refusing to allow a predisposition toward an economic system to dictate political alliances. As the late Mozambican leader Samora Machel succinctly put it, "Africans must use Marxism, but Marxism must not be allowed to use Africans."[90] One tragedy of postcolonial Africa is that Africans *have* been manipulated, not by a single ideology but by the East–West power struggle.

The map of Africa today is a colonial creation. The borders that divide ethnic groups in half and bring together disparate peoples into one nation derive from the arbitrary decisions of imperial powers. After the withdrawal of these powers in the 1950s and 1960s, hopes for pan-African unity gradually faded as many ethnic groups resumed age-old rivalries both within and between newly independent coun-

Africa

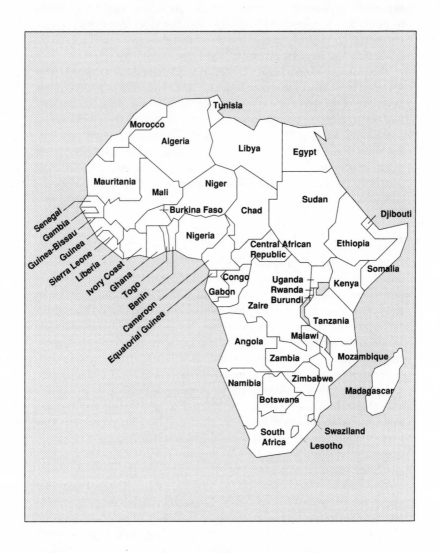

tries. To make matters worse, long into the postcolonial era, the United States, the Soviet Union, and several European nations continued to exploit the tensions among these ethnic groups. In turn, such groups have imported large supplies of military technology, thus escalating the violence of various struggles over the right to rule.

During the 1970s, these African ethnic groups and their political representatives took advantage of a marked upsurge in arms sales worldwide. From 1970 to 1978, global arms transfers increased from $9.1 billion annually to $19.1 billion.[91] It was a burgeoning market, with the United States providing 39 percent and the Soviet Union 29 percent of shipments.[92] From 1978 to 1982, African nations and movements alone imported *$31 billion* in military hardware, reflecting a dramatic increase in purchases.[93] War had certainly not left the continent with the colonial rulers.

Despite Soviet willingness to provide arms and other forms of aid, postcolonial African leaders have generally expressed ambivalence toward the U.S.S.R., forcing the Soviets to pursue some improbable strategies to gain influence. Consider, for example, the Soviet role in the Nigerian Civil War.

In 1967, the Ibo people seceded from postcolonial Nigeria, calling their new territory Biafra. Since the Ibos were self-styled progressives seeking "national liberation" from a relatively conservative military government, the U.S.S.R. would, according to conventional wisdom, back the Ibos. It backed the Nigerian government instead, joining Great Britain against Biafra's supporters—France, Israel, and China.[94] For several years after putting down the Biafran rebellion, the Nigerian government maintained close ties with the U.S.S.R., but it eventually turned back to the United States (which had remained neutral in the civil war), providing oil during the 1970s oil crisis and adopting the U.S. constitutional model of government.[95] Soviet support for the status quo had brought few advantages.

Elsewhere, the Soviets have met with similar fickleness. Since 1979, Congo (Brazzaville) has turned away from Soviet military support and toward Western investment (the United States is Congo's top trading partner).[96] The Marxist Mozambique Liberation Front (Frelimo) used Soviet money to build the economy and used Soviet arms to fight a South African–sponsored insurgency, but President Samora Machel always kept Mozambique's foreign policy independent[97] and in 1983 steered government policy toward encouraging private enterprise.[98] In Zimbabwe (formerly Rhodesia), the U.S. State Department long accused current President Robert Mugabe's insurgents of being Soviet clients. Mugabe was a popular politician with support from the majority Shona people, and it was his opponent Joshua Nkomo who, among Zimbabwean politicians, had Soviet backing. Since being elected to office, Mugabe has guided Zimbabwe to a firmly nonaligned position.

A relationship that promises to grow more problematic over time is that between the Soviets and the formerly strident anti-Communist Muammar Qadafi, of Libya. In the 1970s, Qadafi combined Islam and nationalism to forge a "third way" between capitalism and Communism. *The Green Book,* Qadafi's statement of principles, criticizes equally Soviet party politics and Western representative democracy. Despite casting a pox on both houses, Qadafi has sought to normalize relations with the United States and, to continue his war against Chad, has secured substantial Soviet arms deals.[99] Continued U.S. antagonism toward Libya might push Qadafi even closer to the U.S.S.R. despite the fundamental differences between Soviet Communism and Islamic nationalism.[100]

In other African countries, the Soviet Union has remained aloof from several wars of national liberation, most notably from the struggle by the Polisario Front to establish a government free of Morocco. Although continuing to support the anti-apartheid struggles of the African National Congress (ANC) in South Africa, the U.S.S.R. unexpectedly began high-level discussions with South African government leaders in April 1989.[101] The contradictions inherent in the remaking of the Soviet image stand out in relief in this example. Soviet leadership wants to appear to be talking to both sides in a conflict, but it has historically refused to negotiate with the apartheid regime. For the moment, at least, Soviet diplomats must be nimble, supporting traditional allies while making this transition to mediating power brokers.

The situation of Angola and Namibia exemplifies the newfound commitment to diplomatic solutions. During Angola's struggle for independence from Portugal, the U.S.S.R. funded the Popular Movement for the Liberation of Angola (MPLA) (after the MPLA failed to receive funds requested from the United States in 1962).[102]

Soviet aid increased when the United States, China, and South Africa began pouring money into rival groups of insurgents. In 1975, Cuban troops intervened in the conflict (spelling the end of détente, according to many U.S. policy makers) but only after South Africa and Zaire had invaded from the north and south (with U.S. encouragement).[103] That year, after Portugal had granted independence to Angola, the MPLA defeated its rivals sufficiently to declare itself a government in Luanda.

But the civil war continued, primarily between this new Cuban-backed Angolan government and Jonas Savimbi's Unita faction, which was backed by the U.S. and South Africa. Meanwhile, in neighboring Namibia (at the time, a territory administered by South Africa), the South West Africa People's Organization (SWAPO) was fighting for independence from South Africa, operating from bases in Angola. Angola (and the Namibian people) demanded independence for Namibia; South Africa maintained that it had to control the territory for reasons of national security. The conflict was indeed complicated: two civil wars and various insurgents backed by Cuba, the Soviet Union, the United States, Zaire, or South Africa. This long-term regional crisis absorbed arms at an alarming rate and appeared to be resistant to diplomatic solutions.

Over the past decade, several multinational negotiating frameworks have failed to produce any effective agreements on either the Angolan civil war or the status of Namibia. Working behind the scenes and in conjunction with the United States, the U.S.S.R. put whatever pressure it could on its allies in Cuba and Angola to support a negotiated solution. Funding the Angolan government, whether directly or indirectly through Cuba, was an economic drain for the U.S.S.R., and it preferred a face-saving withdrawal. A late 1988 proposal to resolve the crisis called for the withdrawal of Cuban and South African troops from Angola and independence for Namibia. Under the auspices of the United Nations, the plan was carried out, and Namibian elections are scheduled for November 1989. The Angolan civil war, despite several recent cease-fires, continues.[104]

The Gorbachev administration has inherited a very mixed foreign policy legacy in Africa. The Soviet Union has poured money into the continent but won few allies. It has supported leaders of virtually every political stripe but secured few stable relationships. Every country it supplies insists on trying to establish friendly relations with the West. Changing strategies, the Gorbachev administration, with its newly acquired parsimony, has sought to establish joint ventures and secure reciprocal trade agreements that take advantage of potentially large African markets. [105] Neither military aid nor the presence of Soviet troops guaranteed these relationships under Brezhnev; support for national liberation movements under Khrushchev likewise met with variable success. The Gorbachev administration seems willing to try the new tactics of diplomacy and economic cooperation.

SOUTHWEST ASIA

President Carter's national security adviser Zbigniew Brzezinski referred to this region—the Middle East in the center, the Horn of Africa to the west, Afghanistan and Iran to the northeast—as the "arc of crisis," less a coherent geographic area than a U.S. strategic preoccupation. In the late 1970s, a series of events challenged U.S. interests in the area: upheavals in Ethiopia and Yemen, revolution in Iran, coups in Afghanistan, a deteriorating situation in Lebanon. Some U.S. policy makers presumed that the Soviet Union instigated these crises in order to control Middle Eastern oil, at the time a major concern for U.S. policy makers.

With the precipitous hike in oil prices in 1973, the decline in exclusive U.S. corporate control over oil supply and distribution, and the increased power of the Organization of Petroleum Exporting Countries (OPEC) cartel, U.S. foreign policy under Nixon, Ford, and then Carter made a priority of guaranteed access to the Persian Gulf oil supply and favorable relations with the countries that control that supply. In 1980, the "Carter doctrine" was declared: the United States would use military force if necessary to defend its "vital" interests in the Middle East. At the same time, U.S. policy makers expanded their focus to include countries bordering the Middle East that could theoretically serve as stepping stones to the oil wells. Consequently, the arc of crisis spanning the Middle East and parts of Asia and Africa—known more generally as "Southwest Asia"—attracted considerable resources and a renewed U.S. commitment to intervention.

Southwest Asia

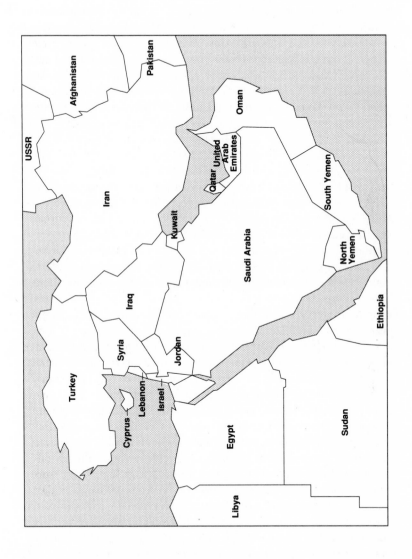

Was an oil-obsessed Soviet Union behind these disparate conflicts? What are its policy objectives in the region today?

Afghanistan is a good place to begin. A conservative monarchy bordering the Soviet Union to the south, Afghanistan conducted relations with the U.S.S.R. since the Russian Revolution. In the 1960s, it attracted significant aid from the Soviets (but little from the United States, which was afraid of offending another U.S. ally, Pakistan).[106] While supplying the government, the Soviets also supported the People's Democratic party of Afghanistan (PDPA). In 1978, this Communist party seized power in a coup. The Soviet Union was but one of several players behind the scenes. Of equal influence was the Shah of Iran, who had been pressuring then President Mohammed Daud to move closer to Iran.[107] When Daud tried to arrest the PDPA leadership in April 1978, the Communists struck back, seizing power. With a new Marxist government on its borders, the Soviet government increased its support, as anti-Marxist opposition increased in the Afghan countryside in mid-1979.[108]

In a move that the Soviet government has publicly regretted, Soviet troops invaded Afghanistan in December 1979, with the rather weak justification that the new Afghan government had invited them. Many U.S. policy makers interpreted the move as a Soviet attempt to get within striking distance of Persian Gulf oil and gain a warm-water port. Afghanistan, in other words, was simply a first step. But the Persian Gulf is no closer geographically to Afghanistan than it is to the Soviet Union. More compelling is the argument that the Soviets took such an extreme step to avoid having a hostile government at its doorstep. In accordance with the Brezhnev doctrine, the invasion of Afghanistan represented an attempt to ensure a pro-Soviet defensive perimeter, a ring of friendly countries on its borders to safeguard national security. The U.S.S.R. acted first to preserve its own national interests, second to assist an ally.

Rather than achieving either of these goals, the Soviet Union instead demonstrated that its army was far from invincible. In May 1988, Gorbachev announced that the Soviet Union would pull out of Afghanistan within nine months. That process, interrupted by Soviet complaints over continued U.S. and Pakistani funding of the Afghani opposition, was nevertheless completed in February 1989. The Soviets had kept their word, though they continue to supply arms to the

Afghan government (which, contrary to Western expectations, did not immediately fall to the Afghan rebels).

Two other frequently cited examples of Soviet aggression in Southwest Asia are the Red Sea countries of Ethiopia and South Yemen. In Ethiopia, a coup toppled the pro-Western government of Haile Selassie in 1974. Although a self-styled socialist government came to power, no evidence has been found that the Soviet Union financed or otherwise supported the action.[109] Following a common pattern in East–West relations, Ethiopia turned to the Soviet Union after the United States turned away in 1977 (in the same way that new governments in Cuba, Nicaragua, Grenada, and Jamaica turned to the U.S.S.R. after U.S. snubs).[110] As in the case of Angola, the Soviets and Cubans militarily intervened in Ethiopia only after the country was invaded, this time by Somalia in 1977. In a painful irony for the Soviets, Somalia had, until this invasion, also been an ally. Becoming increasingly friendly with conservative Saudi Arabia, however, Somalia grew ever more disenchanted with its Soviet patron. The invasion of Ethiopia brought a switch in Soviet allegiance—in certain respects, a strategic loss to the Soviets. Ethiopia's military potential was less important than Somalia's (Ethiopian naval bases on the Red Sea can be easily blockaded at the Gulf of Aden). Further, its economic hardships and costly civil war nullified any potential value Ethiopia might have as a trading partner.[111]

A remarkably similar set of events occurred in South Yemen. A 1978 coup (which was anti-Soviet but in which the Soviets were accused of being involved) led to destabilization by a Western ally (Saudi Arabia) and regional war with North Yemen (a former Soviet ally), into which the Soviets intervened militarily. As in Ethiopia, Soviet meddling brought only occasional rewards, despite an enormous military commitment.[112]

From the U.S. perspective, the conflicts in Afghanistan, Ethiopia, and South Yemen were not simply discrete conflicts. Rather, like a pointillist painting, they resolved themselves at a distance as the bigger picture of a Soviet assault on the Middle East. On the contrary, the evidence suggests that Soviet involvement occurred on a case-by-case basis. Further, given the Soviets' limited power, these activities were straining their capacity to make any additional commitment in the Middle East. Most critical, the U.S.S.R. gained little in the Middle East proper through activities on its periphery. The events of the late 1970s did not significantly improve Soviet standing among Middle Eastern countries; in fact, Soviet standing was hurt.

Until 1974, the most consistent Soviet ally in the Middle East was Egypt. Gamal Abdel Nasser, Egypt's leader in the 1950s and '60s, combined nationalism, anti-imperialism, and socialism in drawing his country away from the West. In 1955, casting around for funds to build the Aswan dam, Nasser had first approached the United States. Rejected, he turned to a more willing Soviet Union. His successor, Anwar Sadat, accepted additional Soviet military advisers and weapons, and large sums of economic and military aid to build Egypt's reputation in the Arab world and its military forces for its 1973 war with Israel.

But as in so many Third World relationships with the Soviet Union, Egypt considered its allegiance practical, not ideological. Even before its decision to undertake the '73 war, Egypt began to view its relationship with the Soviet Union as a liability, since it alienated several Arab countries and decreased the possibility of help from the West (especially from the United States). In 1972, Egypt unceremoniously expelled all Soviet troops and advisers and later declared that it would not repay its debts.

Other Soviet alliances forged in the Middle East—with Sudan, Iraq, Syria, the Palestine Liberation Organization—suffered from similar problems. Although Syria and Iraq never cut themselves off completely from the Soviet Union (they needed the aid), both of these countries behaved independently of Soviet policy. Soviet disapproval of Syria's invasion of Lebanon in 1976 and of Iraq's conflict with Iran did not prevent these countries from pursuing their own policies. Iraq's case is a good example of a deeply ambivalent Soviet ally. According to one commentator, "Iraq has been so far from a Soviet client state that it has arguably caused Soviet diplomats more headaches in the last decade than any other state in the region."[113]

As this history of unreliable alliances shows, the Soviet Union has not wielded effective influence in the Middle East and did not gain in the region by its activities elsewhere in Southwest Asia.[114] Under Gorbachev, the U.S.S.R. is attempting to increase its influence in the region, though not through the traditional means of arms, advisers, and economic aid. The Israeli–Palestinian conflict is a case in point.

Gorbachev has joined other leaders in calling for an international peace conference to resolve this issue.[115] Such a conference reflects Soviet interest in having all sides participate in resolving the conflict (including, of course, the U.S.S.R.). To that end, the U.S.S.R. has encouraged its allies to compromise. The Soviets used their influence over both mainstream and leftist factions of the PLO to help Palestinian leaders reunify the PLO in 1987.[116] The 1988 decision of the Palestine National Council to accept U.N. resolutions 242 and 338, accept partition of Palestine, and give de facto recognition to Israel was achieved with considerable encouragement from the Soviet Union, culminating a long process of change occurring within the PLO for over a decade. The U.S.S.R. has also wooed Israel, a country with which it broke off relations in 1967. In June 1987, Soviet diplomats visited Israel for the first time in twenty years.[117] In late 1988, a consular-level Soviet delegation went to Israel and Israeli representatives went to Moscow, indicating that official diplomatic ties might be forthcoming. In February 1989, Eduard Shevardnadze toured the Middle East, meeting with feuding leaders (PLO's Yasser Arafat and Israel's defense minister, Moshe Arens, on the same day). The Soviet foreign minister repeated many Middle East peace proposals: withdrawal of foreign navies from the Persian Gulf, another call for an international conference, on-site inspections of Israeli and Arab military installations.[118] Once limited to pressuring independently minded allies in the region, the U.S.S.R. has in effect dealt itself into the Arab-Israeli conflict by exploiting both old and new diplomatic connections.

In June 1989, more channels of communication were opened when Iranian Speaker of the House Hojatolislam Rafsanjani visited Moscow and secured the reopening of railroad links between the two countries. This at a time when Iran, because of Ayatollah Khomeini's death threat against Salman Rushdie, the author of *The Satanic Verses,* has drifted further from the West. With relations established with most actors in the region, the U.S.S.R. appears interested in resolving another hornet's nest: Lebanon. With that country torn by factional fighting, Moscow has been putting pressure on its allies Iraq and Syria to be more cooperative in ending the crisis.[119]

Rather than relying on military intervention, the U.S.S.R. has since sought to engage diplomatically as many countries as possible in the Middle East. Far from trying to control the region through escalating crises, the Gorbachev administration seems more concerned with resolving crises, whether it be the Iran–Iraq war or the Israeli–Palestinian conflict. Unanticipated conflicts in Ethiopia and Yemen yielded few benefits for the U.S.S.R.; escalating crisis in Afghanistan brought only a protracted defeat. As elsewhere, the Soviet reformers would prefer to gain influence in this vast region through trade and activist diplomacy, not through confrontation or military means.

ASIA/PACIFIC

Ironically, the U.S.S.R. is perhaps weakest militarily in its own backyard, at least in its territorial waters. Historically, the U.S.S.R. has had few military bases, limited air power, extremely restricted access to sea lanes, and a relatively small submarine force in this region. This lack of offensive firepower and the means to deploy it throughout the region has led to an almost de facto "defensive defense" strategy intended to protect home waters rather than to patrol the high seas.[120]

Instead of attempting to improve its capabilities at sea, the Gorbachev administration has cut back. In 1987, naval deployments overseas decreased 6 percent over the previous year, according to the U.S. Navy's own calculations.[121] The authors of *American Lake* point out, however, that the lack of Soviet conventional might in the region is potentially destabilizing: in the event of an attack (or even perceived aggression), the U.S.S.R. might feel compelled to use some of its considerable stock of nuclear weapons.[122] The U.S.S.R. is the prisoner, paradoxically, of its greatest military weakness and its most profound military strength.

The question of nuclear weapons is critical in the Asia/Pacific region and applies not only to Soviet land- and sea-based missiles. India and Pakistan have unofficially joined the nuclear club; U.S. nuclear submarines also routinely patrol the Pacific; in South Korea, the U.S. government deploys 150 tactical nuclear weapons (the only nuclear weapons on Korean soil). The region also figures prominently in nuclear war-fighting plans. The U.S. Pacific fleet, in a crisis situation, would attempt to cut off the Soviet fleet in the straits near Japan.

Asia and the Pacific

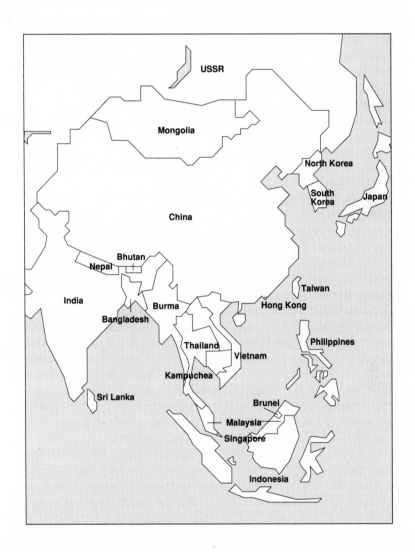

As one military strategist notes, "The danger is that geography and strategy will combine to bring nuclear war to Asia, even though not a shot had been fired first anywhere else."[123]

The Gorbachev administration clearly recognizes the relevance of the nuclear question to the region. When Gorbachev offered a major concession in July 1987 during the INF negotiations, he did so in comments to the editor of an Indonesian newspaper. In the *Merdeka* interview, Gorbachev announced that he would include 100 Asian-based medium-range missiles in the INF agreement; he also reiterated previously stated desires to reduce nuclear-capable aircraft in Soviet Asia and limit even further naval exercises in the Pacific and Indian Oceans. At one stroke, Gorbachev revealed the priority Asian countries held for the Soviet government and the connections between the region and nuclear weapons issues.

Soviet "new thinking" on Asia/Pacific issues is not confined to nuclear weapons. Though often underreported in the U.S. press, new initiatives toward the region constitute perhaps the most significant turnabout in Soviet foreign policy.

The first indication of a shift in Soviet policy came in July 1986 in a major speech at Vladivostok (in the Soviet Far East). In that speech, Gorbachev outlined a five-point plan for regional cooperation, closer ties with China, and the withdrawal of six regiments of Soviet troops from Afghanistan. (The latter point is especially important, because it reveals that the U.S.S.R. viewed Afghanistan not simply as a conflict peculiar to U.S.–Soviet relations or as part of an arc of crisis, but rather as an Asian issue, one that has hindered efforts to improve relations with many Asian countries.) The regional cooperation plan also included a call for an end to nuclear proliferation in the area, reductions in military forces and in naval activities, confidence-building measures, and improved economic ties.[124]

In September 1988, Gorbachev outlined another series of initiatives for the region that included an offer to turn the controversial Krasnoyarsk radar over to international control (which was rejected by the United States). Gorbachev also proposed removing Soviet bases from Cam Ranh Bay in Vietnam in exchange for the removal of U.S. bases from the Philippines. In addition, Gorbachev proposed unprecedented economic links to South Korea and repeated previous proposals such as a Sino-Soviet summit, limited naval exercises in the Pacific, reduced military activities in the Sea of Japan and the Yellow Sea, and a freeze on nuclear weapons in the region. Perhaps the most intriguing comments, however, concerned the possibility of the U.S.S.R. establishing a free-trade zone in the Soviet Far East that would take advantage of the economic success of the region.[125]

The success of these regional initiatives depends a great deal on relationships that the U.S.S.R. has fostered with particular countries, relationships that have been, to put it mildly, tempestuous. China and Indonesia broke off relations in 1962: both devastating blows to Soviet prestige. North Korea, allied with the Chinese in 1969, has been playing the Soviet Union and China off against each other ever since. Vietnam has proven anything but docile, invading Cambodia in 1978 and skirmishing with the Chinese in 1979.

In order for the U.S.S.R. to stabilize its relations with the region, however, it must clarify its ties with the two ideological poles: China and Japan.

Present-day China illustrates how nonmonolithic Communism really is. A strong ally of the U.S.S.R. after Mao Zedong's forces drove the Kuomintang off the mainland in 1949, China gradually drew away from 1960 to 1962 over questions of de-Stalinization, Yugoslav economic reform, warming U.S.–Soviet relations, and Soviet policy toward national liberation. The Chinese condemned Khrushchev for moving closer to the "imperialists" and away from Third World revolutions.[126] In an early anticipation of Gorbachev's foreign policy, *Pravda* criticized the Chinese for "a very dangerous form of sectarianism," singling out the export of revolution and the imposition of external social systems for particular censure.[127] Border skirmishes between the Communist giants followed throughout the 1960s.

After the death of Mao in 1976, China shifted direction in its domestic policies, decollectivizing agriculture and increasingly adopting market mechanisms. While its economic policy has not been entirely consistent, China nonetheless views the present Soviet reforms favorably.[128] And Gorbachev apparently pays close attention to changes in Beijing policy: "We are greatly interested in reforms of the economic mechanism and political system currently under way in the People's Republic of China," he said in a 1988 interview.[129] The lessening of tensions between the countries has led the Soviet government to withdraw 10,000 troops from Mongolia and the Chinese government to pursue its own unilateral disarmament (in 1985, it demobilized 20 percent of its troops). In June 1989, Gorbachev visited China, and the two countries re-established diplomatic relations after thirty years. This dramatic foreign policy event was then overshadowed by the Chinese government's violent suppression of demonstrations in Tiananmen Square, shortly after Gorbachev had left the country.[130] Despite China's internal crisis, détente with the Soviet Union seems secure.[131]

One sign of Sino-Soviet détente is the handling of the Cambodian conflict. In 1979, Soviet ally Vietnam invaded Cambodia and deposed Chinese ally Pol Pot. China has continually called for Vietnam to withdraw and has pressured the Soviet government to influence *its* ally. In line with its new policy of military disengagement from regional conflict, the U.S.S.R. did just that. In September 1989, Hanoi declared that its last troops had left (though the Cambodian government of Hun Sen remains closely tied to Vietnam). With the breakdown of negotiations between various Cambodian factions, an escalating civil war unfortunately appears likely. With its clarified stance on regional conflicts, the U.S.S.R. will probably not become militarily involved, either directly or indirectly.

In addition to courting the world's most populous country, the Soviet Union has recently attempted to move closer to Japan, now the world's largest creditor nation. The two countries have been long-standing adversaries, dating from the 1905 Russo-Japanese War, through the Russian civil war and World War II and into the postwar era. The Kuriles—a group of islands north of the Japanese island of Hokkaido that are part of territory seized by the Soviets from Japan at the end of World War II—have been at issue for the past forty years. Since the 1960s, the Soviet government has used these islands as military bases to monitor sea traffic in and around Japan (which claims the territory as its own). Because of the crucial military importance of the Kuriles—without them, the Soviet Navy would be even more bottled up than it is now—an agreement will be very difficult to reach.

Beyond territorial issues, the Soviet government has had two major concerns in dealing with Japan. The Soviet Union worries about Japan's recent decision to spend more than 1 percent of its GNP on the military, its development of an antisubmarine warfare capability, and the possibility that Japan might acquire nuclear weapons.[132] Second, the Soviet Union would like to take advantage of Japan's proximity to develop closer economic ties.[133] Its attention fixed on the economic success of the region, the Soviet Union participated in the November 1986 meeting of the Pacific Basin Community and was an observer in the Asian Development Bank in 1987.[134] As the major economic power in the region, Japan can play a role in laying the groundwork for Soviet entry into the world economy. It has, to date, provided a larger line of credit to the U.S.S.R. than any other nation.[135]

As the Asia/Pacific region becomes more important on the international scene for both strategic and economic reasons, the Gorbachev reformers are increasingly taking advantage of the U.S.S.R.'s part-Asian identity to secure closer ties with the region. As it has in the Middle East and elsewhere—through a series of remarkable proposals, concessions, and diplomatic overtures—the Soviet Union is playing an activist role that de-emphasizes military relations while emphasizing diplomacy and trade.

The U.S.S.R. of course remains a superpower. That is, it continues to attempt to exert influence in numerous countries proportional to its geographic position and size, economic strength, and military power. Although its power-projection scarcely compares with that of the United States, the U.S.S.R. still retains its nuclear trump card. There are still large Soviet ground forces facing Europe and Asia. The U.S.S.R. still maintains and supports political allies in various parts of the world.

For the most part, however, the Gorbachev contribution to Soviet policy toward these regions is the pragmatic recognition that military force has not yielded the U.S.S.R. great advantages in the past and will probably not do so in the future. The reformers use roughly the same argument to promote arms control with the West and undercut support for military spending within the government.

In downplaying the usefulness of force in external relations, the Soviets have not simply employed a cost-benefit analysis and determined that their previous policies registered losses. Rather, the new thinking questions the notion that in today's world, a single country can successfully impose its wishes on other countries. Soviet policy toward the Third World reflects a new conception of international relations and the role of multipolarism.

International Organizations

Since the United Nations' Palme Commission produced the report "Common Security" in 1982, the concept of security as multipolar—having many centers of importance—has gained wider acceptance. "There is one overriding truth in this nuclear age—no nation can achieve true security by itself," former secretary of state Cyrus Vance wrote in the introduction to the U.S. edition of the book.[136] Gorbachev, it would seem, has lifted the new Soviet attitude toward security virtually word for word from the U.N. document. Compare Vance's quotation with the following remark from a television address given by Gorbachev in August 1986:

> Today one's own security cannot be ensured without taking into account the security of other states and peoples. There can be no genuine security unless it is equal for all and comprehensive. To think otherwise is to live in a world of illusions, in a world of self-deception.[137]

While Soviet rhetoric of common security is certainly pleasing to hear, is the Soviet Union prepared to give more than rhetorical support?[138]

An important measure of this commitment to common security is the Soviet role in the United Nations. In the past, relations have been stormy: General Assembly members have denounced the U.S.S.R. over its invasions of Hungary (1956), Czechoslovakia (1968), and Afghanistan (1979); many Soviet motions in the past (such as the proposal to oust Israel from the U.N.) have never generated much support; a nonaligned bloc of nations within the U.N. has often sided with neither the United States nor the Soviet Union on critical economic and political votes.

Under Gorbachev, the Soviet Union has adopted a conciliatory attitude toward the international body. While the United States refused to participate in a 1987 U.N. Conference on Disarmament and Development (alleging that there was no connection between the two), the Soviet Union participated fully. At the conclusion of the conference, the U.S.S.R. proposed a U.N. summit on disarmament and economic aid, thus reviving an often-stated proposal to shift money spent on armaments in the Northern Hemisphere to economic assistance for developing countries in the Third World. In September 1987, in an article for the Soviet newspaper *Izvestia*, Gorbachev called for greater powers for the U.N., including a wider peace-keeping role, greater jurisdiction for the International Court of Justice, creation of a U.N. tribunal to investigate international instances of terrorism, the creation of a world space organization, and an increase in authority for the International Atomic Energy Agency. [139] Finally, in October 1987, giving a financial basis to its common-security rhetoric, the Soviets paid the $197 million owed in dues payments to the United Nations. One year later, the United States paid only part of its enormous debt (it still owes $402 million as of January 1989; the Bush administration has proposed $27.5 million toward paying back this sum).

In October 1988, the U.S.S.R. submitted a proposal for strengthening the U.N., specifically calling for additional peace-keeping troops and improved training. Such empowerment of the U.N. fits in with other Soviet foreign policy initiatives, such as multilateral verification of arms control treaties or perhaps even a code of nonintervention. For instance, the Soviet government views U.N. observer teams as a key element to protect borders and to monitor potential hot spots that might encourage intervention. [140] The U.S.S.R. has even begun to accept international rulings that affect its internal affairs—for instance, the March 1989 decision to abide by World Court jurisdiction on five key human rights regulations.

The Soviet decision to appeal to international norms and standards and support multilateral institutions such as the U.N. is both strategic and ultimately inevitable. By embracing multipolarism, the Soviets speak to all the countries that have felt locked out of East–West relations. Soviet rejection of the bipolar map of the world also reflects the geopolitical reality that political and economic power is more widely distributed.

* * *

Since 1985, the number and variety of foreign policy initiatives undertaken by the Gorbachev administration demonstrate an important new conception of the role of the U.S.S.R. in the world. The INF treaty, on-site verification, scaled-back naval exercises, unilateral conventional-weapons cuts for Europe, the withdrawal of troops from Afghanistan, support for the resolution of conflicts in Angola and Cambodia, calls for strengthening the United Nations—these indicate a concrete and clear Soviet commitment to more peaceful international relations.

Again, these proposals reflect not a burst of global benevolence but a conscious recognition of a military inability to compete for influence in the Third World and an economic inability to maintain the arms race. The Soviet Union certainly remains a military power: it still maintains large armies and an enormous arsenal of nuclear weapons. But the Gorbachev administration realizes that these military advantages do not result directly in economic or diplomatic gains.

The Gorbachev camp relies for its political position within the Soviet government on its ability to transform foreign policy into concrete domestic gains. The enormous costs of maintaining the military balance in Europe and competing for influence in the Third World have led Gorbachev and his supporters to seek agreements with the United States and its Western allies. Though the agreements are still few in number, an undeniable lessening of tensions in East–West relations has taken place.

But what about the future? Will this lessening of tension in East–West relations become permanent? Or will it simply join previous détentes in being all too temporary?

3

Détente

Détente is the process of the easing of tension between states whose interests are so radically divergent that reconciliation is inherently limited.[1]

THE UNITED STATES and the Soviet Union have, since 1986, entered a period in which the tensions so pervasive in the earlier part of the decade have considerably lessened. This present relationship has yielded a successfully negotiated arms control treaty, an increase in economic and cultural exchange, and a general softening in mutual rhetoric. The Soviet leadership has, for instance, announced that it no longer considers the United States an imperialist enemy;[2] President Reagan, in turn, publicly retracted his contention that the U.S.S.R. was an "evil empire." According to polls conducted by the Americans Talk Security project, Gorbachev now receives more favorable ratings from the U.S. people than any international leader except British Prime Minister Margaret Thatcher.[3] This reversal in East–West relations has been so dramatic that it has prompted several political leaders, including the conservative Thatcher, to declare the Cold War to be over.[4]

Such judgments may be premature. If the present period of relations is only a détente, then the Cold War is by no means over. According to conventional wisdom, a détente is a period of peace that has every possibility of becoming permanent. But viewed historically, détentes have been no more than one stage in the predictable rhythms of the Cold War, much as a period of prosperity (or "boom") is part of the boom/bust cycle of a market economy. Détente, after all, implicitly assumes a deep ideological division between the United States and the Soviet Union, one that necessarily limits the degree to which cooperation is possible. In other words, détentes are destined by definition to be temporary.

On the other hand, the United States and the Soviet Union may truly be breaking the cycles of the Cold War. If this is the case, the present warming trend in U.S.–Soviet relations would not be a détente, because the two superpowers are at a point of realizing a permanent relaxing of tensions. Such an achievement has its precedents. The United States and Great Britain, once implacable enemies that fought two wars against each other, are today the closest of allies. It took a mere ten years for France and Germany, in opposing trenches in both world wars, to join together in a military alliance. Ideological differences, no matter how deep, are not eternal.

Which situation presently faces the United States and the Soviet Union? Will the period after 1986 appear in the history books as simply another brief détente, or will this era be considered a true watershed in U.S.–Soviet relations? There are several indications that we are experiencing only a continuation of the Cold War, not its last rites:

- the present period in several important respects closely resembles détentes of the past;
- several long-standing U.S.–held Cold War myths about the Soviet Union, though perhaps in varying stages of dormancy, still have currency and could be revived in the near future to trigger or hasten a worsening of relations;
- the relationship between industrialized nations and the Third World is still economically and militarily destabilizing and may adversely affect East–West relations.

To characterize and put into context present U.S.–Soviet relations, previous U.S.–Soviet détentes will be explored in this chapter. Thus, it is necessary to analyze some of the myths concerning the Soviet

Union that have undergirded U.S. policy over the past forty years and that have been maintained across the cycles of the Cold War, as well as to speculate on the implications of détente for countries outside the East–West axis. Finally, arms control—an emblematic expression of détente—will be explored, in order to evaluate whether it can meet the challenges that this period of international relations presents.

Cycles of Détente

Even before the terms *détente* and *Cold War* became fashionable in defining East–West conflict, U.S.–Soviet relations from 1917 to 1945 obeyed a cyclical pattern of alternating peaks and troughs. At the very inception of the Bolshevik government, for instance, U.S. policy vacillated considerably. In 1917, reflecting a general U.S. policy-making sentiment toward the Bolshevik Revolution, the *New York Times* editorialized, "The Bolsheviks have put Russia outside the pale of civilized, recognizable government."[5] Yet, in early 1918 President Wilson, reluctant to lose Russian military support in World War I, offered the U.S.S.R. "a sincere welcome into the society of free nations under institutions of her own choosing; and, more than a welcome, assistance also of every kind that she may need and may herself desire."[6] Within the same year, however, U.S. forces had joined other countries in intervening *against* the Bolsheviks in the Russian Civil War.

During the 1920s, U.S. policy reversed again, as substantial economic resources flowed to the Soviet Union. Herbert Hoover's American Relief Administration provided millions of dollars in famine relief in 1921 and 1922.[7] In 1929, the Ford Motor Company set up a plant in Nizhni-Novgorod.[8] In 1933, the Roosevelt administration finally recognized the Soviet Union, making official through diplomacy what had been an economic fact for over a decade.

World War II brought another quick reversal in relations. In 1939, the Soviet Non-Aggression Pact signed with Germany drew strong protest from the United States. But after Germany attacked the U.S.S.R. in 1941, the United States and the Soviet Union became close allies.[9] In the tumultuous years following the end of World War II, relations between the United States and the Soviet Union quickly hardened. The Soviet Union consolidated its gains from the war in Eastern Europe and Asia. The United States developed the policy of containment to complement its new activist role in world affairs and, in the most critical test of this activism, to counterbalance the Soviet Union.

Containment began, as George Kennan conceived of it, as a means to protect certain key geographic areas from Soviet control. As it was translated into concrete policies, however, containment grew in scope. In 1947, Truman inaugurated the Marshall Plan, a massive package of aid sent to pivotal war-torn countries, ostensibly to help them rebuild but at least in part to ensure their non-Communism. Congress established, in the same year, the cornerstones of the national security state: the Central Intelligence Agency and the National Security Council. By 1950, the remaining Cold War touches were in place with National Security Council memorandum 68 (NSC-68), a measure that discouraged negotiations with the Soviet Union, pushed for both the development of the hydrogen bomb and an upgrading of U.S. conventional forces, proposed raising taxes to pay for these military modifications, and established anti-Communism as the yardstick of American patriotism.[10] As Truman hyperbolically justified these extensive precautions, "The assault on free institutions is worldwide and a defeat anywhere is a defeat everywhere."[11] The process by which the U.S. government established these mechanisms, however, was anything but free and democratic. The debate that led to the construction of the national security state took place within high policy-making circles and involved virtually no public discussion.

Through both words and actions, the Soviet Union shares responsibility for dividing the world into East and West. A year and a half after Churchill's famous Iron Curtain speech, Leningrad party boss Andrei Zhdanov offered the official Soviet position—the "two-camp" speech of September 1947—promoting the idea of a life-and-death struggle between Communism and capitalism. The Cold War—a battle waged through words, threats, and political and military proxies—was firmly established with the help of both governments.

Roughly four periods of détente have alleviated Cold War tension.

Following Stalin's death in 1953, the two powers achieved a treaty on Austria's neutrality. In 1959, a new but brief bilateral effort toward nuclear disarmament emerged. In 1963, the two countries negotiated two important arms control treaties—the Hot Line Agreement and the Limited Test Ban Treaty. From 1972 to 1974, trade relations improved dramatically, and the first strategic arms limitation treaty was successfully concluded.[12] Each of these détentes came after a period of particularly heightened tension, whether as a result of the Korean War (1950), the Soviet suppression of the Hungarian uprising (1956), the Bay of Pigs (1961) and the Cuban missile crisis (1962), or the Soviet invasion of Czechoslovakia (1968). As each détente began, policy makers of both sides expressed their fervent belief that East–West relations had entered a new age—of trust and cooperation. While each détente indeed left a mark on relations—whether in the form of treaties or the memories of less fractious dialogue—new eras were conspicuously absent.

The post-1986 détente, like its predecessors, followed a hostile stretch of U.S.–Soviet relations that began in 1974 over the Angola conflict and became overtly antagonistic in the late 1970s. After the Soviet invasion of Afghanistan in 1979, U.S. politicians expunged the term détente from their vocabulary.

During the 1980 presidential election campaign, Republican party candidate Ronald Reagan accentuated perceptions of U.S. global weakness by constantly referring to the Soviet invasion of Afghanistan, the Iranian revolution and the seizure of American hostages, the Nicaraguan revolution, the civil wars in Angola and El Salvador, and the regional conflict in Ethiopia. Reagan, however, viewed the inability of the United States to exert global power unilaterally as a temporary phenomenon. To halt the drift, Reagan argued that the United States has to display its military muscle, especially toward the "advancing" Soviet Union. Reagan was not alone in this opinion. The late 1970s witnessed a resurgence of Cold War posturing. President Carter, who early in his administration pursued relatively conciliatory policies, responded to this thunder on the right, growing hawkish in his final two years in office, with a boycott of the 1980 Moscow Olympics, a grain embargo of the Soviet Union, and a reinstatement of military draft registration.[13]

When Reagan assumed the presidency in 1981, he consistently

implemented the anti-Sovietism of his campaign.[14] Although keeping his promise to U.S. farmers to end the grain embargo, the new president otherwise was unremittingly antagonistic toward the Soviet Union. Reagan accused the Soviet Union of being an "evil empire," a repository for everything antithetical to the American way: the center of international terrorism, the architect behind the attempt to kill John Paul II, the destabilizer of numerous Third World governments, the country holding Western Europe under constant fear of invasion. This Reagan onslaught successfully exploited U.S. fears of a Soviet threat and frequently ignored more level-headed analyses and contrary evidence.[15] In an atmosphere poisoned by accusation and counteraccusation, arms control negotiations came to a virtual standstill.

Anti-Sovietism neared fever pitch in the wake of the U.S.S.R.'s downing of Korean Airlines 007 in September 1983. The Reagan administration immediately seized upon the incident as proof of the evil nature of the Soviet government, a country with which negotiations were obviously useless.[16] The U.S. invasion of Grenada in 1983 and the consequent Soviet boycott of the 1984 Los Angeles Olympics further heightened tensions between the two countries.

During the late Carter and early Reagan years, Soviet policy making was virtually paralyzed by the extreme age and ill health of Kremlin leadership. By 1980, it seemed, senility had overtaken Leonid Brezhnev. When Yuri Andropov became general secretary in 1983, improving U.S.–Soviet relations figured high on his agenda, but he died before achieving any measurable change. His successor, Konstantin Chernenko, a Brezhnevite, was either unwilling or simply too ill to overcome U.S. resistance (and resistance within his own ranks) to détente.

Yet, the present détente emerged from this nadir in relations. Several factors have contributed, perhaps the most important being the remarkable changes in Soviet foreign policy. In accordance with the new thinking, the present Soviet leadership realizes that an improvement in relations with the United States can lead to considerable trading advantages and can free substantial funds to be diverted from the military to economic activities. Thus, U.S.–Soviet relations have a high priority on the Gorbachev administration's agenda. Other aspects of the multilateral Soviet foreign policy—reflecting the greater global integration of economic, political, military, and environmental factors—are *dependent* to a great extent on U.S. cooperation. Although moving toward an essentially nonprovocative relationship with allies and enemies alike, the U.S.S.R. would probably not move toward a *total* demilitarized relationship with the Third World without similar U.S. initiatives. The U.S.S.R. cannot participate in the world economy unless the United States lends its support through its leading role in GATT, in the IMF, and in the formation of its allies' economic policies. The U.S.S.R. cannot help strengthen multilateral institutions such as the United Nations unless the United States and its allies share a similar commitment. Détente then, for the Soviet reformers, is a necessary first step in realizing the aims of their entire domestic and foreign policy agenda.

Soviet initiatives have not alone created the present détente. In the United States, the Reagan administration was struggling in the foreign policy realm, especially in the aftermath of the Iran-contra scandal of 1986 (in which U.S. government officials traded arms to Iran in exchange for the release of U.S. hostages; the profits from the arms deal were then sent illegally to fund the contras working to overthrow the Nicaraguan government). Meanwhile, the staggering costs of the arms race and the pressures it placed on the U.S. budget made possible a certain flexibility in the U.S. policy-making establishment. Finally, the U.S. public, fearful of a deteriorating economy, weary of the threat posed by nuclear weapons, and increasingly concerned with domestic problems (such as budget deficits and drug use), by and large supported an improvement in bilateral relations.

Though both governments have found some common ground, they nonetheless see the present détente very differently. For the U.S.S.R., it is a necessary first principle. Without U.S. diplomatic support, the Gorbachev program will be in serious economic and military straits. For the United States, however, détente is a tentative policy: the government has not linked any domestic programs to détente, nor has it announced any major shift in military spending or policy.[17] This asymmetry may ultimately prove to be the undoing of U.S.–Soviet cooperation.

But an asymmetry in intentions and goals is not the only troubling sign. U.S.–Soviet relations, despite recent improvements, are far from idyllic. In the United States, for instance, certain Cold War myths about the U.S.S.R. continue to shape political discourse. These myths have carried across previous détentes only to be reactivated in times of escalating hostility.[18] That the following six myths still influence the contemporary analyses of politicians, scholars, and journalists does not bode well for the future of constructive U.S.–Soviet relations.

Six U.S. Myths About the Soviet Union

Myth 1. The Soviet Union is bent upon global conquest.
Ever since the forged testament of Peter the Great was "uncovered" in the nineteenth century, "proving" that the Russians had designs on India, various schemes of global conquest have been attributed to the rulers of Russia.[19] Given the territorial acquisitions made under the tsars and the stated desire of the Bolsheviks for world proletarian revolution, the belief in the concoction of a "master plan" is at least understandable. But Russian expansion before the twentieth century was more arbitrary than planned, and Bolshevik calls for world revolution were soon muted by internal problems.

The myth of Soviet expansionism breaks down into a series of assumptions. The Soviet-sponsored North Korean invasion of South Korea was *assumed* to be a springboard to Japan. With allies in the Middle East—Syria, Iraq, and Egypt—the Soviets were *assumed* to be building a "land bridge" to Africa, the ultimate goal being South Africa's riches. Afghanistan was *assumed* to be a first step toward the Persian Gulf.[20] Poland, Czechoslovakia, East Germany were all *assumed* to be mere appetizers before a Western European entrée. As it turned out, none of these assumptions was correct. The U.S.S.R. only hesitantly supported North Korea's push southward[21] and never subsequently threatened Japan. No land bridge was ever built to Africa, no Persian Gulf position has been gained, and no Western European countries have been swallowed up. More important, no plans for any of these schemes have ever been unearthed. Whether or not these assumptions had any basis in reality, U.S. leaders constantly predicated U.S. global activities on *perceptions* of Soviet actions, not on the actions themselves.

In fact, since the 1950s, Soviet geopolitical momentum has steadily declined. Thirty years ago, the U.S.S.R. had significant influence in one out of seven countries; now, despite decades of military and economic aid, it influences only one in ten.[22] In the mid-1980s, the Soviet Union had significant influence, according to one source, in only eighteen countries.[23] Regardless of these diminishing returns, did the U.S.S.R. expand influence worldwide through planned aggression?

The countries of Eastern Europe, as we have seen, were divided quite deliberately by East and West. U.S. Cold War policies helped push the U.S.S.R. away from supporting coalition governments and toward instructing Eastern European Communist parties to seize power. Nonalignment was never an option for Bulgaria, Rumania, East Germany, Czechoslovakia, Poland, or Hungary. Subsequent Soviet interventions in Poland, Czechoslovakia, and Hungary were attempts to *maintain*, not *expand*, influence.

Revolutions in Cuba, Nicaragua, Ethiopia, and South Yemen were unexpected by the Soviet government and did not figure in any Soviet plan to increase its influence in these areas of the world. After the fact, the U.S.S.R. seized the opportunities to win allies, especially when the United States had thoroughly alienated each country in turn.

Through massive arms sales, the U.S.S.R. has tried to woo Syria, Libya, Mozambique, and Angola, but these countries still conduct independent foreign and domestic policies. (In 1988, Soviet arms sales declined by 47 percent, while U.S. sales increased by 66 percent; in that year Moscow exported $9.9 billion in arms, while the United States exported $9.2 billion.[24]) Further, the U.S.S.R. never intervened militarily in these countries, although in Mozambique and Angola it supported particular insurgents, as did the United States. Cuban troops have been instrumental in African conflicts (Angola, Ethiopia), as well as in a primarily advisory capacity in Latin America and the Caribbean. But Havana and Moscow do not see eye to eye, either on the role of revolution or on domestic reform. Cuba's relationship with the U.S.S.R. appears to be increasingly like Israel's relationship with the United States: strategic ally but independent-minded.

In Asia, perceived Communist expansion engendered not only the domino theory but the alliances SEATO (South East Asia Treaty Organization) and CENTO (Central Treaty Organization). "Viewed in the cool light of history," writes Asia specialist Paul Kreisberg in *Foreign Policy* magazine, "a coherent and continuous communist front against the United States and the non-communist countries of Asia probably never existed."[25] The bases that the Soviets established in Somalia, South Yemen, Diego Garcia, and Vietnam, Kreisberg continues, were not used to intimidate, nor were they cause for alarm for the non-Communist countries in the region.[26] The U.S.S.R. is left with two chief allies in the region—Vietnam and North Korea. Yet both countries have remained independent, with North Korea occasionally drifting closer to China.

The U.S.S.R. may not have followed a grand design to conquer the world, but still it may not be as peace-loving (and practicing) as its various pronouncements and constitutions have suggested. In 1921, the Soviet Union imposed Communist rule in Mongolia. The Non-Aggression Pact with Nazi Germany brought the previously independent Baltic states into the U.S.S.R. in 1939. In the same year, the U.S.S.R. attempted an invasion of Finland. Policy toward Eastern Europe has entailed extensive violence and loss of life (several thousand Hungarians dead, for instance, in the 1956 uprising). Soviet tanks rolling into the streets of East Berlin and Prague could only be interpreted as aggression, as were Soviet troops moving into Afghanistan in 1979, whether invited by an increasingly isolated government or not. Arms sales, covert funding of insurgents, use of proxies—the U.S.S.R. has employed all these techniques, as superpowers are unfortunately inclined to do. Nevertheless, these examples do not constitute a pattern consistent with a strategy of expansion. To quote Kennan, the father of containment:

> I saw no evidence at that time [1950], and have seen none since, of any Soviet desire to assume the burdens of occupation over any extensive territories beyond those that came under their occupation or control as part of the outcome of World War II.[27]

Despite Kennan's certitude, it is difficult to say whether Soviet reticence has derived from a lack of desire or a lack of capability. Historically, the U.S.S.R. has simply not had the means to extend power much beyond its territorial limits.[28] Today, the U.S.S.R. is in no better position, according to Director of U.S. Naval Intelligence Rear Admiral William Studeman:

> Soviet forces abroad, such as those of Cam Ranh Bay, Vietnam or in Ethiopia, South Yemen, Cuba or the South Atlantic, are still too few and too weak to enable the Soviets to engage in any significant power projection, particularly over a prolonged period.[29]

While such comparisons can be tricky, it is nonetheless worth noting that U.S. global strategy, in the name of preventing Soviet expansion, has been quite expansive in its own right. U.S. post–World War II interventions and destabilizations have included Angola, Cambodia, Chile, Congo, Cuba, Dominican Republic, El Salvador, Grenada, Guatemala, Indonesia, Iran, Laos, Libya, Nicaragua, Vietnam, the Western Sahara, Zaire, and Zimbabwe. As has been often observed, we frequently construct our enemies in our own image.

Myth 2. *The Soviet Union enjoys nuclear superiority over the United States.*

The speed with which the U.S.S.R. followed the development of its first atom bomb in 1949 with the explosion of a hydrogen bomb in 1954 thoroughly surprised U.S. scientists. These same scientists no longer considered the Soviet H-bomb a fluke when in 1957 the U.S.S.R. tested the first intercontinental ballistic missile (ICBM) and launched the first orbiting satellite (Sputnik), thus charging ahead of the United States in the space race. Many in the West then assumed that the Soviets would surpass the United States in the arms race as well. This assumption gave birth to a number of potent misconceptions.

The first imagined Soviet threat was President Truman's "bomber gap." In 1950, the air force predicted that the Soviets would have 600 to 700 bombers by 1959. In fact, by 1961, the Soviets would have only 190.[30] Under President Eisenhower, a "missile gap" appeared, later to be promoted by Democratic presidential candidate John Kennedy. Paul Nitze, formerly of the National Security Council, estimated that the Soviet Union would have 500 ICBMs by 1961, but the Soviets by that time could only manage four ineffectual ones.[31] In the 1960s, an "antiballistic missile (ABM) gap" was perceived, but the Soviets succeeded in building only one ABM site to protect Moscow (a later treaty restricted deployment).[32]

Following a brief period of détente during the Nixon years, the Cold Warriors resurfaced to take the offensive. Paul Nitze and his organization, the Committee on the Present Danger, led a neo-conservative attack on President Carter's foreign policy, using inflated estimates of the Soviet nuclear threat. Their most important distortions concerned the Soviets' superiority in missile launchers, missile throw-weight, and degree of military spending: all misleading assessments peddled successfully by the Reagan administration.[33] While the hawks could point to actual Soviet numerical superiorities, they neglected to point out that launchers are not as strategically important as deliverable warheads, in which the U.S. still has the lead; that although Soviet missiles are heavier in throw-weight, U.S. missile makers *chose* to produce lighter, more technologically efficient models; that the Soviet GNP is half that of the United States, and hence comparisons of military spending as a percentage of GNP lead to misleading conclusions.[34]

In one field, that of innovations in weapons development, the United States has maintained a conspicuous superiority. The U.S.S.R. has been the leader in weapons innovation only twice—with the intercontinental ballistic missile (ICBM) and the antiballistic missile system (ABM). On every other new development, from the atom bomb to the Cruise missile to SDI, the United States has established the precedent. Of thirty-nine major weapons developments since World War II, according to military analyst Tom Gervasi, the United States has pioneered thirty-seven.[35]

Further, since 1968, the Soviet Union has been exceptionally responsive on several nuclear arms issues. In 1970, military analyst Michael MccGwire notes, the Soviets abandoned construction of 70 ICBM silos and in 1979 dropped plans to convert 100 ICBM silos from third-generation to fourth-generation systems.[36] These unilateral decisions signaled a clear interest in pursuing the two SALT agreements. The United States, meanwhile, showed no comparable commitment, developing MIRV technology (a major technical spur to the arms race which enabled missiles to carry multiple warheads) and deliberately not including it in negotiations.[37] From 1970 to 1975, at a time when limits were being negotiated on strategic nuclear weapons, U.S. nuclear warheads increased from 1,775 to 6,800, while Soviet warheads increased from 1,700 to 2,700.[38]

Every perceived "gap" between the U.S. and Soviet nuclear arsenals has proved to be either imagined or deliberately manufactured. Even if gaps existed, they would now be largely irrelevant. Both sides possess an enormous number of weapons—in the multiple overkill range. Both sides also possess a virtually impregnable sea-based deterrent (though both sides are researching antisubmarine weapons systems that may eventually undermine this deterrent).

Are there degrees of nuclear deterrence? Can one side ever accumulate sufficient missiles to justify, in a strategic military sense, their deliberate use? During the 1961 Berlin crisis, when President Kennedy considered using nuclear weapons against the Soviet Union, his analysts calculated that a Soviet response would probably kill 15 million Americans. Journalist Andrew Cockburn writes:

> It is an indication of the irrelevance of the enormous arsenals currently maintained by both the Soviet Union and the United States to deterrence that even the minimal threat of Soviet retaliation was enough to deter the United States from launching an attack on Russia at a time when it possessed the maximum nuclear advantage over the Soviets.[39]

The question of nuclear superiority has no purely military significance at the level of weapons both sides possess. The use of "superiority," though, has blocked critical nuclear arms control negotiations and distorted East–West relations.

Myth 3. The Soviet Union can successfully conquer Western Europe with its conventional forces.

In 1967, on the eve of the fiftieth anniversary of the Russian Revolution, the Soviets were planning a dramatic display of their military strength. As one of their showpiece demonstrations, a complement of tanks was to cross the Dnieper River—*beneath* the water. Unfortunately for the Soviets, they discovered during trial runs that halfway across the river the tanks ran amok, knocked off course by trapped air and difficulties in steering. Soviet engineers set to work—and laid concrete guides entirely across the riverbed. When the celebration day came, the tanks made their trip safely, kept in place by grooved paths. Oblivious to the Soviets' feat of conjuring, the Western media photographed the exhibition and it became but one more example of irrefutable Soviet conventional superiority.[40]

As this anecdote suggests, the myth of the Soviet threat is a collaborative fiction—neither the Soviet leadership nor the U.S. leadership wants the U.S.S.R. to appear weak. For the Soviets, the matter is one of national security. For the Americans, the Soviet threat has frequently justified aggressive countermeasures. From 1981 to 1984, for instance, the Reagan administration used the myth of a Soviet military threat to justify the largest peacetime increase in military strength in U.S. history.

Behind this perception of Soviet military superiority is another Soviet reality: poorly paid and disgruntled conscripts, technically faulty machinery, outdated command and control centers, unreliable Eastern European units, limited naval access to important sea routes, and costly and ineffective civil defense units. When the U.S. military runs mock exercises using captured Soviet weapons and armored transport vehicles, the Soviet systems often have to be significantly modified or even replaced by American systems—either because the Soviet hardware does not work or because it endangers the lives of the American soldiers using it.[41] Soviet SAMs (surface-to-air missiles) and tanks were grossly ineffective against the Israelis in both the Yom Kippur War (1973) and in Israel's 1982 invasion of Lebanon.[42] When the Soviets were considering a move into Poland in 1980, the call-up of Soviet reservists was in many cases a fiasco.[43] In its only major military campaign since 1945, the Red Army lost 13,000 to 15,000 Soviet soldiers in failing to subdue Afghani insurgents between 1979 and 1989.

These are the weapons and the personnel that have been compared favorably with U.S. systems and troops. To use Defense Department parlance, these are the Soviet "beans." The Reagan administration has made much of the "bean count" because it shows that Warsaw Pact forces contain more tanks, more personnel, and more planes than NATO forces. On paper, the Soviets do have advantages, in some cases overwhelming: for instance, they have nearly three times as many tanks and artillery pieces stationed in Europe. But sheer numbers do not an invincible army make. One indication of the military value of these forces is the Soviet willingness to scrap them.

Recently, many U.S. policy makers have expanded their focus to include more than just beans. Perhaps the most dramatic of these analyses is Senator Carl Levin's report "Beyond the Bean Count," submitted to the Senate Armed Services Committee in January 1988. Just looking at beans, Levin argues, obscures many crucial and hard-to-quantify elements: terrain, troop morale, quality of weapons, leadership experience, emerging technology. Taking these elements into consideration, Levin concludes that a rough parity exists between NATO and Warsaw Pact forces.[44]

The House Armed Services Committee in late 1988 was even more emphatic in disposing of the myth of Soviet conventional superiority. It concluded that NATO forces in Europe were simply better prepared than Warsaw Pact forces.[45]

Myth 4. Only "hard-line" policies work with the Soviet Union.
While hard-line policies may work when a large country bullies a smaller country into submission, such policies rarely resolve conflicts between two powerful nations (short of the all-out military defeat of one side). When the Soviets have attempted hard-line policies against the United States—in the 1948 Berlin blockade, for instance—they have failed dramatically. Stalin had hoped that by starving the population of West Berlin, he could remove the Western enclave. Intent upon achieving this goal, he even ignored U.S. threats to use the atom bomb on Moscow. His hard-line policy—which had worked earlier on the smaller Baltic countries—met its match and more in Berlin. Stalin simply provoked the West into unity, and Berlin remained divided.[46] Similarly, when Khrushchev confronted the United States with the placement of nuclear missiles in Cuba in 1962, Soviet brinkmanship again accomplished little more than to spur U.S. defiance and outrage.

U.S. policy toward the U.S.S.R. has suffered from equally misinformed premises. The hard-line rhetoric of Eisenhower's Secretary of State John Foster Dulles and his vigorous support of West German re-armament only strengthened the hands of Soviet conservatives and in part prevented Georgi Malenkov from more radically de-Stalinizing Soviet foreign policy.[47] The Jackson-Vanik amendment, a 1974 piece of legislation linking favorable trade terms to increased emigration rates, did not force the Soviets to ease restrictions. From 1975 to 1977, emigration rates instead dipped considerably. Only in 1978, when the Soviets wanted the SALT II treaty to pass the Senate, did the rates rise.[48] In the anti-Soviet first term of the Reagan administration, the rates plummeted again. Yet, as relations warmed in the latter Reagan administration years, rates of emigration rose once again.[49]

When the Carter administration wanted to punish the Soviets for invading Afghanistan in 1979, it pulled the United States out of the 1980 Olympics and levied a grain embargo. Only mildly put off by the U.S. rebuff, the Soviets hosted the Moscow games anyway and then boycotted the U.S. Olympics in 1984. Though distressed at the loss of good rates for grain from the United States, the Soviets turned to Canada and Argentina and maintained their import levels. In both cases, the Soviets did not suffer particularly, but U.S. farmers and U.S. Olympic athletes did. Even Reagan realized the foolishness of the grain embargo and repealed it in his first term.

Unilateral U.S. trade sanctions during the late 1970s and Reagan's first term only helped the trade balances of Western European countries. Germany expanded its trade with the Soviets by 30 percent in the first six months after the Soviet invasion of Afghanistan; in the first nine months of 1980, French–Soviet trade jumped by 60 percent.[50] The United States may criticize its European allies for opportunism or ethical laxity, but the fact remains: without a concerted international response, U.S. hard-line policies only rebound painfully. During the 1982 pipeline controversy, when the United States once again reduced trade with the Soviets, it was only U.S. companies that were punished: the Caterpillar company, for instance, lost hundreds of millions of dollars and consequently laid off part of its work force.[51]

Cold Warriors in the United States only reinforce Soviet Cold Warriors.[52] The latter argue that it is fruitless to negotiate with the United States; the former develop policies that prove the accuracy of that contention. It would seem that U.S. hard-liners do not want the

U.S.S.R. to become conciliatory. As Eurystheus devised the impossible twelve labors for Hercules, so have U.S. hard-liners set increasingly difficult tasks for the Soviet Union in order to ensure that it will fail. The continued presence of a Soviet enemy also allows hardliners to push for more military expenditures, to justify U.S. interventions in the Third World, and to discredit domestic opposition to those policies. An interventionary foreign policy can only sustain itself by feeding on fear. For the last forty years, the Soviet Union has supplied that fodder.

Did the hard-liner Reagan produce the soft-liner Gorbachev? During Reagan's first term, four years of unrelenting hostility from Washington only produced similarly uncooperative responses from Moscow. Given this less-than-constructive record, it would seem more logical that the soft-liner Gorbachev produced a new, softer Reagan. As we have seen, furthermore, Soviet reform did not begin with Gorbachev; he merely synthesized past programs, added charisma, and had the great fortune to be at the height of his political life at a time when more conservative Politburo members were nearing the end of theirs. To repeat: A complex set of Soviet domestic concerns, innovative Soviet leadership, and international pressures, not the aggressive and often irresponsible muscle-flexing of the United States, has produced flexible Soviet negotiating positions.

Myth 5. The Soviet Union seeks détentes only as "breathing spells" before consolidating and overpowering the United States.

According to this "boxing match" theory of international politics, countries square off against each other with the objective of knocking out the opponent or winning through attrition. If an adversary appears to be resting, it is only a stratagem, a breathing spell before the resumption of the fight. At the end—and there will always be an end in such scenarios—only one winner will remain. Draws are anathema.

William Hyland, editor of the influential journal *Foreign Affairs*, recasts the argument as it relates to U.S.–Soviet relations:

> The first objective for American policy . . . is to create the circumstances that will make it difficult for the Soviet Union to

resume the offensive if and when Gorbachev or his successors have rebuilt Soviet power.[53]

Hyland implies that the U.S.S.R. is inherently offensive and incorrigibly dishonest about its intentions. The U.S.S.R., in other words, is fixed in a Cold War posture, incapable of changing to fit a new set of international conditions.

This view also ignores the inescapable fact that the positions held by the United States and the Soviet Union in the immediate postwar world cannot be regained. Since that time, other nations have acquired nuclear technology, other nations have become economic powers, and the utility of military force has declined (though not disappeared). The Soviet Union is concerned with renovating its own policy, not vis-à-vis the United States but in line with its own domestic imperatives and in accord with these new international conditions.

Furthermore, the "breathing spell" argument assumes a consensus between civilian reformers and the Soviet military, that the politicians will give the green light to the generals when economic success has been guaranteed. The Gorbachev camp, however, has a less than sanguine attitude toward "old school" militarists and leans toward military planners conversant in "reasonable sufficiency" and a *permanently* streamlined military.[54] Nor does it seem that the Soviet reformers view foreign policy initiatives simply as a means to an end. Reductions in military capacity are not seen *solely* within the context of domestic savings. Rather, the reformers seem to be approaching foreign policy in the same way they are approaching domestic issues. Thus, if and when the Soviet economy improves, there is no reason to expect that any major reversal in Soviet foreign policy will take place. Even in the highly improbable case of the U.S.S.R. doubling its GNP, it would still have only achieved parity with the present United States GNP (and that presumes no growth in the U.S. economy). Even with parity, the U.S.S.R. would hardly be in a position to overpower the international economic system or to assert its political will unilaterally.

With its breakneck pace, military competition between the two superpowers by its very nature necessitates these "breathing spells" or détentes. The Soviet Union seems to have realized that superpower competition is no longer economically or politically tenable and wants to make arms reductions permanent—not a fourth-round rest in a ten-round battle to the death. Whether the United States arrives at the same realization will, in part, determine the ultimate longevity of Myth 5.

Myth 6. The United States can neither help nor hinder Soviet reform.

Recent U.S. analyses of the Gorbachev reforms have indeed recognized their significance. Often the analysts endorse the changes. Yet, an increasingly popular conclusion has been: though perhaps in the world's best interest, these reforms are essentially internal and cannot be influenced by outside forces. "There is little Western governments can do to speed up the reform process," argues Soviet analyst Ed Hewett. "The fate of *perestroika*—and of Mr. Gorbachev himself—will be determined in Moscow, not Washington or Bonn."55

While the burden of responsibility for success lies primarily on the shoulders of Gorbachev and his colleagues, the notion that the United States cannot influence the process is rather odd. As we have seen, domestic reform in the Soviet Union is intimately connected to foreign policy, especially U.S.–Soviet relations. Whether redirecting money from the military to consumer industries or fostering more advantageous trade relationships, the Soviet reformers recognize that positive Western response is critical—at the negotiating tables with U.S. representatives in Geneva and Vienna, in the U.S. Congress, in the boardrooms of U.S. corporations, in the commodity markets on Wall Street, in the meetings of the IMF, the Group of Seven, and GATT. In a world in which domestic economic and political decisions are becoming inescapably international, the Soviet Union's internal situation depends a great deal on the attitudes and programs of other countries, particularly the United States. Gorbachev has so indicated; Western European governments have so acted.

Then why the sudden shrugs from U.S. analysts, the perplexed "gosh, there's nothing we can do" attitudes? Whether consciously or not, the analyses admirably justify the present stance of the Bush administration toward the Soviet Union. Half the President's advisers prefer an activist policy; half favor a passive, wait-and-see policy. This deadlock has produced a nonpolicy that advocates label "pragmatism" and critics call "indecision."[56] The official title is "status quo plus," with the "plus" thrown in more for rhetorical effect than to indicate a verifiable policy.

Although several government reports have maintained that Gorbachev and his allies are likely to remain in power, influential Bush aides such as Secretary of Defense Richard Cheney believe otherwise.[57] In one statement from which the White House eventually had to distance itself, Cheney predicted: "I would guess that [Gorbachev] would ultimately fail; that is to say that he will not be able to reform the Soviet economy and when that happens, he's likely to be replaced by somebody who will be far more hostile."[58] Although White House officials consistently maintain that this view is held only by Cheney and Vice President Quayle, the possibility of a failed Soviet reform acts as a deterrent to formulating clear foreign policy objectives.

There are two critical problems with both Cheney's view and the lukewarm Bush approach. On the one hand, the "wait-and-see" attitude is self-fulfilling: if the administration believes that Soviet reform will not succeed and acts according to these assumptions, Soviet reform has that much less chance of succeeding. On the other hand, the Bush administration has not yet realized that reform is, in certain key respects, inevitable—whether by Gorbachev or by his successors—particularly in the realm of foreign policy. "Moscow simply has no resources for costly global exploits," maintains Soviet analyst Dmitri Simes.[59]

True, there could be a conservative resurgence in the Soviet Union, uniting ambitious party members, neo-Stalinists, and traditional Russian nationalists against the Western-oriented Gorbachev camp. A similar resurgence occurred in China in June 1989, bringing widespread government repression. While political reform and human rights suffered, the Chinese government has not retreated substantially on its economic reform, and its foreign policy has remained reasonably consistent. Should a similar situation result in the Soviet Union, the key elements of the Gorbachev reform—economic reform and military disengagement—would probably remain in place. In the case of a conservative backlash, many groups that are now ambivalent toward Gorbachev—whether Baltic nationalists or striking coal miners—would suddenly embrace the Gorbachev platform and demonstrate, through collective strength, that the U.S.S.R. simply has no other choice but to continue *perestroika*. In the face of these challenges—considerably better organized than ever before in Soviet history—it is not altogether clear whether a conservative bloc could maintain power in Moscow.

Rather than sit back and wait for such a scenario to unfold, the U.S. government would do well to think deeply about what can be done to facilitate reform and improve the lives of Soviet citizens. U.S. policy makers will soon discover that such policies—whether in the form of arms control treaties or trade agreements—could improve the lives of U.S. citizens as well.

These six myths testify to the durability of Cold War attitudes. Détente for the United States remains, in part because of these attitudes, a very fragile state of international affairs. Similar Cold War myths concerning the United States exist in the Soviet Union and in many cases are mirror images: the United States has large nuclear superiority, or only hard-line policies work with the United States. Anti-Americanism is not, however, as strong a force within U.S.S.R. as anti-Sovietism traditionally has been in the United States (most tourists returning from trips to the U.S.S.R. are surprised at how pro-Western the average Soviet citizen is). Further, such myths have been substantially rejected by the present Soviet leadership. Given entrenched conservatism within the party and throughout Soviet society, these myths concerning the United States should not, however, be casually dismissed.

If the present détente is not undermined by the logic of its own history or the myths that persist even during periods of greatest cooperation, a final challenge remains—and by most accounts, it is the most intractable.

North-South Relations

The Third World has traditionally been well insulated from the positive effects of détente. Improved U.S.–Soviet relations during the

Nixon–Brezhnev years did not preclude major wars in Vietnam, the Middle East, and Bangladesh; nor did they prevent superpower confrontation in Angola and the Horn of Africa; nor did they alleviate indirect military and economic manipulation in Chile or Poland; nor did they, in general, encourage self-determination for the peoples of these regions. Furthermore, détente did not close the economic gap between the Northern Hemisphere's prosperity and the Southern Hemisphere's poverty: Third World trade deficits did not markedly improve, famine increased, and fertile lands became barren. In at least one instance, détente even directly aggravated these problems in the Third World: The massive 1972 grain deal between the United States and the U.S.S.R. caused world wheat prices to double within months and in part provoked famine to reappear in India and Africa after a twenty-five-year absence.[60] For all the sighs of relief in the United States and the Soviet Union, détente accomplished little with regard to the Third World. Nor was it designed to apply outside East–West relations. As Henry Kissinger, the principal architect of the Nixon–Brezhnev détente, remarked in 1969: "Nothing important can come from the South. The axis of history starts in Moscow, goes to Bonn, crosses over to Washington, and then goes to Tokyo. What happens in the South is of no importance."[61]

The South came back to haunt Kissinger as conflicts in the 1970s negatively affected U.S.–Soviet relations. Superpower confrontation in the Middle East and Angola hastened the end of détente. The last initiative of this period, SALT II, foundered in the Senate in 1979 because of at least three Third World situations: the Soviet invasion of Afghanistan, East–West conflict in Ethiopia, and a Soviet unit "discovered" in Cuba (they had been stationed there in one form or another since 1962).[62]

A détente in U.S.–Soviet relations, while diminishing the twin threats of superpower nuclear and conventional confrontation in Europe, does not begin to address the competition for influence in the Third World or the economic relationship between North and South. These very problems that détente has ignored have proved its undoing. Poverty and war in the Southern Hemisphere offer many opportunities for manipulation by the economically powerful and arms-exporting countries of the North.[63] These opportunities in turn produce competition—for political influence, military contracts, economic trade—which inevitably has a deleterious effect on East–West relations (not to mention the economic health and general well-being of the Third World countries in question).

The Soviet reformers have presented clear proposals: military disengagement from the Third World, negotiated solutions to regional conflicts, and international actions to correct the disparity in wealth between North and South. In calling for diplomatic and economic negotiations, the reformers have had very practical motives: Soviet military interventions have generally proved unsuccessful, and economic relations with peaceful and prosperous nations bring more immediate advantages.

The West has also presented clear proposals on North–South relations and for the last decade has, unfortunately, been carrying them out. Since 1980, Western military and economic intervention in the Third World has taken the forms of "low-intensity warfare" and the global debt crisis. The following section outlines these particular military and economic challenges to détente.

Low-intensity conflict (LIC) doctrine is the Pentagon's answer to U.S. military failure in the Vietnam War, an intervention that cost 55,000 U.S. lives, resulted in an unambiguous retreat, and undercut the U.S. electorate's support for military intervention in the Third World. As political analyst William Schneider points out, most U.S. citizens today feel, concerning future military campaigns, that the United States "should either win or get out."[64] This attitude, in part, explains the apparently contradictory response of the U.S. public to the invasion of Grenada (thumbs up) and the potential invasion of Nicaragua (thumbs down).

In contrast to full-scale military invasion, current military doctrine relies for the most part on proxies, nonmilitary pressures, and military threats. Although LIC has evolved into a military doctrine in the Reagan years, its lineage extends back much further. Truman, for instance, established the precedents for key LIC elements such as covert operations. Eisenhower's "New Look" emphasized "making containment work more efficiently at less cost."[65] In the 1960s, President Kennedy updated LIC, refining the role of counterinsurgency in Laos, South Vietnam, and Cuba. In response to events in the Arc of Crisis, the Carter administration introduced the Rapid Deployment Force (RDF), military units that could intervene quickly in dangerous situations.

Like a crime syndicate that conceals an illegal operation across a series of seemingly legitimate enterprises, the Reagan administration divided LIC strategy into various "respectable" components: insurgency (support to anti-Communist guerrillas), counterinsurgency (support to governments fighting insurgent movements), antidrug operations (destruction of Peruvian, Bolivian, and Colombian crops), terrorism counteraction (bombing of Libya), and "peace-keeping" operations (invasion of Grenada). The CIA grew in size to accommodate the need for additional intelligence.[66] The undeclared wars involving the United States in El Salvador, Afghanistan, Angola, and Nicaragua operated as testing grounds for the Reagan administration's version of the New Look.

The 1988 Defense Department publication *Discriminate Deterrence* indicated that the revived containment doctrine would not leave the White House with the Reagan administration. This analysis of U.S. foreign policy interests for the 1990s, commissioned by the Defense Department and written by a group of conservatives and *Realpolitik* enthusiasts, advocates a shift in U.S. policy from East–West conflict in Europe to East–West conflict in the Third World.

The Atlantic alliance, these authors argue, has "outlasted all multilateral peacetime alliances in modern history." The Soviet threat has been effectively countered in Europe, and there is little likelihood of war breaking out across the East and West German border. The *real* tinderbox, they maintain, is the Third World, and U.S. policy makers are not paying sufficient attention to the erosion of U.S. influence throughout this vast area. Steps must be taken to shore up U.S. interests abroad and deter Soviet (and to a lesser degree, Chinese and Japanese) expansionism. Cold War assertions abound in *Discriminate Deterrence:* the domino theory is alive and well and operating in Central America; the U.S.S.R. has surpassed the United States militarily; the U.S.S.R. is planning an invasion of the Persian Gulf; low-intensity warfare is being directed *against* the United States; an "advisers gap" exists in the Third World. All of these "facts" necessitate continued U.S. intervention.[67]

The corollary to military intervention is economic manipulation.

Colonial strategy was relatively transparent: industrializing countries used their colonies for raw materials and cheap labor. The decline of colonialism and the establishment of a world economy in the postwar period were supposed to end this direct exploitation and replace it with responsible development: to borrow President Kennedy's image, the Third World boats would be lifted by the rising tide of Western prosperity.

Has this goal been achieved? The West has certainly prospered. But the Third World? A papal encyclical on the social concerns of the Church reflected on the differences between 1968 and 1988: "The first fact to note is that the hopes for development, at that time so lively, today appear very far from being realized."[68] The United Nations estimates that almost *1 billion* rural people in the Third World are today without land.[69] The notion entertained by many in the 1960s of an ever-widening circle of prosperity encompassing the countries of North and South alike cannot in the 1990s be reconciled with the reality of chronic underdevelopment in the Third World: the result of war, debt, and corruption. As one analyst succinctly concludes, "the shame of the 1980s is that the poor are still getting poorer and the rich richer."[70]

No issue puts this problem of global economic inequality in starker contrast than the international debt crisis. In 1982, when Mexico threatened to default on its loan payments to Northern banks, the security of the international financial system was suddenly at risk. A mere three years earlier in 1979, the signs had been seemingly healthy. OPEC countries were profiting from six years of increased oil prices, putting windfall profits into U.S. and European banks, which in turn loaned the money to Third World countries who needed help with trade imbalances. But these loans had become risky during the late 1970s and early '80s. Often, the loans were spent imprudently by Third World elites. Equally important, U.S. interest rates were rising and commodity prices for Third World exports precipitously falling in real terms in 1981–1982 to their lowest levels since the 1940s.[71] Impoverished countries turned to multilateral financial institutions such as the IMF for money to pay back earlier loans, and the IMF imposed austerity programs for the recipients (high exports, low imports, social spending cuts) that only imposed hardships on the poorest and did not solve debt problems.[72] Protests connected with austerity programs have cost lives in Morocco, Egypt, Liberia, Sudan, Peru, Ecuador, Bolivia, and Jamaica, to name just a few.[73] In 1989, Venezuela and Argentina joined this growing list.

Through these austerity programs, Western banks and international lending agencies have essentially managed the economies—and in some cases even the political decisions—of many Third World countries. Less-developed countries (LDCs) are told what to plant, what to sell, whom to sell it to. With banks exchanging debts for controlling interest in LDC enterprises (debt-equity swaps), the manipulation is even more blatant. Such an economic relationship has made postcolonial Third World countries more dependent on the Northern countries, rather than less.

Under the guise of sending money to LDCs, the North has actually extracted resources. According to Carol Barton, in Latin America, for example,

the net transfer of wealth . . . to creditors has been US $110 billion, equivalent in real terms to one and a half times as much as the Marshall Plan transferred to Europe. That is, Latin America has financed a Marshall Plan aid program to the North, and not vice versa as most Americans believe.[74]

The net negative flow of money from the seventeen most indebted nations has been $31 billion. In net terms, the World Bank has gone from lending $2.6 billion in 1985 to extracting $350 million in 1987.[75] Given the extent of continued Third World impoverishment at the hands of Northern banks and governments, it is not surprising that policy analyst Susan George calls the debt crisis "FLIC," or financial low-intensity conflict.[76]

The manipulation of Third World economies by the North is certainly not new. Western companies have previously held controlling interests in Third World economies: United Fruit in Guatemala, U.S. copper companies in Chile, U.S. oil companies in Iran, Belgian mineral concerns in the Congo, British mines in South Africa. In Central America, threat of nationalization of such concerns brought American marines to Nicaragua between 1912 and 1933, Guatemala in 1954, the Dominican Republic in 1965. During the 1960s, however, military means of securing markets became less expedient than the sophisticated use of international economic pressures. In Chile from 1970 to 1973, when Salvador Allende's socialist government began to nationalize the U.S. copper industries, the United States withdrew all aid and influenced the IMF and World Bank to do likewise. When its economy collapsed through the loss of international credits, Allende's democratically elected government succumbed to a military coup from the right. Even food aid, supposedly humanitarian, has been used to pressure Third World governments.[77]

Industrialized countries are not the only cause of Third World poverty. Inequality within developing countries—exemplified by rich aristocracies, wealthy landowning classes, or bureaucratic elites—has also hampered economic development. Instead of working to equalize these internal disparities, however, industrialized countries have generally sided with Third World elites. The Belgian government, for instance, has supported the Zairan *nomenklatura* through military sales and economic aid; U.S. corporations have enriched the wealthy classes in Chile. Whether exploited by outside forces or by indigenous groups, the peoples of the Third World have not witnessed the sustainable economic development so often promised to them over the past several decades.

As Netherlands premier Joop den Uyl noted in 1975, it is not simply a question of choosing between a free-enterprise system and a centrally planned economy.

> The real choice we have to make is between sticking to our present system, which is largely guided and manipulated for the benefit of the rich countries, and opting for a system directed towards finding solutions to the problems of an equitable division of income and property, of scarcity of natural resources and of despoliation of the environment.[78]

These are not simply Third World problems. As we have seen, Eastern Europe too is part of the debt crisis. *Nomenklaturas* in these regions have often expropriated multilateral loans for their own purposes (most notably, the Gierek government in Poland in the 1970s).

More critically, several countries in the region—as well as the Soviet Union—are strongly considering IMF solutions to their economic problems: rapid privatization, slashed social spending, greater disparities in wealth, austerity for the least-protected segments of society. Equitable solutions to the debt crisis must then take into account, to modify Kissinger, *both* axes of history.

Because of low-intensity warfare and the debt crisis, changes in Soviet foreign policy are not unambiguously positive for Third World peoples. The decrease of Soviet influence in the Third World may simply open the way for other countries to rush in to fill the void (with its counterterrorism and antidrug campaigns, the United States is a leading candidate). Soviet eagerness to embrace international capitalism, meanwhile, will lend that much more authority to the current IMF formula for success. Although the U.S.S.R. has indicated that its attitudes conform more to Joop den Uyl's perspective than Milton Friedman's, it is not yet clear whether Soviet leaders will remain so enlightened if and when they have significant input into international economic decision making. Once again, détente and superpower cooperation have their potential negative aspects, especially for the Third World.

Why is the present détente fragile? Wars continue in an increasingly impoverished Third World. East–West questions of deterrence and European conventional war have not lost any importance—few nuclear weapons have actually been dismantled, and large armies still stand ready in Central Europe. Our myths about the U.S.S.R., furthermore, are still operative, whether latent within the policymaking apparatus or explicitly blocking important arms control treaties.

Are traditional techniques of encouraging and preserving détente capable of dispelling Cold War myths and addressing North–South relations? For twenty-five years, arms control has been the major tool in tempering East–West hostilities—bringing the superpowers together at the bargaining table, if only to disagree.

After nearly three decades of only moderate success, has arms control outlived its usefulness?

Arms Control: Meeting the Challenge?

Arms control treaties have occasionally contributed to a lessening of tensions between the two countries, as the Hot Line Agreement and the Limited Test Ban Treaty did during the Kennedy–Khrushchev years, or SALT I during the Nixon–Brezhnev years. They have also occasionally prevented destabilizing technology, through the ABM treaty and the Biological Weapons Convention, or have circumscribed the arms race geographically, as in the Antarctic Treaty, the Latin American Nuclear-Free Zone Treaty, and the Non-Proliferation Treaty.

But these successes are limited, disappointing even analysts within the arms control community. "Arms control negotiations are rapidly becoming the best excuse for escalating, rather than toning down the arms race," Herbert Scoville, Jr., former deputy director of the CIA, has said.[79] This tendency to encourage escalation is not simply the result of politicking on both sides of the East–West divide but rather derives from characteristics intrinsic to the arms control process.

For instance, the arms control framework assumes an adversarial relationship between the negotiating parties and does not address that relationship except in military terms. Even when arms control is successful, political tensions between the countries do not necessarily improve, and these underlying tensions often lead once again to military buildups sustained by technological innovation and/or treaty loopholes.[80]

Arms control does not address these political questions. Or economic issues. Or North–South problems. It is simply not designed for these tasks. It is ironic that these factors contribute to ending détente, and yet the chief method of initiating and preserving détente—namely, arms control—simply ignores them. Instead, arms control negotiations focus only on weapons, most often nuclear weapons. Even judged according to this narrow criterion, however, arms control comes up lacking.

Through loopholes, arms control treaties have often permitted more weapons than they ban. The Outer Space Treaty, for instance, bans orbiting space weapons but not ballistic missiles (which enter outer space but do not orbit) and not potential SDI systems (which are not themselves weapons of mass destruction). The Sea Bed Treaty bans nuclear weapons on the seabed but allows nuclear submarines and "creeping" weapons such as submarines on treads. SALT I does not cover MIRVs (which permitted a massive increase in nuclear warheads during the 1970s). The INF treaty eliminates intermediate-range *missiles*, but not the *warheads*, which can simply be transferred to other weapons.

Other treaties are weakened because major countries are not signatories: Limited Test Ban Treaty (France and China); Non-Proliferation Treaty (Argentina, Brazil, India, Pakistan, Israel, and South Africa[81]); Latin American Nuclear-Free Zone Treaty (Cuba[82]); SALT II, Threshold Test Ban Treaty, and Peaceful Nuclear Explosions Treaty (not ratified by the U.S. Senate).[83]

Given this spotty record, can arms control offer a significant improvement in U.S.–Soviet relations? In a limited sense, the answer is yes: arms control can help to control nuclear weapons and, potentially, conventional forces in Europe as well.

One promising sign on nuclear issues is the increasing acceptance within the arms control community of the concept of minimum deterrence, which permits paring down nuclear arsenals to, for instance, a force of impregnable sea-launched ballistic missiles (SLBMs).[84] An important step toward minimum deterrence is the Strategic Arms Limitations Talks (START), which, experts expect, will lead to a 50 percent reduction in intercontinental ballistic missiles. Until the INF treaty, arms control negotiations simply limited increases in arsenals; START, if passed, would mandate a dramatic decrease in numbers of nuclear weapons. The arms control framework can also address the remaining nuclear weapons of both sides in Europe—the short-range nuclear forces.

Arms control can also effectively restrict technological improvements in nuclear weapons through the Comprehensive Test Ban Treaty (CTBT). A CTBT was to have been the next priority after the 1974 Threshold Test Ban Treaty (TTBT),[85] but the U.S. Senate never ratified TTBT, and CTBT has remained in arms control limbo. Given repeated Soviet offers—and previous unilateral test bans—a CTBT might be quickly negotiated.[86]

Arms control may, in the next decade, finally achieve successes in limiting nonnuclear or conventional weapons such as tanks and aircraft as well as demobilizing troops. A key obstacle facing nonnuclear arms control is "burden sharing," a proposed U.S. policy of forcing U.S. allies to accept a greater share of the military burden. Burden sharing has already won bipartisan support in Congress. NATO is already considering a multinational airborne strike unit designed to ease U.S. military expenditures in Europe.[87] But burden sharing is more than a political expedient to maintain the same level of military forces. Increasing allied military commitment to the European and Pacific theaters potentially allows the United States to redeploy forces in the Third World, where many military analysts advise greater force projection. Moreover, behind the egalitarian message ("each country must pay its way") is the attempt of the United States to impose on its allies, particularly Japan and West Germany, the economic consequences of Reaganism: rising military budgets accompanied by larger trade and budget deficits and higher unemployment. Japan has already devoted more to its military than its post–World War II limit of 1 percent of GNP. A more precipitous rise in Japanese military expenditures will inevitably cut into its social programs and the research and development resources now devoted to civilian industry.

The same budgetary constraints that make burden sharing popular in the United States may force the scaling back and even cancellation of specific weapons systems—the Stealth and B-1 bombers, MX or Midgetman missiles, and D-5 Trident missiles.[88] But even under conditions of zero military growth, the Pentagon budget will remain large enough to sponsor a variety of offensive weapons. Advocating one system over another, which is what arms control often amounts to, will do little to end the arms race or decrease the economic burden weighing on the government budget. (Those arms control negotiations that reduce *offensive* weapons, however, could constitute an improvement—as we shall see in the next chapter).

Arms control negotiations, according to one military analyst,

should not be viewed as potential means of economic salvation. Savings can be made in the defense budget, to be sure, but they are more likely to result from greater efficiency in Defense

Department management and from lowered threat perceptions which could follow continued improvements in U.S.–Soviet political relationships, than from arms control measures.[89]

The post-INF policy of the Bush administration is a case in point. In the wake of the most important arms control treaty in a decade, no change has occurred either in the defense budget or in types of appropriations. All new weapons systems were included in the proposed 1990 defense budget (except for the IU-22 Osprey tilt-rotor aircraft, which many in Congress are trying to reinstate).[90] Although the proposed 1990 defense budget shows a 1.2 percent decrease in real terms, the budgets for the next four years average roughly 2 percent annual increases.[91]

Will the process of arms control yield urgently needed treaties? Perhaps, but even that would not be sufficient. The historical record indicates that arms control alone does not create opportunities and improved relations. In many cases, too, arms control has only served to fuel the arms race. For these reasons, arms control must be pursued, but only as one strategy among many, not as the only goal.[92]

Because of its limited guiding purposes, arms control is simply incapable of answering the critical questions today facing international relations, whether around the global economic system or around military conflicts and economic development in the Third World. These challenges plainly call for "new thinking," to borrow a Gorbachevism. The next chapter will address some of the outlines of this new thinking that may bring the world out of the Cold War and beyond cycles of détente and antagonism.

4

Beyond Détente

DÉTENTE DOES NOT WORK. The United States and the Soviet Union still look at each other through the prism of the Cold War. The Southern Hemisphere is filled with guns and starvation, for which the North is in part responsible. Arms control will not help.

The previous chapter offered a rather pessimistic outlook on the present state of international affairs. Because of lingering hostility and misperceptions and an inequitable relationship between countries of the Northern and Southern Hemispheres, the present state of U.S.–Soviet affairs may be only a détente—a temporary warming in relations within a more encompassing Cold War pattern.

There are many reasons, however, not to be so pessimistic.

The 1990s promise to be years of great flux in international relations, perhaps as critical as the decade following World War II. Certain factors point to an optimistic outcome, toward permanently relaxed East–West tensions and equitably restructured North–South relations. These factors suggest a trend toward dispersion of international power that may spell the end, after more than forty years, to the superpower dualism of the Cold War.

The following examples, though discrete, together indicate that the dynamic of U.S.–Soviet relations is assuming a more modest role in international relations.

Challenges to the exclusive importance of détente have come from both the Third World and from industrialized countries. In the Third World, the most important grouping has been the Nonaligned Movement, which, since 1955, has challenged bipolarism by championing the rights of nations historically subordinate to both the U.S. and the U.S.S.R. Despite fluctuations in their political fortunes and differing political perspectives, the over one hundred nations constituting this movement continue to meet and develop alternative policies. Organizations such as the Southern Africa Development Coordinating Committee (SADCC) (and the proposed Central American parliament) bring together Third World countries on a regional basis and may be expected to assume greater importance in the coming years. Whether any of these efforts will approach the level of success that OPEC initially achieved in challenging the economic stability of the North in the 1970s is an open question. Trends among industrialized nations are also leading to greater multilateralism. In an era of détente, the Nixon administration recognized China as a significant power, and the Trilateral Commission brought Western Europe and Japan into the East–West dialogue. The nations of Western Europe, their national boundaries gradually dissolving, are moving toward political and economic unity in 1992. Pacific economies have, in the 1980s, risen to prominence: Tokyo now rivals New York as a financial center.

With redistribution of global power, the relative power of the United States and the Soviet Union will decline. In other words, the two superpowers could both grow economically and yet, in comparison to the growth of other countries, they would still decline in importance. The same holds true for political power. In the United States, recognition of diminishing global dominance has only recently begun to filter through the policy-making establishment. In his best seller *The Rise and Fall of the Great Powers*, historian Paul Kennedy has argued that the United States has engaged in "imperial overstretch," extending militarily what it can no longer support economically.[1] No less a defender of America's role as world policeman than Jeane Kirkpatrick has expressed her concerns:

Have we, almost without realizing it, arrived at the end of the post–World War II era and entered a new, far more dangerous period of international relations? . . . Have American economic power and governmental authority so eroded that the United States truly has lost the ability to hold its own in the international sphere?[2]

To halt the erosion, some U.S. pundits have called for a new bipartisan consensus on the formation of a Pax Americana.[3] Although recognizing a new era in international relations, many influential policy makers continue to cling to the global strategies of previous eras.

The U.S. public, meanwhile, clearly wants a new foreign policy. According to polls conducted by the Americans Talk Security (ATS) project in 1988, 71 percent of U.S. citizens consider the arms race too expensive and 79 percent think it detracts from domestic spending. Forty-nine percent believe the United States should spend less on its allies, 46 percent believe it should spend less on conventional forces in the Third World, and 84 percent believe it should reduce financial commitments overseas and spend more of those dollars at home.[4] Such dissatisfaction, coupled with trade and budget deficits, has already slowed the growth of the U.S. military budget in the period 1985 to 1987. In Fiscal Year 1988, military spending actually declined.[5]

At the same time, the Soviet Union has fostered a new foreign policy that attempts to conform to international realities and domestic pressures. It has reformulated its positions on the arms race, the bloc system, intervention in the Third World. Soviet reformers do not view international affairs as an East–West tug-of-war and therefore are more attuned to the potential of global cooperation in solving mutual problems. As the *New Republic* encapsulates the Gorbachev view:

Nations . . . are increasingly faced with common problems that are best addressed internationally: environmental threats, terrorism, the cost of mutual military buildup, the prospect of nuclear apocalypse, or of economic apocalypse in a financially integrated world. Increasingly, we're all in the same boat.[6]

In short, Gorbachev and his allies, through foreign policy, are challenging the Cold War model.

To challenge is one thing, to replace is another. What can substitute for the traditional policies that, when successful, lead to conditional détentes and, when unsuccessful, perpetuate the worst of the Cold War?

Certain policies—such as economic conversion of military industries, alternative defense, and increased social and economic contact—build upon growing U.S.–Soviet cooperation. Since East and West are still wary of each other, and reinforce that insecurity with instruments of mass destruction, these confidence-building strategies are critical.

But we must also begin looking beyond U.S.–Soviet issues and toward a different set of problems—often overlooked, considered irrelevant, or deemed secondary to questions related to the East–West axis. For instance, what will be the future relationship between the North and South? And what mechanisms will administer the conduct of international relations? These questions too must be addressed as international relations become less dominated by the confrontation between East and West.

Alternative Policies

ECONOMIC CONVERSION

Economic conversion is an easy concept to imagine. Companies that now produce nuclear missiles would switch to, say, computer production: from ICBMs to IBMs. Of course, much more is at stake than simply dropping a letter. As economist Seymour Melman points out, 20 million people in the United States are dependent on the military-industrial complex.[7] This situation is not unique to the United States—the Soviet Union, China,[8] and many Third World countries all possess similarly profitable arms-producing industries. Even neutral Sweden relies heavily on its major arms manufacturer, Bofors, to bring in revenues and boost employment. Because of this dependency, a major disruption in economies and an enormous displacement of workers and their families would take place if the need for nuclear and conventional weapons was suddenly and dramatically lessened.

Easing the transition from military-oriented to civilian-oriented production is the starting point of economic conversion. The rationales behind such a strategy vary. Some experts argue that the military-industrial complex is a huge, uncontrolled mechanism, subject to cost overruns, inefficient production schedules, and unchecked greed.[9] Reports of grossly overpriced military hardware and Pentagon procurement scandals lend weight to this assessment. Advocates of conversion also argue that nonmilitary government spending employs more workers, produces more socially useful goods, sponsors more efficient research and development for the civilian sector, and provides the critical resources for machine retooling that can make U.S. industry more internationally competitive.[10]

The climate of opinion in the United States around conversion appears to be changing. Three bills have been introduced in Congress, and various site-specific initiatives have achieved some success in transforming military-related production into civilian production.[11] In order to streamline the military budget, the Pentagon has already announced a number of domestic military base closings and has allocated $1 million for establishing civilian uses for these facilities.[12] Although this allocation is undeniably small, a decreasing military budget may well produce more such government-sponsored programs.

The challenge of economic conversion for its supporters is not so much intellectual, since the retooling and retraining processes have been well researched. The real problem is political.

Conversion advocates in the United States have to confront perhaps the strongest Washington lobby: defense contractors. And at least three government bureaucracies—the Pentagon, the Department of Energy, and the National Aeronautics and Space Administration (NASA)—are heavily involved in the military industry. To sell conversion to the business and government community, economic arguments, though eminently logical, are insufficient. Companies will continue inefficient production so long as inefficiency remains profitable; government will support such practices when policy makers believe that the interests of national security are served (especially when they receive major campaign contributions from defense contractors).

But a conversion program based on self-interest might produce a workable coalition sufficiently powerful to restructure the military-industrial complex. Military reformers disgusted with overpriced and inefficient machinery could find common cause with cost-conscious politicians desperate to make popular budget cuts; peace activists focusing on international security could join with trade unionists and community activists worried about job loss and neighborhood decay. Together these groups could take advantage of present international trends and begin to transform the U.S. defense industry.

One of those international trends is the new Soviet perspective on conversion.[13] Soviet foreign policy initiatives in East–West relations are aimed at creating and supporting the political will to turn military resources to food production, high-technology research, and job retraining. When targeting the inefficiency of particular plants within the Soviet military-industrial enterprise, the reformers find economic arguments persuasive. But they must push conversion plans through an industrial system that historically has been skewed toward the military. The Soviet government's transformation of the Votkinsk machine plant, where the missiles destroyed under the INF were made, into a new facility that produces baby carriages is one new initiative. Using defense industry money and personnel in the food-processing sector is another. The Soviet military-industrial complex remains, nonetheless, well entrenched; the reformers have an uphill struggle, though improved U.S.–Soviet relations would provide considerable leverage for change.

Only when weapons manufacturing and capital in both countries become reoriented toward civilian use will détente be likely to last. Without this structural shift, the threat of large-scale re-armament will always be present. Third World countries, once assured that the superpowers are less of a military threat, are more likely to feel that much more secure in accomplishing their own conversion processes.

ALTERNATIVE DEFENSE

Industrial conversion must resolve the economic dislocation associated with demilitarizing U.S.–Soviet relations. But what can substitute for the dismantled offensive weapons in preserving national security? International agreements and paper assurances are by no means enough.[14]

One limited but concrete step involves a change in the type of weapons deployed. The concept is alternative defense, and the theory is straightforward: limiting the militaries to defense. Rather than structuring a military force in an offensive posture (which encourages one's adversaries to do likewise and thus stimulates an arms race), a military force can be structured defensively, so as not to threaten the security of others. The central assumption of this theory is that deterrence is achieved not through the threat of retaliation but rather through an ultimately insuperable defense. Congressman Les Aspin, Wisconsin Democrat serving on the House Armed Services Committee, has articulated what the hardware implications would be. The United States should restrict its armed forces, he said in a September 1987 speech, to rely more on antitank barriers, antitank weapons, close air support, and mobile artillery, in order to lead to "a world where, if our adversaries attack first, they will gain minimal military advantage at best, but risk devastation to their forces."[15]

The world Aspin had in mind and the world in which alternative defense functions best is Central Europe. NATO and Warsaw Pact forces now face off along the border between East and West Germany, their postures unquestionably offensive. NATO fighter-bombers are ready to strike deep into Eastern Europe;[16] Warsaw Pact tanks are prepared to attack West Germany. Both sides also deploy tactical nuclear weapons, which, given their destructive capabilities, can only be described as offensive (their use defensively would be literally self-defeating).

A composite picture drawn from the work of several analysts provides one possible configuration of an alternative or "nonprovocative" defense posture.[17] A weapons-free corridor runs through Central Europe, containing tank barriers, sensors, and other static defenses—verified by satellite photography. Military units range up and down on both sides of this corridor, relying only on light infantry, antitank guided weapons, and mobile anti-aircraft weapons. Finally, at a considerable distance from the corridor, are stationed tanks, troops, and aircraft ready to repulse any invasion, which, given the time it would take for the attackers to cross the corridor, would be well telegraphed. Arms control negotiations would concentrate on eliminating the long-range missiles that would destabilize such an arrangement and would gradually reduce the backup forces until no offensive weapons were stationed in Europe.

Lutz Unterseher and the Study Group on Alternative Security Policy (SAS) offer perhaps the most comprehensive alternative defense variant, which they liken to a spider in a web. In this analogy, the spider is lethal only within its web, but the web is so constructed that any intrusions into the spider's realm are fatal. The SAS proposal consists of three parts: (1) a containment force of decentralized infantry; (2) a rapid commitment force of mechanized troops; (3) a rear protection force of light infantry.[18]

The history of alternative defense is diverse and dates back to the turn of the century; its proponents come from both within and outside the military establishment. Alternative defense theories have been put into practice in several countries, most notably Yugoslavia, Sweden, and Switzerland. The Yugoslavs, after breaking with the U.S.S.R. in 1948, restructured their military to defend against a possible Soviet invasion. Yet, they were careful not to introduce any threatening offensive weapons into their arsenals for fear of encouraging the U.S.S.R. to attack first.[19] The Swedes have successfully stayed out of European conflicts since 1815 and have, since World War II, structured their military in a nonthreatening manner. The Swiss have clung to neutrality since the Napoleonic Wars, relying on a large army of reservists, a distinctively defensive terrain of forested high mountains, and sophisticated defensive weapons.

Most alternative defense analysts restrict their models to Central Europe and the NATO–Warsaw Pact confrontation. Some, like the advocates of civilian-based defense, have a more generalizable theory. Civilian-based defense puts minimum emphasis on institutionalized military response to threats and puts a premium instead on civilian actions: civil disobedience, work stoppages, boycotts, and overall noncompliance with the invading army and occupation government.[20]

With the exception of nonviolent civilian-based defense, much of the alternative defense debate is still preoccupied with high-tech weaponry and complex military strategy. Alternative defense also shares with arms control the assumption of a Soviet threat, institutionalizing such a threat not in a negotiating framework but in actual military restructuring. To the degree that alternative defense goes beyond the mere redefining of armed defense in Europe, however, it can function as a temporary stage eventually leading to a demilitarized East–West relationship.[21]

Developments in Soviet foreign policy may improve the chances of alternative defense.[22] The Soviet Union has already announced a shift in military doctrine, from offensive to defensive. This announced shift has been accompanied by the unilateral pledge to reduce tanks and troops in Central Europe and willingness to scale back dramatically in these areas within the arms control framework. With a willing Soviet Union, alternative defense could be a powerful companion to arms control. Theoretically, the two can mutually support one another: the incremental defensive restructuring of NATO and Warsaw Pact military positions can provide the necessary climate to build confidence for conventional-weapons cuts, troop disengagement, territorial denuclearization, and reductions in sea-based nuclear weapons.

Conversely, weapons reductions presently being considered in the Conventional Forces in Europe (CFE) talks might compel both sides to restructure their remaining forces in the most logical and efficient manner. NATO's offensive posture may, for instance, become simply too thin after successful arms control negotiations, and alternative defense would remain a "better buy for the buck."[23]

Alternative defense remains a rarefied topic in the U.S. debate: Greater cooperation between European and American activists might eventually change that situation. A number of organizations have recently increased their efforts toward just that end.[24] Can alternative defense become popular? It must, according to peace researcher Dietrich Fischer:

> We should not depend on the traditional political and military elites to find a way out of the nuclear predicament. That would be as if the abolitionists had waited for the slave traders and slave owners to take the lead in abolishing slavery. If we want to regain our security we must seize the initiative and build an irresistible popular movement for global survival.[25]

HUMAN RIGHTS

In order truly to institutionalize détente, East–West relations must become more than a matter of military disengagement. Better relations between the U.S. and the U.S.S.R. must extend into the economic, scientific, and cultural spheres.[26] Only then will mutual stereotypes begin to disintegrate.

One aspect of cultural relations that has played an ambiguous role in détente is the question of human rights. In the Brezhnev–Nixon years, some U.S. policy makers used the human rights situation in the U.S.S.R. to jeopardize arms control and trade relations (e.g., the Jackson-Vanik amendment). This "linkage" of international agreements with internal developments has often been used by hard-liners in order to ensure the failure of détente.

The issue of human rights has been misused in other ways—for instance, when U.S. policy makers have applied the human rights standard inconsistently. The violations of the Salvadoran government and paramilitary apparatus (12,500 Salvadorans killed in 1981 alone[27]) have not stood in the way of millions of dollars of U.S. aid. Nor have violations in Chile, the Philippines, South Korea, Guatemala, South Africa, or Haiti been excoriated at the same length as the violations in Communist or Soviet-allied countries.[28] The Polish security police's murder of a priest in 1984 received far greater attention from the U.S. government (not to mention the U.S. press) than the hundreds of religious victims killed by Latin American governments.[29] The United States is not, of course, the only government that is cynical about human rights. The Soviet Union has also supported political activists in other countries when its own dissidents languished in prisons and mental hospitals.

Despite their highly political use by governments, human rights are critical to détente and the future of peaceful East–West relations. European activists have eloquently restated this crucial relationship:

We oppose any tendency to play off peace against freedom or vice versa. A lasting détente cannot be bought at the cost of civil liberties and human—political and social—rights. Peace and security, détente and cooperation, basic rights and self-determination of peoples have to be achieved together. Set-backs in any of these spheres have their negative effects on all others.[30]

There can be no peace that does not respect human rights; a government that *fundamentally* respects human rights—those of its own citizens as well as those of citizens of other countries—is a peaceful government. As such, concern for human rights should be a first principle, a consistent policy not to be used as a bargaining chip. Governments may manipulate human rights issues, but those interested in going beyond the Cold War should not play the same game.

The Soviet Union has demonstrably improved its record in this area. The Gorbachev administration has relaxed state controls on civil liberties, releasing hundreds of political dissidents, easing restrictions on emigration, and permitting freer expression through the press and other cultural outlets. But there is certainly room for further improvement. The U.S. decision to participate in the 1991 human rights conference in the U.S.S.R. indicates that both countries are at least willing to discuss the question.

Human rights are a contested point in East–West relations, but self-determination for people in the Third World (and Eastern Europe for that matter) is no less a human right than freedom of speech or religion. To guarantee this right of self-determination, however, global powers must begin to question their traditional policy of interference and intervention into the affairs of other countries.

NONINTERVENTION

Intervention can take many forms, from military engagements to economic manipulation to political pressuring. *Non*intervention alternatives are likewise diverse, whether pledges not to interfere militarily or guarantees respecting political and economic autonomy.

Compared with the United States, the U.S.S.R. has been relatively isolated from the Third World. Certainly the Soviet government is complicit through arms sales and support for various proxies, but Soviet power projection pales beside the U.S. capability, and the lack of substantial Soviet participation in international finance renders the

U.S.S.R. comparatively powerless in affecting Third World economies. A policy of nonintervention would then differentially affect the conduct of foreign affairs of the two powers. The U.S.S.R. might simply continue its present policy of scaled-back military commitments. The United States would have to re-evaluate fundamentally the nature of its role in the world.

Given the U.S. government's history of intervention and its current fascination with low-intensity conflict and nonmilitary destabilization in the Third World, what are the prospects for U.S. support of nonintervention alternatives? Advocates of such policies can point to historical examples, even enlisting the support of former U.S. policy makers of the Cold War era. For instance, President Truman initially maintained that the United States would not "pursue a course which would lead to involvement with civil conflicts in China." Certain U.S. politicians, notably Senator John Connally of Texas, cautioned against military interference in Korea.[31] Even George Kennan, an architect of U.S. Cold War doctrine, expressed mixed feelings about the issue of interference in foreign affairs. By 1948, Kennan was arguing that the United States should not be primarily concerned with the internal organization of other countries.[32] "With regard to other nations, let us not judge, that we not be judged. Let us not attempt to constitute ourselves the guardians of everyone else's virtue; we have enough trouble to guard our own," he wrote to John Foster Dulles in 1952.[33]

A joint report issued in May 1988 by the American Committee on U.S.–Soviet Relations and the Soviet Union's U.S.A.–Canada Institute recalls many of Kennan's iconoclastic concerns in calling for concrete steps to improve U.S.–Soviet relations and leave the Cold War era behind once and for all. These steps include: an end to the use of military force by either superpower in the Third World, whether direct or by proxy, and a decrease in weapons transfers to Third World nations. Such recommendations are less startling than the list of those making them, including former CIA director William Colby, former undersecretary of state George Ball, and former CIA covert operations specialist Arthur Macy Cox.[34]

A similar call, from one of the architects of the Nuclear Freeze, Randall Forsberg, elaborates the notion of a "nonintervention" regime. Forsberg's plan provides for a formal regime under which the nations of North America and Europe plus the U.S.S.R., China, Japan, Australia, and New Zealand would undertake explicitly never to send more than, say, 1000 military personnel (or civilians performing military tasks), for any purpose, into the territory or the territorial waters of any nation in Latin America, Africa, the Middle East, South Asia, or the Far East.[35]

Although the specifics of this plan are controversial, Forsberg has nonetheless considered nonintervention as important as nuclear disarmament and conventional restructuring.

Several recent developments give these plans special relevance. Soviet pledges of noninterference in the affairs of Eastern Europe bode well. Its withdrawal from Afghanistan indicates that the Soviet Union has realized that military interventions are costly and counterproductive. The phased withdrawal of Soviet troops has also presented the model of disengagement that was followed by Vietnam in its pullout from Cambodia. Furthermore, the current attempt at resolving the conflict in Angola—in which Angola, South Africa, and Cuba have negotiated the withdrawal of foreign troops and a process for the independence of Namibia—might serve as another model for superpower military disengagement from the Third World.

A concrete first step in ensuring nonintervention is engaging in relations with "pariah" countries. The Reagan administration moved closer to North Korea and the PLO; the Gorbachev administration, meanwhile, has tentatively reached out to South Korea and Israel. Both superpowers can undertake further measures. In 1988, Ethiopia explicitly sought U.S. support,[36] and the recognition of Cuba by the United States is an opportunity waiting to be seized by the Bush administration.[37] Countries so often criticized in the United States, such as Libya or Iran, should also be approached—diplomatically, not militarily. The U.S.S.R., if it desires a greater role in Middle Eastern affairs, must eventually re-establish ties with Israel. Such recognition would bring greater political and economic ties and reduce the two-bloc mentality, as well as the risk of military intervention.

Restricting military interventions and extending diplomatic recognition are necessary but not sufficient. Neither of these options precludes any number of equally effective economic pressures, such as trade sanctions, the withholding of aid, or the extension of risky loans. And as the nonaligned countries have consistently argued for more than thirty years, the inequity of the international economic system functions like an interventionary threat. At their 1970 summit in Lusaka, for instance, Tanzanian President Julius Nyerere argued that the economic threat of underdevelopment was more dangerous to Third World countries than any military threat.[38]

Working for higher wages for workers around the world and giving more power to Third World countries in the IMF and other financial organizations would both be possible ways of diminishing the threat of underdevelopment.[39] Additionally, the countries of the North must acknowledge that trade is a zero-sum game and that the Third World will always have balance-of-payment problems as long as in-dustrialized countries generate large trade surpluses. Such surpluses should be used to overcome the debt crisis.[40]

Nonintervention cannot simply be legislated. Countries respect such laws until perceived national security interests dictate their abrogation.[41] But nonintervention pacts can work within the context of a security system providing greater distribution of power interna-tionally. As long as the superpowers possess the economic and mili-tary power to bend smaller countries to their will, they will try to do so. If, however, a system can be established that shares power among countries, then a new page in the history of international relations will have been turned. Intervention will, of course, continue. Altru-ism is not, after all, generally practiced in international relations. But given more democratic international institutions, the worst abuses of intervention visited on the most vulnerable might be contained; and the positive acts of intervention (for instance, economic and political pressures on the South African government to end apartheid) will be undertaken collectively. Such an international system involves multi-lateral—that is, multigovernment—solutions.

MULTILATERALISM

In a 1985 article, the president of the Carnegie Endowment for International Peace declared internationalism dead. In view of the Reagan administration's persistent U.N. bashing and such decisions as its withdrawal from UNESCO (United Nations Educational, Scientific, and Cultural Organization), this pessimistic assessment appeared to fit the facts, at least when it came to U.S. attitudes.

But as foreign policy analyst Tom Farer points out, despite much "go it alone" rhetoric from the neo-conservatives, the Reagan administration did not stem the tide of internationalism. Whether authorizing U.S. participation in multilateral efforts to prevent ozone depletion or calling for the U.N. Security Council to end the Iran–Iraq war, Reagan found himself appealing to international norms and regulations as frequently as his predecessors had.[42] In October 1988, the Reagan administration even suggested to the Soviet Union that their disputes should be arbitrated in the World Court—a response to Gorbachev's appeal for strengthening that institution.[43] This from an administration that not only defied the World Court's decision two years previously on the U.S. mining of Nicaraguan harbors but also unilaterally announced that the institution's rulings were not binding on the United States. At the beginning of 1989, the United States participated in the international reaffirmation of the ban on the use of chemical weapons, joining 140 other nations.[44]

The Reagan administration had not suddenly converted to internationalism. Rather, international pressures have forced the United States to re-evaluate its unilateralism. Those same pressures have affected the Bush administration, which submitted a case to the World Court in February 1989, the first time since Reagan's 1986 repudiation of a court decision. In August, the Soviet Union and the United States decided to allow the court to arbitrate in seven treaties. Bush has also reinstated U.S. payments of current assessments to the United Nations.

Renewed U.S. approval is but one of the many signs of the improved health of the U.N. Despite a long period of financial problems, the U.N. has been increasingly active in world affairs, mediating in the Iran–Iraq war, offering to administer the Western Sahara, participating in resolving conflicts in Afghanistan and Angola, reinstating negotiations between Turks and Greeks in Cyprus, supervising the Namibian independence process, and monitoring elections in Nicaragua. So highly valued have U.N. peace-keeping forces been in recent years that they were awarded the 1988 Nobel Peace Prize.

Internationalism is not only reflected in institutions. More generally, it is an approach, a way of addressing problems that cannot be solved otherwise. Many problems once thought to pertain only to certain clusters of countries are now seen as global. With few exceptions, *all* countries must combat famine, soil erosion, air pollution, ozone depletion, vested military interests, debt, vulnerability to nuclear weapons attack, energy crises. The 1985 Chernobyl accident brought home the realization that environmental issues are *global* issues that do not pertain to any particular axis.[45] Radiation from a nuclear reactor meltdown, like fallout from a nuclear war, respects no political boundaries. Acid rain cannot be stopped by plugging the smokestacks of only one country. Ozone depletion will not end because of the cessation of production of chlorofluorocarbons by only one country. Other environmental problems are also nationally indiscriminate: the topsoil is in danger of erosion, forests are being decimated for fuel and profit, the oceans cannot support the dual function of food producer and waste receptacle.[46] There are indeed several current and potential ecological crises that could unseat nuclear war as the leading candidate for world apocalypse.

Or, to twist the argument slightly, as Jonathan Schell does in *The Fate of the Earth*, the two situations are related: ecological doom and nuclear annihilation both result from man's attempts to master nature. Stressing this intimate relationship, many analysts maintain that steps taken toward ecological security are in effect steps toward international security: in short, toward a more responsible *stewardship* of the Earth.[47]

Such stewardship cannot be conducted by only one or two stewards. Solutions to these international problems must emerge from a global democratic process. A recent initiative, India's "Action Plan for Ushering in a Nuclear Weapon-Free and Non-violent World Order," introduced at the U.N. Third Special Session on Disarmament in June 1988, makes precisely this argument. In the document's most powerful language, India's Prime Minister Rajiv Gandhi appeals for an end to the bipolar view of the world:

A world order crafted out of outmoded concepts of the balance of power, of dominance of power blocs, of spheres of influence and special rights and privileges for a select group of nations, is an unacceptable anachronism. It is out of tune with the democratic temper of our age.[48]

From Ideas to Results

These, then, are samples of ideas and concrete proposals that can contribute to a restructuring of international relations. These options can also form part of the U.S. response to the challenge of Soviet reform: economic conversion would meet Soviet concerns over military spending; alternative defense would mesh with new Soviet military doctrine; campaigning for human rights takes advantage of *glasnost* and greater Eastern European independence; a nonintervention policy might succeed in light of the new explicitly nonconfrontational Soviet foreign policy; strengthening of international institutions is greatly facilitated by new Soviet multilateralism.

But what does it really mean for the two superpowers to go "beyond" détente?

Détente, as we have seen, both recognizes and preserves a certain balance of power in the world. The Soviet Union and the United States, being superpowers, have the right, according to the logic of détente, to dictate military and economic terms to their respective alliances and to the rest of the world. During détente, the two blocs have together justified their dominance; at frostier moments of the Cold War, the United States and the U.S.S.R. have worked unilaterally and through their alliances to ensure a mutually beneficial bipolar world that primarily benefits the two superpowers. Therein lies the ambiguity of détente: preserving the alliance system even as it points beyond. Arms control ensures superpower domination even as it defuses superpower rivalry. Thus, the major instrument of détente has, in a perverse fashion, legitimated the arms race; East–West accords have precluded neither military confrontation in the Third World nor economic manipulation of developing countries. To go beyond détente means to challenge not only the bloc system but also the privilege of industrialized nations to determine how the rest of the world should live.

The United States and the Soviet Union are superpowers and will no doubt remain so for quite some time. But the age in which they are the *sole* superpowers has passed. Both countries must recognize this international fact and begin to develop policies that take into account the increased power of competing centers, whether Japan, a united Europe, the Third World, or various international organizations.

One superpower, through its actions, suggests that it is developing such policies. The Soviet Union under Mikhail Gorbachev has vigorously sought to reduce its nuclear and conventional weapons, withdrawn its troops from Afghanistan, scaled back on its activities on the world's oceans, encouraged its allies to resolve regional conflicts, and shifted its support more generally from military to diplomatic solutions. This is not to suggest that the Soviet Union has resigned as a military power. Simply put, it has decided to increase its cooperation with other nations rather than enforce its rule unilaterally.

What about the United States? When Jimmy Carter constructed a foreign policy to reflect an "age of limits"—one that was multipolar, recognized the autonomous importance of the Third World, granted human rights a central role in foreign policy, and valued the diplomatic over the military—he was roundly criticized, forced to adapt his positions, and promptly voted out of office in 1980.[49] Seven years later—after a massive military buildup and an "America First" public relations campaign by neo-conservatives had failed to establish U.S. unilateralism—the "age of limits" has returned. A spate of recent books chronicle the decline of U.S. global power and an equal number of articles search for a new "grand strategy" to preserve U.S. interests.

The Cold War produced a bipartisan foreign policy that lasted roughly from 1945 to 1968. Carter attempted a premature multilateralism, Reagan an anachronistic unilateralism. Bush offers "status quo plus." Given new international circumstances and a growing recognition of the relative decline in U.S. global power, a new post–Cold War foreign policy is clearly necessary.

How can concerned citizens speed this process along?

Some of the ideas that can contribute have been outlined in this chapter. Yet, however morally compelling and logically coherent, ideas of themselves do not convince politicians to change policies.

Our leaders, in order to maintain their offices, respond to the power that backs up ideas. Unity across constituencies, and even national boundaries, can generate the power necessary to project issues into the policy-making arena.

Political power would, of course, be greatly increased if ties were not simply made among constituencies at home but also among like-minded political groups internationally. Opportunities have presented themselves. The founding principles of the Nonaligned Movement, the Panshilah, or Five Principles, formulated in 1954 by China and India, could serve as the core of a noninterventionist position, but they are rarely invoked.[50] In Belgrade in 1961, the Nonaligned Movement issued its first call for a world disarmament conference (unheeded for nearly two decades). In Cairo in 1964, the assembled countries adopted an eleven-point Program for Peace and International Cooperation that does not differ in substance from calls made by the U.S. peace movement in 1988.[51] Nor is the Nonaligned Movement alone. The six-nation (formerly five-continent) peace initiative, the New International Economic Order, the Cologne Declaration, and many other international documents have consistently and repeatedly provided multilateral frameworks for military and economic reform.

But these governmental proposals are not sufficient. Internationalism should also entail the joining together of *citizens* from various countries. Activists from Eastern European countries are beginning to work together on the issues that affect all of them, both domestically and regionally. If U.S. *and* European activists unite on a platform for NATO reform and pressure all the governments involved, the action of all the parts will create a powerful consensus for change. Better yet, activists East and West could cooperate on a program targeting both NATO and the Warsaw Pact. Similarly, activists in the Third World and in industrialized countries should work in concert over the debt issue. The developing world already contains movements of remarkable size and strength: for instance, 12,000 independent development organizations in India, 16,000 women's groups in Kenya, 100,000 Christian-based communities in Brazil.[52] The success of these groups ultimately depends on international factors: loans, trade policies, political agreements. The most intractable foreign policy problems are global; to effect change, the organizing must take place on a global scale.

The role that organized U.S. citizens can play in the restructuring of international relations may ultimately be (and should be) no greater than the roles of activists from other countries. Impetus for change may well come from citizens of debt-ridden Third World countries who join together to challenge the economic interests of the North. Or perhaps activists from within the Soviet Union or Eastern Europe will ultimately determine the political geography of the post–Cold War world (if Poland and Hungary are indications, such activists are well along on that path). Just as the United States is slowly learning that it can no longer dictate through foreign policy, so must U.S. nongovernmental organizations and movements realize that their brand of reform cannot be imposed upon the world.

In restructuring international relations, then, U.S. citizens—from peace activists to the American Legion—may discover that there is a good deal more to learn than there is to teach.

What are the chances of an alternative foreign policy replacing the still current U.S. Cold War perspective? The times are right. This book has detailed how the Soviet Union is taking advantage of these circumstances to transform its domestic situation. Whether activists in the United States can capitalize upon these same trends depends on the kind of power mobilized.

Issues of peace and justice have mass appeal in the United States. The popularity of the Nuclear Freeze and the longevity of New Deal legislation attest to this fact. The strength of the civil rights and anti–Vietnam War movements also indicates the potential for social and political action. Those who desire an alternative foreign and domestic policy in the United States must form powerful coalitions involving unions, religious congregations, community organizations, women, and people of color. These coalitions should think not only of *influencing* but of *producing* policy makers. Only then will there be a possibility that alternative policies will make that all-important leap from idea to reality.

Only then will we have a chance to go beyond détente, beyond the Cold War, beyond the destructive legacy of World War II—and begin to address the challenges of a new era of international relations.

Notes

INTRODUCTION

1. The best anticipation of the Gorbachev reforms was Stephen F. Cohen's *Rethinking the Soviet Experience* (New York: Oxford University Press, 1985). The Kremlin government is not simply an inflexible bureaucratic dictatorship, Cohen argues. This Cold War picture of a monolithic Soviet state ignores crucial differences of opinions among high policy makers. Although missing the Gorbachev succession by scant months, Cohen contributed to laying the conceptual groundwork for understanding how such reform could take place within the Soviet system. Only later have other Sovietologists begun to embrace Cohen's insights, especially his subsequent analyses of the significance of Gorbachev's reforms. For an indication of the turn-around in the profession of Sovietology see, e.g., Thomas Friedman, "Soviet Watchers Now Say Gorbachev Is 'For Real,'" *New York Times*, 5/8/89.

2. *New York Times*, 3/12/85.

3. Such Gorbachev allies include Vadim Medvedev, Eduard Shevardnadze, and Alexander Yakovlev in the Politburo, Boris Yeltsin in the Supreme Soviet, sociologist Tatyana Zaslavskaya and economist Abel Agan-

begyan, poets Yevgenii Yevtushenko and Andrei Voznesensky, and commentators such as Fyodor Burlatsky. It should be stressed that the division between Gorbachev allies and opponents is not always distinct, with many individuals keeping feet in both camps and going either way, depending on the issue. An illuminating Soviet article on the subject describes a meeting of Soviet and U.S. intellectuals on the subject of reform in the U.S.S.R.: "Perestroika: Kto Protiv?" *Ogonek*, no. 50 (12/88), pp. 10–14. Some of the Soviet champions of reform at this meeting were historian Yuri Afanasyev, writer Alexander Gelman, *Ogonek* editor Vitaly Korotich, and economist Nikolai Shmelev.

4. For early skepticism of Soviet reform see, e.g., Natan Sharansky, "Gorbachev Plays a Double Game," *New York Times*, 1/14/87; Edwin Yoder, "What Soviet 'Glasnost' Conceals," *Philadelphia Inquirer*, 6/30/87; John Hughes, "Glasnost Redux," *Christian Science Monitor*, 8/28/87; Hugh De Santis and Dimitri Simes, "Beware of Wishful Thinking About Gorbachev," *New York Times*, 10/25/87; William Safire, "Danger: Gorby Fever," *New York Times*, 12/2/87; and essays in both *Mesmerized by the Bear: The Soviet Strategy of Deception* (New York: Dodd, Mead and Co., 1987) and *Perestroika: How New Is Gorbachev's New Thinking?* (Washington, D.C.: Ethics and Public Policy Center, 1989). For recent "Gorbophobia," see, e.g., Richard Nixon, "Dealing With Gorbachev," *New York Times Magazine*, 3/13/88; Edward Luttwak, "The Alliance, Without an Enemy," *New York Times*, 2/3/89; and Zbigniew Brzezinski, "Will the Soviet Empire Self-Destruct?" *New York Times Magazine*, 2/25/89. Also see Michael Massing's brief but excellent analysis of the issue in "Gorbophobia," *The Nation*, vol. 247, no. 2 (12/26/88), pp. 713–16.

5. Michael Gordon, "Bush Urged to Find a Middle Course on Soviet Changes," *New York Times*, 4/9/89. The skeptics in the administration are said to include Secretary of Defense Richard Cheney and Robert Gates, deputy national security adviser.

6. Bill Keller, "New Soviet Ideologist Rejects Idea of World Struggle Against West," *New York Times*, 10/6/88.

7. After drug trafficking, domestic problems, nuclear proliferation to the Third World, terrorism, economic competition from Japan, acid rain, and the greenhouse effect. *Americans Talk Security: A Series of Surveys of American Voters*, no. 9 (October 1988), p. 40. In a later poll by the same organization, it was found that only 26 percent of U.S. citizens in 1989 considered the U.S.S.R. a growing military threat and immediate danger to the United States, down from 64 percent in 1983. R. W. Apple, Jr., "Polls Find That Gorbachev's Role Eases American Minds on Soviets," *New York Times*, 5/16/89.

1 : THE DOMESTIC ROOTS OF SOVIET FOREIGN POLICY

1. Quoted in Robert Legvold and the Task Force on Soviet New Thinking, *Gorbachev's Foreign Policy: How Should the United States Respond?* (New York: Foreign Policy Association, 1988), p. 10.

2. It should be noted that in pre-Soviet history, many Russian leaders (including Peter the Great and his "Westernization" of Russian society) made similar links between domestic and international policy.

3. Quoted in Wolfgang Leonhard, *The Kremlin and the West* (New York: W. W. Norton and Co., 1986), p. 7.

4. Those domestic changes that have little or no effect on Soviet foreign policy will not be examined. For example, issues of gender, religion, and culture, though unquestionably important in understanding Soviet society, will receive less attention in this book.

5. According to the Julian calendar that Peter the Great brought to Russia in 1700, the Bolshevik Revolution took place on October 25, and hence is known as the October Revolution. According to the Gregorian calendar that the Bolsheviks instituted in the Soviet Union, however, the Bolshevik Revolution occurred on November 7.

6. These local councils gave the new state a name: Union of *Soviet* Socialist Republics or the *Soviet* Union.

7. For instance, in 1918, the workers' and peasants' soviets elected only 175 Bolsheviks out of 707 delegates to the Constituent Assembly, a government organ established after the February revolution. At the time, workers and peasants voting through their local soviets preferred the Socialist Revolutionary and Menshevik parties to the Bolsheviks, an embarrassing political situation that led Lenin to rethink his "All Power to the Soviets" tactic and dissolve the Constituent Assembly.

8. The political structure of the Soviet Union consists of an interrelated and interacting series of party and state (or *soviet*) organizations that extend from the national to the local level. The lower echelons of both party and state structures are filled by elected representatives, who in turn choose leaders to occupy upper posts. Some party and state offices are appointed.

9. For a description of this crucial interplay between party and government in the early days of the Soviet Union, see, e.g., Charles Bettelheim, *Class Struggles in the U.S.S.R.: 1917–1923* (New York: Monthly Review Press, 1976), pp. 99–126.

10. The Bolshevik party's new name after 1918.

11. For an excellent description of these factional disputes, see, e.g., Stephen F. Cohen, *Bukharin and the Bolshevik Revolution* (New York: Vintage Books, 1975). Cohen outlines the disagreements within the Bolshevik party over industrialization, agricultural policy, foreign relations, and political organization, using the figure of Nikolai Bukharin as a focal point. Since Bukharin's ideas in many ways prefigure those of Gorbachev, Cohen's biography provides important historical background useful for interpreting contemporary Soviet reform.

12. Conservative Sovietologists (e.g., Adam Ulam, Richard Pipes) tend to project Stalinism back through the 1920s (arguing that Lenin was the logical predecessor to Stalin) and forward into the 1960s and 1970s (arguing that no Soviet leader can escape the legacy of Stalinism). The result of this historical manipulation is the equation of the entirety of the Soviet experience with the experience of Stalinism.

13. Mark Field, "Soviet Society and Communist Party Controls: A Case of Constricted Development," in *Understanding Soviet Society*, ed. by Michael Paul Sacks and Jerry Pankhurst (Boston: Unwin Hyman, 1988), p. 123.

14. Lionel Kochan and Richard Abraham, *The Making of Modern Russia*, 2d ed. (New York: Penguin, 1983), p. 473.

15. For a detailed description of this privileged class, see Michael Voslensky, *Nomenklatura: The Soviet Ruling Class* (New York: Doubleday and Co., 1984).

16. Brezhnev awarded himself the highest award for bravery four times. Soviet writer Viktor Astafyev writes, "To the accompaniment of smarmy words, unctuous smiles, and stormy applause, Brezhnev was being given another award that he didn't earn." Quoted in Paul Quinn-Judge, "Kremlin Renews Its Attacks on Brezhnev Years," *Christian Science Monitor*, 10/8/87.

17. By 1982, agricultural failure was so pronounced that it appeared likely that the then secretary of agriculture would lose his job because of it. But Brezhnev's death in 1982 saved Mikhail Gorbachev: "It became more natural to make the deceased responsible for the agricultural and economic failures than to blame those who were still alive and well." Zhores Medvedev, *Gorbachev* (New York: W. W. Norton and Co., 1986), p. 118.

18. When Gorbachev directed agriculture in the provinces, his Moscow patron was Fyodor Kulakov; brought to Moscow in 1981, Gorbachev came under the influence of Yuri Andropov and Mikhail Suslov; on the eve of assuming the position of general secretary, Gorbachev found an ally in Andrei Gromyko, the long-standing foreign minister.

19. Gorbachev made a key speech at a Central Committee conference on December 10, 1984, shortly before assuming the position of general secre-

tary. Here he introduced many of the words and strategies that would later become elaborated into policy. See a description of this speech in Anders Aslund, *Gorbachev's Struggle for Economic Reform* (Ithaca, NY: Cornell University Press, 1989), pp. 26–27.

20. The three Brezhnevites were Vitaly Vorotnikov, Vladimir Shcherbitsky, and Dinmukhamed Kunaev.

21. Medvedev, *Gorbachev*, p. 6.

22. Stalin did not completely eliminate his political opponents by 1929: numerous Trotskyists remained active in party life through the early collectivization campaigns (although Trotsky himself was exiled in 1929); Bukharin re-emerged in political life in the 1930s before his trial and execution in 1938. For a description of Stalin's rise to power, see, e.g., Isaac Deutscher, *Stalin* (New York: Oxford University Press, 1969), pp. 228–93.

23. Martin McCauley, "Gorbachev as Leader," in *The Soviet Union Under Gorbachev*, ed. by Martin McCauley (New York: St. Martin's Press, 1987), p. 19.

24. Ibid., p. 21.

25. At least two Soviet interceptors tailed the West German pilot Mathias Rust and did not shoot him down—whether in an example of incompetence or humanity, it is difficult to say. James E. Oberg, *Uncovering Soviet Disasters: Exploring the Limits of Glasnost* (New York: Random House, 1988), p. 49.

26. In 1988, on the centenary of his birth, Soviet journals began the process of rehabilitating the most important of these figures, Bukharin, and gave extensive coverage to his alternative economic theories. See, e.g., L. K. Shkarenov, "Nikolai Ivanovich Bukharin," *Voprosi Istorii* (7/88), pp. 59–79 (this Bukharin profile is juxtaposed with interesting resonances with a feature on Thomas Paine); N. Bukharin, "Zliye Zametky," *Voprosi Literaturi*, no. 8 (1988), pp. 220–25; G. A. Bordugov and V. A. Kozlov, "Povorot 1929 goda i alternativa Bukharina," *Voprosi Istorii KPSS* (10/88), pp. 73–78; "Pisma N. I. Bukharina," *Voprosi Istorii KPSS* (11/88), pp. 42–51; "Duumvarit: Bukharin i Stalin," *Ogonek*, no. 45 (11/88), pp. 29–31. Even Trotsky, vilified for over fifty years in the U.S.S.R., has received more positive treatment. See, e.g., Craig Whitney, "The New Trotsky: No Longer a Devil," *New York Times*, 1/16/89.

27. Dale Herspring, "Gorbachev and the Soviet Military," in *Soviet Foreign Policy*, ed. by Robbin F. Laird (New York: The Academy of Political Science, 1987), vol. 36, no. 4, p. 43.

28. Aslund, *Gorbachev's Struggle*, p. 34.

29. The expression "cult of modesty" is borrowed from Herspring, "Gorbachev and the Soviet Military," p. 43.

30. Serge Schmemann, "Gorbachev Warns Fawning Speaker," *New York Times*, 3/2/86.

31. Christian Schmidt-Hauer, *Gorbachev: The Path to Power* (Topsfield, MA: Salem House, 1986), p. 122. Afanasyev has since been replaced by a more reform-minded editor.

32. Bill Keller, "Moscow Says Changes in Voting Usher in Many New Local Leaders," *New York Times*, 9/21/88.

33. Jonathan Steele, "Rebirth of Political Activity," *The Guardian*, reprinted in *World Press Review*, vol. 34, no. 11 (November 1987), pp. 38–39. The name of the organization is "Circle of Social Initiatives."

34. For more on those political clubs that do not call themselves socialist and openly favor different economic and political ideologies, see, e.g., Bill Keller, "Moscow Political Clubs Issue Call for Expanded Freedoms," *New York Times*, 6/13/88. Also James Weinstein, "Living Perestroika," *In These Times*, vol. 13, no. 7 (Dec. 21, 1988–Jan. 10, 1989).

35. According to Boris Kagarlitsky, the supporters of the Popular Front consist generally of the "lower strata of the intelligentsia and, partly, skilled workers and student youth." Kagarlitsky, "A Difficult Hegemony," *Across Frontiers*, vol. 5, no. 2 (Summer 1989), p. 12.

36. Yuri Levada and Victor Sheinis, "1953–1964: Why Reform Didn't Work Then," *Moscow News*, no. 18, 1988, p. 9.

37. Quoted in Michel Tatu, "19th CPSU Conference," *Problems of Communism*, vol. 37, no. 3–4 (May–August 1988), p. 8.

38. Gorbachev has said, for instance, "I have already said recently that we need democracy not to show off and not to play democracy. We need democracy to rearrange many things in our life, to give greater scope to the creativity of people, to new ideas and initiatives." Quoted in Philip Taubman, "Gorbachev Candid About Opposition," *New York Times*, 2/26/87.

39. "A different—and obvious—approach has not apparently been seriously considered: making the Party step back from overseeing the everyday management of society, permitting officers of the state to devise their own ways of administering policy (even if that means they will occasionally make mistakes), and restricting the Party's role to one of general political guidance and leadership. That would indeed be a radical reform, with profound implications for the way the Soviet Union is governed. For that very reason, perhaps, it is unlikely to be contemplated." Ronald Hill, "State and Ideology," in McCauley, ed., *The Soviet Union Under Gorbachev*, pp. 57–58.

40. For an interesting personal account of the conference, see, e.g., Vitaly Korotich's remarks in "Obshchaya Sudba, Obshcheye Dyela," *Ogonek*, no. 28 (July 1988), p. 3.

41. For this argument, see, e.g., Moishe Lewin, *The Gorbachev Phenomenon: A Historical Interpretation* (Berkeley: University of California Press, 1988), p. 133.

42. Jerry Hough and Merle Fainsod, *How the Soviet Union Is Governed* (Cambridge: Harvard University Press, 1979), p. 344.

43. Fyodor Burlatsky maintains that these political changes are designed to prevent individual and group abuse of power: "Experience shows that the concentration of power in the hands of one organ (party or government) leads in the end to what Lenin noted as an excessive convergence of power in the hands of one individual, displayed in tragic consequences in Stalin and in all the ineffectiveness of the Brezhnev era." Fyodor Burlatsky, "O Sovetskom Parlamentarisme," *Literaturnaya Gazeta*, 6/15/88.

44. For a pessimistic analysis of this conflict, see Peter Reddaway, "Resisting Gorbachev," *New York Review of Books*, vol. 35, no. 13 (Aug. 18, 1988).

45. Karl Marx maintained that under Communism, a state would be unnecessary as an organ of mediation of class conflict. As classes disappear, so would the state.

46. Ronald Hill, *The Soviet Union: Politics, Economics and Society* (Boulder: Lynne Rienner Publishers, 1985), pp. 113–14.

47. See, e.g., Philip Taubman, "A Soviet Paradox," *New York Times*, 10/3/88. On the one hand, Taubman mistakenly perceives "democratization" as including decentralized decision making at the highest echelons of Soviet power. On the other hand, he apparently imagines that Gorbachev could, through top-down reform, institute a complex set of rules that would, in a matter of days, endow the Politburo with the characteristics of a parliamentary democracy.

48. See P. Bunich's comments in "Perestroika: Kto Protiv?" *Ogonek*, no. 50 (12/88), p. 13.

49. Seweryn Bialer, "Gorbachev's Program of Change: Sources, Significance, Prospects," in *Gorbachev's Russia and American Foreign Policy*, ed. by Seweryn Bialer and Michael Mandelbaum (Boulder: Westview, 1988), p. 242.

50. Fred Halliday, *Soviet Policy in the Arc of Crisis* (Washington, DC: Institute for Policy Studies, 1981), p. 53.

51. Abel Aganbegyan, *The Challenge: Economics of Perestroika* (London: Hutchinson, 1988), p. 45.

52. Leon Baradat, *Soviet Political Society* (Englewood Cliffs, NJ: Prentice-Hall, 1986), p. 259.

53. Gail W. Lapidus, "Soviet Society in Transition," in *The Gorbachev*

Era, ed. by Alexander Dallin and Condoleezza Rice (Stanford: Stanford Alumni Association, 1986), p. 35.

54. Baradat, *Soviet Political Society,* p. 259.

55. Aslund, *Gorbachev's Struggle,* p. 17.

56. The drop in the price of oil in the 1980s, for instance, squeezed the flow of hard currency to the U.S.S.R.; fewer dollars, yen, and marks meant less imported grain and more important, less high-tech machinery.

57. With Western consumerism came Western decadence, as some NEP-men turned a considerable profit. For a fictionalized look at the excesses of the NEP years, see Alexandra Kollontai, "Vasilisa Malygina," *Love of Worker Bees* (Chicago: Academy Press Limited, 1978).

58. See, e.g., V. I. Lenin, "Six Theses on the Immediate Tasks of the Soviet Government," in *Selected Works,* vol. 2 (Moscow: Progress Publishers, 1977), p. 622. Elsewhere, Lenin defended his tactics thus: "[S]tate capitalism would be a *step forward* as compared with the present state of affairs in our Soviet republic. If in approximately six months' time state capitalism became established in our Republic, this would be a great success and a sure guarantee that within a year socialism will have gained a permanently firm hold in our country"; " 'Left-Wing' Childishness and Petty-Bourgeois Mentality," ibid., p. 631. For a contemporary analysis of Taylorism and Marxism, see Harry Braverman, *Labor and Monopoly Capital* (New York: Monthly Review Press, 1974), pp. 12–14.

59. Moishe Lewin, *Russian Peasants and Soviet Power* (New York: W. W. Norton and Co., 1975), p. 21.

60. The Soviet Union under Stalin was not completely gray and undifferentiated. For the first half of the 1930s, significant resistance to Stalin's collectivization policies brought about a relaxing of controls, an "Indian summer of Communist toleration" (Kochan and Abraham, *Modern Russia,* p. 377). Prokofiev composed *Romeo and Juliet* (1938), and Pasternak wrote his famous poems; religion prospered during the war years; political dissent occasionally survived in outlying areas. But these were beleaguered exceptions to an otherwise tyrannical rule.

61. Kochan and Abraham, *Modern Russia,* p. 463.

62. Jerry Hough, *Russia and the West: Gorbachev and the Politics of Reform* (New York: Simon and Schuster, 1988), p. 93.

63. Quoted in Andrew Nagorski, *Reluctant Farewell* (New York: Holt, Rinehart and Winston, 1985), p. 10.

64. Karen Dawisha, *Eastern Europe: Gorbachev and Reform: The Great Challenge* (Cambridge: Cambridge University Press, 1988), p. 115. For a relatively positive account of the East German economy, see Henry Kamm,

"A Riddle for Communists: Why Does the East German Economy Prosper?" *New York Times*, 3/13/89; for a relatively negative appraisal, see Martin McCauley, "GDR Economy in 1988," *Soviet Analyst*, vol. 18, no. 6 (March 22, 1989).

65. Dawisha, *Eastern Europe*, pp. 53–54.

66. C. Bradley Scharf, *Politics and Change in East Germany* (Boulder: Westview, 1984), p. 78.

67. Ibid., p. 75.

68. Ibid., pp. 68–76.

69. Philip Taubman, "Soviet Overhauls Farm Bureaucracy," *New York Times*, 11/23/85.

70. Bialer, "Gorbachev's Program of Change," in *Gorbachev's Russia*, p. 242.

71. Joyce Kolko, *Restructuring the World Economy* (New York: Pantheon, 1988), p. 128.

72. Ibid., p. 281.

73. Aslund, *Gorbachev's Struggle*, pp. 76–80.

74. Vladimir Treml, "A Noble Experiment? Gorbachev's Antidrinking Campaign," in *Soviet Society Under Gorbachev*, ed. by Maurice Friedberg and Heyward Isham (Armonk, NY: M. E. Sharpe, 1987), p. 54.

75. Unflattering nicknames included "Lemonade Joe" and "The Mineral Water Secretary" (*mineralny secretar* instead of *generalny secretar*).

76. Treml, "A Noble Experiment," p. 61.

77. Philip Taubman, "Moscow Vodka Is Up and, What's Worse, Out," *New York Times*, 8/2/86.

78. Marie Lavigne, "Problems Facing the Soviet Economy," in *The Gorbachev Era*, p. 45.

79. Vladimir Kontorovich, "Labor Problems and the Prospects for Accelerated Economic Growth," in *Soviet Society Under Gorbachev*, p. 31.

80. Ibid., p. 39.

81. See, e.g., the first section of Aganbegyan's *The Challenge*. He begins with a discussion of how better to use resources, labor, and machinery and only then proceeds to the more radical topics of management reform, cooperatives, and market mechanisms. Aslund (*Gorbachev's Struggle*) follows a similar path but from a more critical perspective. For a more informal discussion, see "The Dictatorship of the Consumer," an interview with Aganbegyan in *New Perspectives Quarterly*, vol. 5, no. 4 (Winter 1988–89).

82. Quoted in Bill Keller, "New World for Russians," *New York Times*, 6/27/87.

83. Aslund, *Gorbachev's Struggle*, p. 179.

84. As the Soviet-installed leader of Hungary after the 1956 uprising, Kadar was almost universally reviled within Hungary. With various liberalization campaigns like NEM, he was largely able to turn that sentiment around. As Hungary moved closer to repudiating the one-party system, Kadar once again became a target of abuse, up until his death in 1989.

85. Martin McCauley, "Glasnost in Eastern Europe," *Contemporary Review*, vol. 253, no. 1471 (August 1988), p. 57.

86. Quoted in James Markham, "Gorbachev Cites Hungary as Model, New Leader Says," *New York Times*, 7/10/88.

87. E. Iasin, "Positions on Restructuring and the Price of Competence," *The Soviet Review*, vol. 30, no. 4 (July–August 1989), p. 31.

88. Quoted in McCauley, "Gorbachev as Leader," in McCauley, ed., *The Soviet Union Under Gorbachev*, p. 33.

89. Marshall Goldman, *Gorbachev's Challenge: Economic Reform in the Age of High Technology* (New York: W. W. Norton and Co., 1987), p. 28.

90. Leonhard, *The Kremlin and the West*, p. 41.

91. "Notes From the Underproductive: A Soviet Plant Manager's Blunt Words," *New York Times*, 6/30/88.

92. Aslund, *Gorbachev's Struggle*, p. 95.

93. Genrikh Bazhenov, "The Locomotive Can't Pick Up Speed: Joint Ventures, Two Years On," *New Times*, no. 9 (March 1989), p. 25.

94. An interesting political parallel is the new Soviet fondness for liberalism's guarantees of civil and political rights. See, e.g., Burlatsky, "O Sovetskom Parlamentarisme," op. cit.

95. "Give a Dog a Bad Name," *Soviet Analyst*, vol. 18, no. 10 (May 17, 1989), p. 1.

96. See Bill Keller, "Soviets Curbing Private Business," *New York Times*, 12/5/89; Myra Salikova, "Kooperativy Zakrivayutsa," *Ogonek*, no. 8 (February 1989); Tamara Kuznetsova, "Cooperatives: Pros and Cons," *New Times*, no. 28 (July 1989), pp. 32–33.

97. Bill Keller, "Gorbachev's Plan to Revise Farms Produces Opposition in Kremlin," *New York Times*, 3/15/89.

98. Boris Rumer, *Soviet Central Asia* (Boston: Unwin Hyman, 1989), pp. 125–27.

99. Bill Keller, "Gorbachev Urges Freeing of Farms from Collectives," *New York Times,* 10/14/88.

100. Bill Keller, "Moscow Importing Consumer Goods to Appease Public," *New York Times,* 4/17/89.

101. "The Soviet Economy in 1988: Gorbachev Changes Course," A Report by the Central Intelligence Agency and the Defense Intelligence Agency to the Subcommittee on National Security Economics of the Joint Economic Committee (April 14, 1989), p. 14.

102. Ibid., p. 21.

103. Aslund, *Gorbachev's Struggle,* p. 16.

104. "The Soviet Economy in 1988," C.I.A. and D.I.A., p. 7. For an interesting analysis of Soviet computers, albeit both anecdotal and polemical, see David Wellman, *A Chip in the Curtain* (Washington, DC: National Defense University, 1989).

105. All three figures come from Wilson P. Dizard and S. Blake Swensrud, *Gorbachev's Information Revolution: Controlling Glasnost in a New Electronic Era* (Boulder: Westview Press, 1987), pp. 1, 4, 26.

106. Bill Keller, "Soviet Critic of Economy in Spotlight," *New York Times,* 6/4/87.

107. The convertibility of the ruble is as inevitable as it is destabilizing for the Soviet economy. Upon embarking on this course, for instance, the U.S.S.R. will undoubtedly find itself with severe balance-of-payments problems and shortages in hard currency as imports flood Soviet markets. First with the Marshall Plan and then with guaranteed U.S. trade deficits until the late 1960s, Europe and Japan eventually could float their currencies (even then, Japan's currency didn't become convertible until 1964). Without the benefits of such protective mechanisms, the U.S.S.R.'s entry into the international market will be even more difficult. For a discussion of how European and Japanese currencies became convertible, see Robert Solomon, *The International Monetary System 1945–1976: An Insider's View* (New York: Harper & Row, 1977). For a Soviet view of the issue, see "When Will the Ruble Be Made Convertible?" an interview with Grigory Khanin, *New Times,* no. 30 (July 1989).

108. See, e.g., Iu. Sukhotin and V. Dementev, "Economic Reform and the Forces of Inhibition," *The Soviet Review,* vol. 30, no. 2 (March–April 1989); Vasilii Seliunin, "A Profound Reform or the Revenge of the Bureaucracy," *The Soviet Review,* vol. 30, no. 3 (May–June 1989); Alexander Polyukhov, "A Free Enterprise Zone," *New Times,* no. 29 (July 1989); Gavriil Popov, "Either Restructure Perestroika or Watch Rebuilding Collapse," *Glasnost,* vol. 2, no. 3 (May–July 1989).

109. Thomas Naylor, *The Gorbachev Strategy: Opening the Closed Society* (Lexington, MA: Lexington Books, 1988), p. 206.

110. "The Soviet Economy in 1988," C.I.A. and D.I.A., p. 2.

111. Kolko, *Restructuring the World Economy*, pp. 244–49.

112. Ibid., p. 53.

113. In October 1988, the Chinese government announced a resumption of price controls and limitations on private traders in an effort to ease the crunch for Chinese workers, primarily in the cities. These moves notwithstanding, the Chinese government decided to push through its stock market plan and was even considering a plan to privatize major industries. Edward Gargan, "China Reining in Economy's Shift to a Free Market," *New York Times*, 10/17/88; Nicholas Kristof, "China, Seeking More Efficiency, Looks to a Stock Market System," *New York Times*, 12/5/88; Nicholas Kristof, "In Beijing, a Bold New Proposal: End State Ownership of Industry," *New York Times*, 1/10/89. The events of June 1989—increased government repression and a swing in favor of party hard-liners—caused the government to readjust its economic policies. While foreign trade, agricultural reforms, and the free-enterprise zones continue relatively unchanged, a new emphasis on eliminating corruption and unequal income distribution through a "rectification" campaign has permeated Chinese articles on the economy. Moves toward privatization of large industries have apparently ended. "China's Foreign Trade Policy Remains Unchanged," *Beijing Review*, vol. 32, no. 30 (July 24–30, 1989); Yao Jianguo, "Hope of China's Agriculture," *Beijing Review*, vol. 32, no. 33 (August 14–20, 1989); Jing Wei, "Fruit of the Open Policy," *Beijing Review*, vol. 32, no. 34 (August 21–27, 1989); Jin Qi, "Why China Will Not Practice Privatization," *Beijing Review*, vol. 32, no. 36 (September 4–10, 1989).

114. For a thoughtful discussion of this topic, see, e.g., Harry Harding and Ed Hewett, "Socialist Reforms and the World Economy," in *Restructuring American Foreign Policy*, ed. by John Steinbrunner (Washington, DC: Brookings Institution, 1989), pp. 158–84. For a favorable Soviet analysis of Western financial thinking on economic internationalism, see, e.g., V. Sheinis, "Strukturniye sdvigi v ekonomike kapitalizma i perspektivi razvivavshchikhsya stran," *Azia i Afrika* (11/88), pp. 20–24.

115. Other countries with centrally planned economies, such as Hungary, Rumania, Yugoslavia, Poland, Vietnam, and China, have preceded the U.S.S.R. in gaining access to the trade privileges and hard-currency loans of the international lending agencies.

116. Kolko, *Restructuring the World Economy*, p. 193.

117. Bazhenov, "The Locomotive Can't Pick Up Speed," *New Times*, pp. 24–25.

118. Foreign assets for the United States dropped from $100 billion in 1980 to $20 billion in 1984, while Japanese assets grew from $7 to $74 billion in the same period. Kolko, *Restructuring the World Economy,* p. 197.

119. In his December 1988 United Nations speech, Gorbachev declared that the U.S.S.R. was willing to place a hundred-year moratorium on certain debt repayments and would consider completely writing off others.

120. For new Soviet thinking on the international economy and the Third World, see, e.g., Nikolai Shmelev, "The Third World and International Economic Relations," *Social Sciences,* 3/88, pp. 165–81.

121. Padma Desai, *Perestroika in Perspective* (Princeton: Princeton University Press, 1989), p. 24.

122. Lavigne, "Problems Facing the Soviet Economy," in *The Gorbachev Era,* p. 56.

123. Ibid., p. 57.

124. "By 1986 about 90 percent of all currency exchange was in the hands of traders, primarily in the banks. They deal in million-dollar blocks, exchanging some $200 billion a day. Traders can buy or sell within minutes rather than within days or weeks as in the past. This tremendous power has effectively eroded the ability of states to control their own economic policies." Kolko, *Restructuring the World Economy,* p. 113.

125. Bill Keller, "One Soviet Paper Rebukes Another," *New York Times,* 5/5/88. It wasn't until August 1989 that *Ogonek* published a profile of Andreyeva. Instead of interviewing Andreyeva personally, the magazine simply translated a piece from the *Washington Post,* introducing the article: "A country must know its heroes. Its anti-heroes as well." "Razyarenniy Kritik Gorbacheva," *Ogonek,* no. 33 (August 1989), p. 25.

126. See, e.g., Bill Keller, "Russian Party Officials Rage at Changes Under Gorbachev," *New York Times,* 4/28/89.

127. Reddaway, "Resisting Gorbachev," p. 40.

128. "Russian Nationalism in the Gorbachev Era: Alive and Well," *Soviet Nationality Survey,* vol. 6, no. 2 (February 1989), p. 2.

129. Yuri Bondarev, "My zhivem v pluralisme, chort vozmi!" *Ogonek,* no. 15 (April 1989), p. 13.

130. A traditional opposition in Russian thought is between "Westernizers" such as Ivan Turgenev and "Slavophiles" such as Fyodor Dostoevsky. The contemporary Russian chauvinists stem from the Slavophile wing.

131. For Pamyat's 1987 appeal see " 'Pamyat': An Appeal to the Russian People," *Soviet-Jewish Affairs,* vol. 18, no. 1 (1988), pp. 60–71.

132. See, e.g., *Soviet Analyst,* vol. 17, no. 10 (5/18/88), p. 6.

133. Schmidt-Hauer, *Gorbachev: The Path to Power,* p. 68.

134. How representative is Pamyat? Alexander Yanov has written extensively on the ascendancy of Russian chauvinism, its links to "legitimate" Soviet conservatives like Solzhenitsyn, and its potential for taking power in the Soviet Union. While Yanov probably exaggerates the political clout of such reactionaries when he compares it to the influence of the Bolsheviks in the decade before the 1917 Revolution, Russian chauvinism has unquestionable support, especially outside urban areas in the Russian Republic. See Alexander Yanov, *The Russian Challenge and the Year 2000* (New York: Basil Blackwell, 1987).

135. Georgians (Shevardnadze), Kazakhs (Kunaev), and Azerbaijanis (Aliev) have all recently served in the Politburo.

136. Paul Goble, "Gorbachev and the Soviet Nationality Problem," in *Soviet Society Under Gorbachev,* p. 80.

137. Aslund, *Gorbachev's Struggle,* pp. 103–4. As Aslund points out, however, Shevardnadze's experiments were reversed by his successor, Dzhumber Patiashvili.

138. In August 1989, on the fiftieth anniversary of the U.S.S.R.–Germany Non-Aggression Pact, which ceded the then independent Baltic republics to Soviet control, hundreds of thousands of Baltic citizens joined hands across the three regions in a demonstration of solidarity and independence. Moscow responded shortly after with a statement condemning nationalism in the area.

139. Esther Fein, "Lativans to Seek a 'Special Status,'" *New York Times,* 9/1/89.

140. See Eduard Gudava, "The Tragedy of Georgia," *Glasnost,* vol. 2, no. 3 (May–July 1989), p. 5.

141. Esther Fein, "Worry Grows for Russians in Estonia," *New York Times,* 8/25/89.

142. "The Georgians themselves came to the conclusion that Abkhazians were used as pawns by some ultra-conservatives in Russia to provoke serious ethnic unrest and compromise Gorbachev's *perestroika.*" *Central Asia and Caucasus Chronicle,* vol. 8, no. 2 (May 1989), p. 1.

143. The conflict between the Baltics and Moscow in August 1989 underscores the Kremlin's resistance to secession. See Esther Fein, "Baltic Communists Press Middle Road on Independence," *New York Times,* 8/29/89; Esther Fein, "Gorbachev Said to Have Approved Baltic Broadside," *New York Times,* 8/30/89.

144. According to one Soviet analyst, however, these intellectuals are

"the weakest possible political allies within the system." Daniel Matu-szewski, "Nationalities in the Soviet Future: Trends Under Gorbachev," in *Gorbachev and the Soviet Future*, ed. by Lawrence Lerner and Donald Treadgold (Boulder: Westview, 1988), pp. 92–93.

145. Although nationalism from the republics perhaps constitutes Gor-bachev's most profound challenge, the various calls for sovereignty are not unified. Most ethnic groups have as much antipathy toward one another as they have for mother Russia. See, e.g., Viktor Aksyuchits' description of "blinkered self-absorption" in "With Malice Towards All and Charity to One," *Glasnost*, vol. 2, no. 3 (May–July 1989), pp. 24, 29. Aksyuchits unintentionally corroborates his position by making the particularly insensi-tive argument that Islam explains Azerbaijani "savagery" and Christianity Armenian "tolerance" in the Nagorno-Karabakh conflict.

146. Boris Kagarlitsky, "Perestroika: The Dialectic of Change," *New Left Review*, no. 169 (May–June 1988), p. 81. The data Kagarlitsky refers to come from research conducted by the Central Economic-Mathematical Institute and *Literaturnaya Gazeta*. For more insights into the independent Soviet left, see, e.g., Kagarlitsky, "A Difficult Hegemony," *Across Frontiers*, vol. 5, no. 2 (Summer 1989).

147. During the Brezhnev administration, Roy Medvedev argued that political and social democracy were essential complements to economic reor-ganization along socialist principles. In the 1970s, Medvedev crusaded for worker self-management and industrial democracy, the key demands of the Soviet "new left." Although supportive of small-scale private initiative, Med-vedev remained skeptical of capitalism. See, e.g., Roy A. Medvedev, *On Socialist Democracy* (New York: W. W. Norton and Co., 1975). Medvedev is now a member of the Congress of People's Deputies. Another pre-*glasnost* organ of dissent was the Moscow Trust group, formed in 1982. The Trust group maintained extensive contacts with the West, functioned as a valuable conduit of information East–West, and conducted numerous demonstrations in Mos-cow. Many of its members were arrested, jailed, or expelled from the country and many more were harassed and lost jobs. For an excellent description of the history of the Moscow Trust group, see Olga Medvedkov, "The Moscow Trust Group: An Uncontrolled Grass-Roots Movement in the Soviet Union," *Mershon Center Quarterly Report*, vol. 12, no. 4 (Spring 1988).

148. Kagarlitsky, "Perestroika," p. 83.

149. Philip Taubman, "Joblessness, in Theory No Issue for Soviet, Is Suddenly Debated," *New York Times*, 1/9/86.

150. Felicity Barringer, "Soviet Is Reporting One Million Jobless in Uzbek Republic," *New York Times*, 3/29/87.

151. Bill Keller, "Moscow Says Changes in Voting Usher in Many New Local Leaders," *New York Times*, 9/21/88.

152. Taubman, "Joblessness," *New York Times*, 1/9/86.

153. Aslund, *Gorbachev's Struggle*, p. 84.

154. Ludmilla Alexeyeva, "Strikes in the Soviet Union," *Across Frontiers*, vol. 3, no. 4 (Summer–Fall 1987), pp. 16–19.

155. "Soviet Says Food Prices Will Rise," *New York Times*, 10/3/87.

156. Bill Keller, "Russians, Fearing Rise in Prices, Hoard Food," *New York Times*, 10/30/87.

157. Francis Clines, "Some of Siberia's Miners Return; Gorbachev Calls Strike a Crisis," *New York Times*, 7/20/89; Francis Clines, "Gorbachev Hails Striking Miners as Aiding Change," *New York Times*, 7/24/89. Also see Zamira Ibragimova, "Ploshchadi Boli," *Ogonek*, no. 32 (August 1989).

158. Abel Aganbegyan, "New Directions in Soviet Economics," *New Left Review*, no. 169 (May–June, 1988), pp. 90–92. Also see Aganbegyan's discussion of the issue in his book *The Challenge: Economics of Perestroika*, pp. 175–91.

159. Aganbegyan, "New Directions," p. 93.

160. Some on the Soviet left distrust government statements on worker democracy: "The Soviet authorities are afraid of worker self-management as the most dangerous of the only real alternatives to its totalitarian rule." Vadim Belotserkovsky, "Soviet Intellectuals and the 'Workers Question,'" *Across Frontiers*, vol. 3, no. 4 (Summer–Fall 1987), p. 21.

161. See, e.g., Hillel Ticktin, "Prime Time Glasnost," *Across Frontiers*, vol. 3, no. 4 (Summer–Fall 1987), pp. 14–15.

162. Bill Keller, "Moscow's Other Mastermind," *New York Times Magazine*, 2/19/89, p. 43.

163. Quoted in Solomon, *The International Monetary System*, p. 25.

2 : THE NEW THINKING IN SOVIET FOREIGN POLICY

1. Naylor, *The Gorbachev Strategy*, p. 128.

2. The Bolshevik in question was Karl Radek. See Kochan and Abraham, *The Making of Modern Russia*, p. 317.

3. Tom Gervasi, *The Myth of Soviet Military Supremacy* (New York: Harper & Row, 1986), pp. 157–58.

4. Jon Connell, *The New Maginot Line* (New York: Arbor House, 1986), p. 172.

5. Gervasi, *The Myth*, p. 53.

6. For this argument on the relationship between START and SDI, see Andrew Goldberg, "Offense and Defense in the Postnuclear System," *Washington Quarterly*, vol. 11, no. 2 (Spring 1988), p. 59.

7. For background on the INF history, see, e.g., Jonathan Dean, *Watershed in Europe: Dismantling the East–West Military Confrontation* (Lexington, MA: Lexington Books, 1987), pp. 91–152. Also, the excellent review of Soviet motivations in Alan Sherr, *The Other Side of Arms Control: Soviet Objectives in the Gorbachev Era* (Boston: Unwin Hyman, 1988), pp. 137–77.

8. Dean, *Watershed in Europe*, p. 133.

9. Ibid., p. 137.

10. The description of Soviet initiatives leading up to the INF treaty draws from the following articles: Seth Mydans, "Gorbachev Ready for Reagan Talks; Freezes Missiles," *New York Times*, 4/8/85; Gerald Boyd, "U.S. and Russians Make New Offers on Nuclear Tests," *New York Times*, 7/30/85; Richard Bernstein, "Gorbachev Urges Arms Agreements with Europeans," *New York Times*, 10/4/85; Serge Schmemann, "Gorbachev Offers to Scrap A-Arms Within 15 Years," *New York Times*, 1/16/86; Serge Schmemann, "Gorbachev Seeks to Talk to Reagan on Atom Test Ban," *New York Times*, 3/30/86; Serge Schmemann, "Gorbachev on Arms Offer," *New York Times*, 6/17/86; Philip Taubman, "Gorbachev Says Soviet Test Halt Is Again Extended," *New York Times*, 8/19/86; Michael Gordon, "Soviet Leads US in Arms-Cut Image," *New York Times*, 6/7/87; Paul Quinn-Judge, "Gorbachev Takes the Initiative," *Christian Science Monitor*, 3/2/87; John Cushman, Jr., "U.S. Is Demanding Wide Verification for a Missile Pact," *New York Times*, 3/12/87.

11. According to some Soviet analysts, even the CIA figures are conservative. In "Soviet Numbers Game Threatens Perestroika," Richard Ericson quotes a Soviet study that the Soviet government directs an astounding 25 to 30 percent of GNP to the military. In comparison, the United States apportions roughly 5 to 6 percent of a GNP twice the size. See *Bulletin of Atomic Scientists*, vol. 44, no. 10 (12/88), p. 25.

12. As Marshall Goldman points out, "A cutback in the heavy industrial sector will necessarily provoke a parallel contraction in the military sector, because heavy industry is the major source of Soviet armaments." Goldman, *Gorbachev's Challenge*, p. 11.

13. For a discussion of the inefficiency of the Soviet military-industrial complex, see, e.g., Andrew Cockburn, *The Threat: Inside the Soviet Military Machine* (New York: Vintage, 1984). For a discussion of the inefficiency of the U.S. military-industrial complex, see, e.g., Seymour Melman, *The Permanent War Economy* (New York: Simon and Schuster, 1985).

14. Even Paul Nitze, the Reagan administration arms control negotiator, has criticized the Bush administration's stance on short-range missiles. Michael Gordon, "Reagan Arms Advisor Says Bush Is Wrong on Short-Range Missiles," *New York Times,* 5/3/89.

15. Jesse James, "Compromise on Missiles Heads Off NATO Rift," *Arms Control Today,* vol. 19, no. 5 (June–July 1989), p. 23.

16. See discussion in Sherr, *The Other Side of Arms Control,* pp. 221ff.

17. For instance, physicist Edward Teller and Lieutenant General Daniel Graham. Connell, *The New Maginot Line,* p. 205.

18. In April 1989, Gorbachev offered to dismantle the disputed Krasnoyarsk radar in exchange for a strict U.S. interpretation of the ABM treaty. In October 1989 the Soviet Union admitted that the radar was a violation of the treaty.

19. Bill Keller, "Gorbachev Promises Big Cut in Military Spending," *New York Times,* 1/19/89; Bill Keller, "Soviet Premier Says Cutbacks Could Reach 33 Percent for Military," *New York Times,* 6/8/89.

20. On this subject see, e.g., Jack Snyder, "Limiting Offensive Conventional Forces," *International Security,* vol. 12, no. 4 (Spring 1988). Similar arguments appear in Michael MccGwire, *Military Objectives in Soviet Foreign Policy* (Washington, DC: Brookings Institution, 1987). MccGwire also shows how these changes in doctrine can be traced to pre-Gorbachev military developments. Also see "The Revised Soviet Military Doctrine," by Makhmut Gareyev, the Deputy Chief of the General Staff of the Armed Forces of the Soviet Union, *Bulletin of Atomic Scientists,* vol. 44, no. 10 (12/88), pp. 30–34; Andrei Kokosin and Valentin Larionov, "Shifting the Emphasis to Defense," *New Times,* no. 10 (March 1989); Alexei Arbatov, "Reasonable Sufficiency," *New Times,* no. 17 (April 1989). Also see the frequent compilations of Soviet high-level views in the U.S. government publication *Strategic Review* in the section entitled "The Soviet Strategic View."

21. John Steinbrunner, "The Prospect of Cooperative Security," in *Restructuring American Foreign Policy,* ed. by John Steinbrunner (Washington, DC: Brookings Institution, 1989), p. 99.

22. For the best explication of Yazov's views, see Yazov's own article, "The Soviet Proposal for European Security," *Bulletin of Atomic Scientists,* vol. 44, No. 7 (9/88), pp. 8–11. For more information on military reshuffling see also Bill Keller, "Soviets Seen Retiring Warsaw Pact Chief," *New York Times,* 1/12/89. In February 1989, Pyotr Lushev replaced Viktor Kulikov as Warsaw Pact chief, another example of reformers in, dead wood out.

23. Paul Lewis, "Soviet Offers to Adjust Imbalance of Conventional Forces in Europe," *New York Times,* 6/24/88. In January 1989, the Soviet

government released its figures and acknowledged superiority in various categories, including troops and tanks.

24. For an analysis of these concessions, see "Gorbachev Announces Unilateral Cuts in Soviet Conventional Forces," *Arms Control Today,* vol. 19, no. 1 (January–February 1989), p. 24. Also, Jack Mendelsohn, "Gorbachev's Preemptive Concession," *Arms Control Today,* vol. 19, no. 12 (March 1989), p. 10.

25. The levels enumerated in the Soviet proposal were 1,350,000 ground troops, 1,500 tactical-strike aircraft, 1,700 helicopters, 20,000 tanks, 24,000 cannons, mortars, and multiple rocket launchers, and 28,000 armored vehicles and armored troop carriers. Thomas Halverson, "U.S., Soviet Proposals Boost CFE Prospects," *Arms Control Today,* vol. 19, no. 5 (June–July 1989), p. 22.

26. Ibid., p. 30.

27. Robert Pear, "35 Nations Issue East–West Accord Assuring a Broad Range of Rights," *New York Times,* 1/17/89.

28. Many Western analysts continue to view this Soviet strategy within the divide-and-conquer framework. See, e.g., Harry Gelman, *Gorbachev's Policies Toward Western Europe: A Balance Sheet,* Executive Summary (Santa Monica: RAND Corporation, 1987).

29. Clyde Farnsworth, "Rise in Allies' Lending to Soviets Divides U.S.," *New York Times,* 10/21/88.

30. Edith Cresson, "France and the European Community," *Harvard International Review* (Summer 1989), p. 28.

31. Michael Farr, "Bonn Sets Credit Line for Soviets," *New York Times,* 10/12/88.

32. The exact figures in the final agreement for Soviet influence in the region were: 80 percent in Hungary, 80 percent in Bulgaria, 90 percent in Rumania, 50 percent in Yugoslavia, and 10 percent in Greece. Charles Gati, *Hungary and the Soviet Bloc* (Durham: Duke University Press, 1986), p. 31.

33. The Teheran and Yalta conferences allowed the Soviet Union to reclaim a large section of Polish territory it had lost after World War I. Advancing through Poland on the heels of the retreating Germans, the U.S.S.R. established the Lublin Committee, a provisional Polish government that leaned heavily in its favor. The Polish government-in-exile in England, still bitter over the boundary issue, initially refused to negotiate with this provisional body over the formation of a new Polish government, despite pressure from the British and the United States. Finally, Stanislaw Mikolajczyk of the Peasant Movement returned to Poland to form a coalition government that lasted from June 1945 to January 1947. Then came a highly undemocratic

election, which gave the Polish Communist party a dubious mandate to create a one-party state. See Gar Alperovitz, *Atomic Diplomacy* (New York: Penguin, 1985), pp. 291–318.

34. Certain U.S. policy makers, notably Franklin Roosevelt, refused to engage in balance-of-power discussions, but this opposition did not prevent the balance from being negotiated anyway; Gati, *Hungary and the Soviet Bloc*, p. 29.

35. Ibid., p. 42.

36. "In the immediate aftermath of war, [Stalin] instructed the Communists of France, Italy, Czechoslovakia, and Yugoslavia not to attempt to take power on their own; only the Yugoslavs turned a deaf ear. Stalin continued to respect the British position in Greece, despite the temptations offered by the civil war there." Kochan and Abrams, *The Making of Modern Russia*, p. 482.

37. Gati, *Hungary and the Soviet Bloc*, p. 69.

38. Albert Resis, *Stalin, the Politburo, and the Onset of the Cold War, 1945–6*, The Carl Beck Papers in Russian and East European Studies, no. 701 (Pittsburgh: University of Pittsburgh Center for Russian and East European Studies, 1988).

39. Soviet historians and essayists have begun attacking not only Stalin's domestic policy, but his foreign policy as well. The Cold War, they argue in departing from Soviet tradition, was also in part Stalin's fault. See Vyacheslav Dashichev, "Vostok-Zapad: Poisk Novikh Otnosheniye," *Literaturnaya Gazeta*, no. 20 (May 18, 1988), p. 14; Nikolai Popov, "Vse My v Odnoy Lodke," *Literaturnaya Gazeta*, no. 9 (March 1, 1989), p. 14.

40. John Lewis Gaddis, *Strategies of Containment* (Oxford: Oxford University Press, 1982), p. 71.

41. Dawisha, *Eastern Europe*, p. 196.

42. According to Chinese documents, Khrushchev vacillated on sending troops into Hungary and only did so after persuasion of the Chinese government. *The Sino–Soviet Dispute*, Keesing's Research Report 3 (New York: Charles Scribner's Sons, 1969), p. 11.

43. Quoted in Dawisha, *Eastern Europe*, p. 164.

44. Ibid., p. 75. On his October 1989 trip to Finland, Gorbachev reiterated this policy.

45. See also Henry Kamm, "Gorbachev Said to Reject Soviet Right to Intervene," *New York Times*, 4/2/89; James Markham, "Gorbachev Spurns the Use of Force in Eastern Europe," *New York Times*, 7/7/89.

46. For indications of Gorbachev's role in the Polish events, see, e.g.,

Francis Clines, "Gorbachev Calls, Then Polish Party Drops Its Demands," *New York Times*, 9/22/89.

47. For an overview of this Polish history, see Norman Davies, *Heart of Europe* (Oxford: Oxford University Press, 1986).

48. William Echikson, "Poland Launches Sweeping Reforms," *Christian Science Monitor*, 10/9/87.

49. Actually, the government proposal won a majority of votes, but low turnout meant that the measure did not gain the needed 51 percent of registered voters. Jackson Diehl, "Reform Plan Loses Vote in Poland," *Philadelphia Inquirer*, 12/1/87.

50. Eric Bourne, "Budapest Party Chief Says Further Reform Is Essential," *Christian Science Monitor*, 3/30/87.

51. For a startling Soviet perspective on Hungarian reform, see Marina Shakina, "Invitation to Power," *New Times*, no. 34 (August 22–28, 1989).

52. *Poland: Reform, Adjustment, and Growth*, A World Bank Country Study (Washington, DC: The World Bank, 1987), p. 40.

53. For instance, in per capita Gross Domestic Product, East Germany and Czechoslovakia exceed Poland, Hungary, and the Soviet Union. Henry Kamm, "A Riddle for Communists: Why Does the East German Economy Prosper?" *New York Times*, 3/13/89.

54. See, e.g., F. Stephen Larrabee, "The Unavoidable 'German Question,' " *New York Times*, 9/21/89; Serge Schmemann, "One Germany: Bonn's Quiet Yearning," *New York Times*, 9/23/89.

55. An interesting document of inter–Eastern European activism is the border declaration signed by Polish and Czech activists following a July 1988 meeting. See "Border Declaration," *East European Reporter*, vol. 3, no. 3 (Autumn 1988), pp. 61–62.

56. George Konrad, *Antipolitics* (New York: Harcourt Brace Jovanovich, 1984), p. 35.

57. Brian Morton and Joanne Landy, "East European Activists Test Glasnost," *Bulletin of Atomic Scientists* (May 1988); Michael Kaufman, "Rights Conference Stirs Warsaw Ire," *New York Times*, 5/14/87.

58. Jackson Diehl, "Poland Weighs Offering Dissidents Alternatives to Military Service," *Philadelphia Inquirer*, 1/21/88.

59. See "Gnomes, Revolution, and Toilet Paper: The Orange Alternative in Wroclaw," *Across Frontiers* (Spring–Summer 1988), vol. 4, nos. 2 and 3, pp. 1–6.

60. See "The Prague Appeal," reprinted in *From Below: Independent*

Peace and Environmental Movements in Eastern Europe and the U.S.S.R., Helsinki Watch (October 1987), p. 211.

61. See Jiri Dienstbier, "Gorbachev and Czechoslovakian Reform," *New Politics*, vol. 2, no. 3 (Summer 1989); Janet Fleischman, "Protest and Political Trials in Prague," *Across Frontiers*, vol. 5, no. 2 (Summer 1989); Craig Whitney, "Prague to Make Changes, but Not Dramatic Ones," *New York Times*, 9/6/89.

62. Elizabeth Pond, "East Germany Shuns Glasnost, Opts For More Censorship," *Christian Science Monitor*, 4/8/88.

63. Serge Schmemann, "Opposition Forms in East Germany," *New York Times*, 9/20/89.

64. See "Special Report on Environmental Politics in Hungary," *Across Frontiers*, vol. 3, no. 4 (Summer–Fall 1987), pp. 7–14.

65. This section on regional relations will consider Soviet attitudes toward the Third World. Once a term connoting a third path between capitalism and Communism, the *Third World* now is used more frequently to describe "developing" countries. Because of its regional focus, this section will often discuss countries that are neither wholly independent (Cuba, El Salvador) nor industrially less advanced (Japan, Israel). For an interesting account of how the Third World became less of a political alternative and more of an economic category, see Nigel Harris, *The End of the Third World* (New York: Penguin, 1986).

66. See, e.g., Bill Keller, "Soviet, in a Shift, Expands Contact with Third World," *New York Times*, 5/25/87.

67. This framework comes from Rajen Menon, *Soviet Power in the Third World* (New Haven: Yale University Press, 1986).

68. For this argument see Milovan Djilas, *Conversations with Stalin* (New York: Harcourt, Brace and World, 1962), p. 132.

69. Erik P. Hoffman, "Soviet Foreign Policy Aims and Accomplishments from Lenin to Brezhnev," in *Soviet Foreign Policy*, p. 15.

70. Menon, *Soviet Power*, p. 104.

71. Jonathan Kwitny, *Endless Enemies* (New York: Penguin Books, 1986), p. 281.

72. See, e.g., Marie Mendras, "Soviet Policy Toward the Third World," in *Soviet Foreign Policy*, p. 173. Also Elizabeth Valkenier, "New Soviet Thinking About the Third World," *World Policy Journal*, vol. 4, no. 4 (Fall 1987), pp. 651–75. For Soviet assessments, see, e.g., V. Kremenuk, "Sovetsko–Amerikanskie Otnoshenia: Regionalnie Konflikty,"*Azia i Afrika*, 3/89; G.

Mirsky, "Deideologizatsia Mezhgosudarstvennikh Otnoshenii," *Azia i Afrika*, 4/89.

73. Jerry Hough has observed that traditionally there were three rules of conduct for Soviet foreign policy analyses: (1) Soviet policy could not be discussed directly; (2) the United States was always aggressive, the U.S.S.R. always peace-loving; (3) the Marxist–Leninist framework could not be challenged. In recent articles in *Azia i Afrika, Latinskaya Amerika, New Times,* and so on, all three of these rules have been consistently broken, revealing that the "new thinking" has spread throughout the academic and political world. It should be stressed here that Hough reveals through a close reading of Soviet foreign policy analyses 1956–1986 that Gorbachev's attitudes can be traced to earlier work on countries in the Third World. Despite working within the guidelines enumerated above, Soviet analysts could nonetheless make unconventional arguments. Jerry Hough, *The Struggle for the Third World* (Washington, DC: Brookings Institution, 1986).

74. Ellen Mickiewicz, "Making the Media Work: Soviet Society and Communications," in *Soviet Society Under Gorbachev*, p. 141.

75. Desai, *Perestroika in Perspective*, p. 58.

76. Andrey Kozyrev, "Why Soviet Foreign Policy Went Sour," *New York Times*, 1/7/89.

77. Bill Keller, "New Soviet Ideologist Rejects Idea of World Struggle Against West," *New York Times*, 10/6/88.

78. For an excellent overview of the mixed history of Soviet involvement in Latin America, see Marc Edelman, "The Other Super Power, the U.S.S.R. and Latin America: 1917–1987," *NACLA Newsletter*, vol. 21, no. 1 (January–February 1987), pp. 11–29. Also John Lamperti, *What Are We Afraid Of?* (Boston: South End Press, 1988).

79. Cole Blasier, *The Giant's Rival: The U.S.S.R. and Latin America* (Pittsburgh: University of Pittsburgh Press, 1987), pp. 103–97.

80. Edelman, "The Other Super Power," p. 22.

81. Blasier, *The Giant's Rival*, pp. 139–53.

82. Joseph Treaster, "Castro Scorning Gorbachev Model," *New York Times*, 1/11/89; Bill Keller, "Gorbachev–Castro Face-Off: A Clash of Style and Policies," *New York Times*, 4/2/89.

83. In 1987, for instance, the Soviet Union cut oil shipments to Nicaragua as a warning that it could not sustain Nicaraguan dependency. Nicaragua turned to Mexico and Venezuela for these resources instead.

84. Lamperti, *What Are We Afraid Of?*, p. 28.

85. Francis Moore Lappé et al., *Betraying the National Interest* (New York: Grove Press, 1988), p. 153.

86. Edelman, "The Other Super Power," pp. 32–35.

87. "Moscow Improving Relations with Latin America," *Washington Report on the Hemisphere*, vol. 9, no. 6 (Dec. 4, 1988), p. 5.

88. Jorge Dominguez, "U.S., Soviet and Cuban Policies Toward Latin America," in *East–West Tensions in the Third World*, ed. by Marshall Shulman (New York: W. W. Norton and Co., 1986), p. 70.

89. The U.S.S.R. is even pursuing the question of trade in services with Latin America through increased data flow. See, e.g., N. G. Zaitsev, "Latinskaya Amerika v mezhdunarodnaya torgovle islugamy," *Latinskaya Amerika*, 6/87, pp. 18–31.

90. Quoted in Zaki Laidi, ed., *The Third World and the Soviet Union* (London: Zed, 1988), p. 24.

91. Andrew Pierre, *The Global Politics of Arms Sales* (Princeton: Princeton University Press, 1982), p. 11.

92. Ibid., p. 8; figure is for 1977.

93. From 1961 to 1971, African imports amounted to only $4 billion. David Albright, "East–West Tensions in Africa," in *East–West Tensions*, p. 137.

94. Bruce Porter, *The U.S.S.R. in Third World Conflicts* (Cambridge: Cambridge University Press, 1986), p. 91.

95. Kwitny, *Endless Enemies*, p. 125.

96. "Soviet Geopolitical Momentum: Myth or Menace?" *Defense Monitor*, vol. 15, no. 5 (Center for Defense Information, 1986), p. 14.

97. According to Willard Depee, ambassador to Mozambique in the late 1970s, "Sure, Frelimo's Marxist, but they keep their distance from Moscow. They're very independent, pro–Third World." Ibid., p. 13.

98. Kwitny, *Endless Enemies*, p. 389.

99. On Libyan attempts to normalize relations with the United States, see, e.g., Jonathan Bearman, *Qadhafi's Libya* (London: Zed, 1986), pp. 227–28.

100. In its statements on Libya, the U.S.S.R. has emphasized its policy of self-determination and Libya's role in fighting Western oil monopolies. Qadafi's previous criticisms of the U.S.S.R. are conveniently forgotten. See, e.g., A. Svedov and V. Rumantsev, *Sovetsko-Liviiskie Otnosheniya* (Moscow: Progress Publishers, 1986).

101. Christopher Wren, "Soviet Diplomats in South Africa After Three Decades of Hostility," *New York Times*, 4/27/89.

102. Kwitny, *Endless Enemies*, p. 135.

103. Ibid., p. 140.

104. Though it receives Soviet aid and is therefore vulnerable to Soviet pressure, Angola has certainly not become a staunch Soviet ally. In fact, Angola has been actively seeking reconciliation with the United States. In late 1987, Angola applied for IMF membership as President José Eduardo dos Santos criticized excessive economic centralization. "This puts the United States in an ironic ideological position, European diplomats here say. With one hand, the United States, a promoter of free-market economics around the world, blocks Angola's move to enter the fund, and with the other gives aid to the rebel group Unita, a movement that has in its program a call for socialism." James Brooke, "Adam Smith Crowds Marx in Angola," *New York Times*, 12/29/87.

105. See, e.g., G. Polyakov, "SSSR-Afrika: Ekonomycheskoye Sotrud-nychestva," *Azia i Afrika*, 6/88, pp. 2–6. On Soviet view of African debt see, e.g., S. Shatalov, "Dolgovoy Krizis: Strategia Razvitia," *Azia i Afrika*, 2/89.

106. Halliday, *Soviet Policy in the Arc of Crisis*, p. 87.

107. Ibid., pp. 85–86; see also Kwitny, *Endless Enemies*, pp. 214–15.

108. Halliday, *Soviet Policy*, p. 88.

109. Ibid., p. 94.

110. Ibid., p. 95.

111. Another switch in alliances appears in the making as Ethiopia continues to woo the United States and Somalia has tentatively approached the Soviets. Jane Perlez, "Ethiopia Asking U.S. for Full Diplomatic Ties," *New York Times*, 4/20/89; Linda Friedman, "Weak U.S.-Backed Somalia Regime Looks Again to Soviets," *Christian Science Monitor*, 8/22/89.

112. Porter, *Third World Conflicts*, p. 89. For an updated analysis of Soviet policy toward South Yemen that covers the 1986 internal crisis, see Fred Halliday, "Moscow's Crisis Management: The Case of South Yemen," *Middle East Report*, vol. 18, no. 2 (March–April 1988), pp. 18–23.

113. Roderic Pitty, "Soviet Perceptions of Iraq," *Middle East Report*, vol. 18, no. 2 (March–April 1988), p. 23.

114. Labeling the U.S.S.R. singularly unsuccessful in the Middle East, Robert Freedman notes the following pattern: (1) the Soviets generally alienate at least one of a pair of allies when they become rivals; (2) Communist parties in the Middle East often prove to be a liability, as in Iran, Iraq, and Sudan; and (3) suddenly rich in petrodollars after 1973, OPEC countries

turned increasingly to the West for investments. Robert O. Freedman, "Soviet Policy Toward the Middle East," in *Soviet Foreign Policy*, p. 178.

115. Brezhnev also proposed such a conference.

116. Paul Quinn-Judge, "Soviets Pursue Enhanced Role in Mideast," *Christian Science Monitor*, 4/24/87.

117. Mary Curtius, "Israeli Hopes Raised by Soviet Officials' First Visit in 20 Years," *Christian Science Monitor*, 7/13/87.

118. The latter proposal had a distinct flavor of self-interest, given that the U.S.S.R. is concerned with the range of new missiles being developed by Middle Eastern countries, missiles that could reach Soviet territory. Thomas Friedman, "Spread of Missiles Is Seen as Soviet Worry in Mideast," *New York Times*, 3/24/89.

119. See Fida Nasrallah, "Soviet Involvement in the Lebanese Crisis," *Middle East International*, no. 356 (August 14, 1989), pp. 17–18.

120. Peter Hayes et al., *American Lake: Nuclear Peril in the Pacific* (New York: Penguin, 1986), p. 298.

121. "South Pacific Deployments Down," *Pacific News Bulletin*, vol. 4, no. 1 (January 1989); Michael Gordon, "Soviets Decrease Use of Navy and Curb Overseas Exercises," *New York Times*, 7/17/88. The U.S. Navy, meanwhile, has not replied in kind. "We don't see naval arms control as offering the U.S. anything," according to one navy captain. Quoted in Michele Flournoy, "Navy Shuns Credit for Cuts," *Bulletin of Atomic Scientists*, vol. 45, no. 6 (July–August 1989), p. 3.

122. Hayes et al., *American Lake*, p. 335.

123. Thomas Robinson, "Soviet Policy in Asia: The Military Dimension," in *Soviet Foreign Policy*, p. 161.

124. For an extensive analysis of the Vladivostok speech, see *The Soviet Union as an Asia Pacific Power: Implications of Gorbachev's 1986 Vladivostok Initiative* (Boulder, CO: Westview Press, 1987). For Soviet analyses, see, e.g., V. Lizun, "Smelyi Proriv v Budushchee," *Azia i Afrika* (2/88), pp. 2–5, or D. Volsky, "Novoe Myshlenie i Azia," *Azia i Afrika* (3/88), pp. 2–6. For a view specifically on Soviet support for the Raratonga Treaty and the nuclear-free Pacific initiative, see Y. Lugovskoy, "Tikhi Okean: Problema Bezyadernoy Zony," *Azia i Afrika* (7/88), pp. 2–5.

125. See "Gorbachev Offers Disputed Radar for Peaceful Exploration of Space," *New York Times*, 9/17/88. For Soviet irritation at Washington's casual disregard of Krasnoyarsk initiatives, see Y. Lugovskoy, "Krasnoyarski Initsiativy: Bezopasnost ATP," *Azia i Afrika*, 2/89; for economic implications, see B. Nikolayev, "Internatsionalizatsia Khozyaistvennoy Zhizn," *Azia i Afrika*, 6/89.

126. Their own experience in 1945 had educated the Chinese about Soviet strategy: Stalin had advised Mao to cooperate with the Kuomintang, not seek revolution. *The Sino-Soviet Dispute*, Keesing's Research Report #3, p. 1.

127. Ibid., p. 25.

128. See, e.g., Pamela Harriman, "In China, Kremlin Watching," *New York Times*, 8/19/87.

129. Quoted in Philip Taubman, "Gorbachev Offers a Summit Meeting with the Chinese," *New York Times*, 1/11/88. See also V. Arkhipov's favorable article on Chinese free-trade zones, "Kytai: Spetsyalnie Ekonomicheskie Zony," *Azia i Afrika* (2/88), pp. 15–19; Vitaly Gonyushkin et al., "China's Road," *New Times*, nos. 1–4 (January 1989); F. Bozhanov, "Konets Bolshoy Razmolvki," *Azia i Afrika*, 8/89.

130. During his trip, Gorbachev praised the student demonstrators: "These processes are painful, but necessary." Bill Keller, "Gorbachev Praises the Students and Declares Reform Is Necessary," *New York Times*, 5/18/89.

131. Donald Zagoria, "China–Soviet Detente: The Long March," *New York Times*, 5/22/89.

132. The Soviets even offered to sign a treaty promising not to use nuclear weapons against Japan if Japan promised not to develop or deploy such weapons. Susan Lesley Clark, "Soviet Policy Toward Japan," in *Soviet Foreign Policy*, p. 143. Also see pp. 136–39.

133. At one point, Soviet–Japanese economic ties became too close for U.S. preferences. A Japanese company, Toshiba, admitted in 1987 that it had sold computer software to the Soviet government that enabled submarine propellers to operate more smoothly. The Japanese government penalized Toshiba.

134. Legvold et al., *Gorbachev's Foreign Policy*, p. 19.

135. For an analysis of recent Soviet policy toward Japan see, e.g., *SSSR i Yaponia* (Moscow: Nauka, 1987), pp. 392–409.

136. Cyrus Vance, Prologue to *Common Security* (New York: Simon and Schuster, 1982), p. vii.

137. Quoted in Legvold et al., *Gorbachev's Foreign Policy*, p. 14. This sentiment was common, especially following World War I. Compare H. G. Wells' utopian final chapter from *The Outline of History* (Garden City, NY: Garden City Publishing Co., 1949) and his prescription: "There can be no peace now, we realize, but a common peace in the world; no prosperity but a general prosperity."

138. For the Soviet view of common security, see, e.g., V. F. Petrovsky's

rather leaden *Sovetskaya Kontseptsiya Bezapastnosty* (Moscow: Nauka, 1986). The following excerpt from the introduction gives an indication of the tone of the book: "The question above all questions of our time—the removal of the threat of nuclear war—is seen in sharpest focus in the problem of security. . . . The Soviet Union does not separate its security from the security of other states, considering the right to security a universal right. In guaranteeing the peaceful development of states in the nuclear/space age, the U.S.S.R. honors only the paths of political negotiations and reasonable compromises based on the principles of common security."

139. Bill Keller, "Russians Urging U.N. Be Given Greater Powers," *New York Times,* 10/7/87. For indications of this new Soviet view, see, e.g., V. Turadzhev, "Inertsia Proshlovo: Novie Realnosti," *Azia i Afrika,* 2/89.

140. Paul Lewis, "Soviets Urge More Soldiers for U.N.," *New York Times,* 10/3/88.

3: DÉTENTE

1. Richard Stevenson, *The Rise and Fall of Détente* (Chicago: University of Illinois Press, 1985), p. 11.

2. Bill Keller, "New Soviet Ideologist Rejects Idea of World Struggle Against West," *New York Times,* 10/6/88.

3. *Americans Talk Security, A Series of Surveys of American Voters: Attitudes Concerning National Security Issues,* no. 8 (September 1988), pp. 37–38.

4. Don Oberdorfer, "Thatcher Says Cold War Has Come to an End," *Washington Post,* 11/18/88.

5. In particular, see editorials from the *New York Times,* 11/17/17 and 11/27/17.

6. From the sixth point in Wilson's "Fourteen Points" speech of January 1918. Quoted in Donald Treadgold, *Twentieth Century Russia* (Chicago: Rand McNally & Co., 1966), p. 154.

7. Kennan, *Russia and the West,* p. 180. The American Friends Service Committee also provided famine relief during this period.

8. Akron Rubber, DuPont, General Electric, and Sperry Gyroscope all provided technical assistance to the Soviets during the 1920s. Such Western concerns, burdened by World War I–influenced overproduction, eagerly sought Russian markets. Ibid., p. 194.

9. Nor was this simply a governmental alliance. In their mutual opposition toward the Nazis, the U.S. and Soviet peoples grew very close. A Soviet

émigré of that period describes his first trip in the United States at the close of the war: "Everywhere I went in America I received more than my due share of the universal and unbounded admiration for 'our brave Russian allies.' The extravagance of the adulation sometimes made me wince." Victor Kravchenko, *I Chose Freedom* (New York: Charles Scribner's Sons, 1946), p. 466.

10. For a discussion of the contemporary implications of NSC-68, see Gore Vidal, "The National Security State: How to Take Back Our Country," *The Nation,* vol. 246, no. 22 (June 4, 1988).

11. Quoted in Christopher Layne, "Requiem for the Reagan Doctrine," *SAIS Review,* vol. 8, no. 1 (Winter–Spring 1988), p. 5.

12. Richard Stevenson makes this case for four periods of détente in *The Rise and Fall of Détente.* Give or take some subtleties, his analysis fits other histories of the postwar era.

13. I borrow this phrase from Alan Crawford's *Thunder on the Right* (New York: Pantheon, 1980), a description of the growth in influence of conservative forces in the 1970s.

14. See, e.g., Fred Halliday, *The Making of the Second Cold War* (London: Verso, 1983).

15. For instance, the Soviet Union has often suffered attacks of terrorism both within the country (including one in 1973 at Lenin's Tomb) and outside (four Soviet officials were kidnapped in Lebanon in October 1985, with one subsequently killed). No evidence has been found to support the claim that Moscow directs terrorist actions, many of which clearly run counter to Soviet interests. (Directing Iranian terrorists, for instance, would not amuse Soviet allies Syria and Iraq). Similarly, no connections have been made between Soviet intelligence operations and the unsuccessful assassination of the pope (see Edward S. Herman and Frank Brodhead, *The Rise and Fall of the Bulgarian Connection* [New York: Sheridan Square Publications, 1986]). The Soviet Union has since the 1970s provided little support for national liberation struggles seeking to unseat the governments of U.S. allies. Finally, the Warsaw Pact's conventional might has been consistently inflated, as Myth 3 explains.

16. Evidence emerging since 1983 has indicated that the Soviet Union probably did not know that KAL 007 was a civilian jetliner. See, e.g., Seymour Hersh, *The Target Is Destroyed* (New York: Random House, 1986). KAL 007 could also very well have been on a spy mission, since the U.S. military knew of the flight's deviation from course and pointedly did not notify the pilot. See R. W. Johnson, *Shootdown: Flight 007 and the American Connection* (London: Penguin, 1987). The U.S. military's downing of the Iranian civilian plane over the Persian Gulf in June 1988 furthermore showed that the United States was not immune to making equally tragic mistakes.

17. Yet, many high-level policy advisers seem to anticipate a long-term détente. For instance, many security analysts are "retooling," placing their concerns with deterrence and arms control on the back burner and boning up on international economics. See, e.g., James Markham, "Unpredictable Russians Boggle West's Brains," *New York Times*, 12/27/88; and the predominantly economic analyses in John Steinbrunner, ed., *Restructuring American Foreign Policy* (Washington, DC: Brookings Institution, 1989). Some elements of the U.S. military establishment, meanwhile, are advocating a shift away from traditional European concerns and toward diverting military resources to power projection in the Third World. See, e.g., Fred Iklé and Albert Wohlstetter (co-chairs), *Discriminate Deterrence,* Commission on Integrated Long-Term Strategy (Washington, DC: Department of Defense, 1988); Andrew Marshall and Charles Wolf (co-chairs), Future Security Environment Working Group, *Sources of Change in the Future Security Environment,* Commission on Integrated Long-Term Strategy (Washington, DC: Department of Defense, 1988); Paul Gorman (chairman), Regional Conflict Working Group, *Commitment to Freedom,* Commission on Integrated Long-Term Strategy (Washington, DC: Department of Defense, 1988); Paul Gorman (chairman), Regional Conflict Working Group, *Supporting U.S. Strategy for Third World Conflict,* Commission on Integrated Long-Term Strategy (Washington, DC: Department of Defense, 1988).

18. An excellent source of analysis of such distortions in the media (and by extension the political realm) is *Deadline,* a bulletin from the Center for War, Peace, and the News Media at New York University.

19. Alexander Dallin, "A Soviet Master Plan? The Non-Existent 'Grand Design' in World Affairs," in *The Gorbachev Era*, p. 167.

20. Ibid., pp. 174–75.

21. There is, furthermore, no evidence that the Soviet Union urged North Korea to invade South Korea and, in fact, much evidence that the U.S.S.R. did not want its ally to interfere: "Senator Smith reported that he was 'also advised [by intelligence sources] that the Northern Koreans tried to get the Russians to intervene directly in taking over Southern Korea but the Russian reply was that they did not wish to initiate World War III by creating an incident in a minor area like Korea.'" Stone, *The Hidden History of the Korean War,* p. 62.

22. "Soviet Geopolitical Momentum," *Defense Monitor,* p. 3.

23. According to the Center for Defense Information (ibid., p. 3), the eighteen countries are: Poland, Czechoslovakia, Hungary, Rumania, East Germany, Bulgaria, Cambodia, Cuba, Laos, Libya, Vietnam, Angola, Ethiopia, South Yemen, Mongolia, Syria, Mozambique, Afghanistan. Seventeen additional countries are no longer significantly influenced by the U.S.S.R.: Albania, Algeria, Bangladesh, China, Congo, Egypt, Ghana, Guinea, India, Indonesia, Iraq, North Korea, Mali, Somalia, Sudan, North Yemen,

Yugoslavia. These lists can certainly be challenged. Are not Nicaragua and India subject to Soviet influence? Is Libya really so close to the U.S.S.R.? With one or two exceptions, the distinctions are helpful in understanding the decline of Soviet influence worldwide.

24. Robert Pear, "U.S. Weapon Sales to Third World Increase by 66 Percent," *New York Times,* 8/1/89.

25. Paul Kreisberg, "Containment's Last Gasp," *Foreign Policy,* no. 75 (Summer 1989), p. 147.

26. Ibid., p. 148.

27. George Kennan, *Memoirs 1950–1963* (New York: Pantheon, 1972), p. 51.

28. See discussion of Soviet power projection in the Third World in Menon, *Soviet Power in the Third World,* pp. 4–18. A table comparing U.S. and Soviet power projection assets, on p. 104, is especially valuable.

29. Quoted in Michael Gordon, "Soviets Decrease Use of Navy and Curb Overseas Exercises," *New York Times,* 7/17/88.

30. Daniel Ford et al., *Beyond the Freeze* (Boston: Beacon Press, 1982), p. 18.

31. Tom Gervasi, *The Myth of Soviet Military Supremacy* (New York: Harper & Row, 1986), p. 217. The 1960 Democratic candidate for president, John F. Kennedy, successfully used this imagined missile gap to discredit the previous Republican administration and its candidate, Richard Nixon.

32. Ford et al., *Beyond the Freeze,* p. 28.

33. Of 100 top officials in the first term of the Reagan administration, 32 were members of the Committee on the Present Danger, including Secretary of State George Shultz and Paul Nitze himself. Alan Wolfe, *The Rise and Fall of the Soviet Threat: Domestic Sources of the Cold War Consensus* (Boston: South End Press, 1984), p. 2.

34. Ford et al., *Beyond the Freeze,* pp. 34–35.

35. Gervasi, *The Myth of Soviet Military Supremacy,* p. 400.

36. Michael MccGwire, "Why the Soviets Are Serious about Arms Control," in *Soviet Foreign Policy,* p. 82.

37. For the story of the lost opportunity of controlling MIRV, see Seymour Hersh, *The Price of Power* (New York: Summit Books, 1983), pp. 147–56.

38. MccGwire, "Why the Soviets," in *Soviet Foreign Policy,* p. 90. The Soviet Union did not get MIRV operational on an ICBM until 1975; Gervasi, *Myth,* p. 402.

39. Cockburn, *The Threat*, p. 303.

40. Ibid., p. 263.

41. Ibid., pp. 183ff.

42. Ibid., pp. 207, 197.

43. Ibid., pp. 178–79.

44. Carl Levin, "Beyond the Bean Count," Senate Armed Services Sub-committee on Conventional Forces and Alliance Defense (Jan. 20, 1988). Journalist George Perkovich concurs with Levin's analysis, writing at the end of his study of European conventional balance: "NATO can defend against short-warning attack, and long-preparation war is both highly unlikely and risky for Warsaw Pact." George Perkovich, *Defending Europe Without Nuclear Weapons* (Council for a Livable World Education Fund, 1987), p. 21. A long assessment of bean counting also appears in "Policy Focus: The European Conventional Balance," *International Security*, vol. 12, no. 4 (Spring 1988).

45. "A Soviet Attack Seen as Unlikely," *New York Times*, 12/5/88.

46. Historian Isaac Deutscher explains: "While [Berlin] was besieged, the Federal German Republic had come into being and the North Atlantic Alliance had been proclaimed. The blockade had provided grist to all the mills of anti-Russian propaganda; and the American and the British peoples, outraged by Stalin's action, acclaimed their governments for the reversal of alliances, the very idea of which had until quite recently been abhorrent to them." Deutscher, *Stalin*, p. 591.

47. Hough, *The Struggle for the Third World*, p. 198.

48. Between 1973 and 1979, levels of Jewish emigration were: 35,000 (1973), 21,000 (1974), 13,000 (1975), 14,000 (1976), 17,000 (1977), 29,000 (1978), 51,000 (1979). From William Korey, "The Jackson-Vanik Amendment in Perspective," *Soviet Jewish Affairs*, vol. 18, no. 1 (1988), p. 38.

49. Rates of emigration have been: 8,149 (1987); 19,343 (1988); 30–40,000 (expected for 1989). Robert Pear, "Some Jews Favor Easing Soviet Trade Curbs," *New York Times*, 2/4/89.

50. James Chace, *Solvency: The Price of Survival* (New York: Random House, 1981), p. 87.

51. Bruce Jentleson, *Pipeline Politics* (Ithaca: Cornell University Press, 1986), pp. 172–214. Soviet economists have also maintained that trade sanctions connected with the pipeline affair only hurt the United States. Aganbegyan, *The Challenge*, p. 154.

52. An interesting development of this notion comes from E. P.

Thompson in "Questions to Caspar Weinberger," in *The Heavy Dancers*, (New York: Pantheon, 1985), p. 57.

53. William G. Hyland, "East–West Relations," in *Gorbachev's Russia*, p. 449.

54. See, e.g., Matthew Evangelista, "Economic Reform and Military Technology in Soviet Security Policy," *The Harriman Institute Forum*, vol. 2, no. 1 (January 1989).

55. Ed Hewett, "An Idle U.S. Debate About Gorbachev," *New York Times*, 3/30/89. Hewett is joined in this sentiment by the eminent French Sovietologist Michel Tatu in "Bush Is Right About Moscow," *New York Times*, 5/30/89; U.S. Sovietologist Stephen Sestanovitch agrees in "Gorbachev: Beyond Our Help," *New York Times*, 9/20/89. Former U.S. ambassador to the Soviet Union Arthur Hartman concurs: "My simple answer . . . is that the United States has one of the poorest records of figuring out how to help other people. I'm not at all sure we're so knowledgeable about Russia and its hundreds of years of history that we can actually design a program to help Gorbachev. After all, this man doesn't know exactly where he's going, and he's the Soviet leader." Arthur Hartman, "Arms Control and American Interests in an Era of Soviet Change," *Arms Control Today*, vol. 19, no. 5 (June–July 1989), p. 10. Even Andrei Sakharov chimes in: see Craig Whitney, "Sakharov in Britain: Jab at Gorbachev," *New York Times*, 6/24/89.

56. See Michael Gordon, "Bush Urged to Find a Middle Course for Soviet Changes," *New York Times*, 4/9/89; Thomas Friedman, "Bush Policymakers Reach Uneasy Balance on an Approach to the Soviets," *New York Times*, 7/2/89. For support of Bush, see William Hyland, "Bush's Foreign Policy: Pragmatism or Indecision?" *New York Times*, 4/26/89. For critics, see R. W. Apple, Jr., "U.S. Urged to Respond to Soviet Initiatives," *New York Times*, 4/7/89; Theodore Sorensen, "Bush's Timid 100 Days," *New York Times*, 4/27/89.

57. One such classified analysis is mentioned in Gordon, "Bush Urged," *New York Times*, 4/9/89.

58. Bernard Weinraub, "Cheney Remarks on Soviet Future Ruffle the White House Feathers," *New York Times*, 5/2/89.

59. Dimitri Simes, "Even If Gorbachev Fails, Détente Will Last," *New York Times*, 3/20/89.

60. Lester R. Brown, *Building a Sustainable Society* (New York: W. W. Norton and Co., 1981), p. 91.

61. Hersh, *The Price of Power*, p. 263.

62. For any analysis of these factors, see, e.g., Raymond Garthoff, *Détente*

and Confrontation (Washington, DC: Brookings Institution, 1985), pp. 842–48.

63. It should be noted, however, that Third World countries such as Argentina, Brazil, India, Israel, and South Africa are increasingly developing their own arms-exporting industries.

64. William Schneider, " 'Rambo' and Reality: Having It Both Ways," in *Eagle Resurgent?* (Boston: Little, Brown, 1987), p. 45.

65. Gaddis, *Strategies of Containment*, p. 158. A 1954 National Security Council directive spelled out the Eisenhower program: "Propaganda, political action; economic warfare; escape and evasion and evacuation measures; subversion against hostile states or groups including assistance to underground resistance movements, guerillas and refugee liberation groups; support of indigenous and anti-communist elements in threatened countries of the free world; deception plans and operations; and all activities compatible with this directive necessary to accomplish the foregoing." Ibid.

66. From the mid-1960s to the end of the Carter administration, covert-operations personnel dropped from 2,000 to 200. Andrew Wilson, *The Disarmer's Handbook of Military Technology and Organization* (London: Penguin, 1983), p. 155. By 1981, however, the number of covert CIA operatives had tripled, and by 1983 the CIA had received a 25 percent increase in budget. Stephen Goose, "Low-Intensity Warfare: The Warriors and Their Weapons," in *Low Intensity Warfare,* ed. by Michael Klare and Peter Kornbluh (New York: Pantheon, 1988), p. 95. For a discussion of the revival of the CIA under the guidance of William Casey, see Bob Woodward, *Veil: The Secret Wars of the CIA, 1981–1987* (New York: Pocket Books, 1987).

67. *Discriminate Deterrence* does differ in some unusual ways from orthodox Cold War policy. It recognizes, for instance, that bipolarism as a concept has ended and it suggests replacing overseas bases with low-cost satellite surveillance. Fred Iklé and Albert Wohlstetter (co-chairs), *Discriminate Deterrence,* Commission on Integrated Long-Term Strategy (Washington, DC: Department of Defense, 1988).

68. "Excerpts from Papal Encyclical on Social Concerns of the Church," *New York Times,* 2/20/88.

69. Lappé et al., *National Interest,* p. 68.

70. Gwyneth Williams, *Third World Political Organizations* (Atlantic Highlands, NJ: Humanities Press International, 1987), p. 110.

71. Ibid., p. 44.

72. In 1987, the Philippines spent 41 percent of government expenditures on debt services. Nigeria is desperately trying to reschedule its $23 billion debt. Zimbabwe's Minister of Finance estimates that the total debt for Africa

will reach half a trillion dollars by the year 2000. *Debt Crisis Network Newsletter,* vol. 3, no. 2 (May 1988), p. 5.

73. Peter Korner et al., *The IMF and the Debt Crisis* (Atlantic Highlands, NJ: Zed Books, 1986), pp. 138–39.

74. Carol Barton, "Lima North/South NGO Conference on Debt" (3/3/88), reprinted in *Debt Crisis Newsletter* (May 1988).

75. Ivan Head, "South–North Dangers," *Foreign Affairs,* vol. 68, no. 3 (Summer 1989), p. 79.

76. Susan George offers some suggestions on how to stop the economic intervention inherent in the debt crisis. She suggests distributing economic power more favorably from North to South through a process of debt forgiveness, gradual debt repayment, and debt swaps for environmental protection, agricultural development, literacy campaigns, and so on. This process would be overseen by new Third World institutions heavily represented by rural peoples. Susan George, *A Fate Worse Than Debt* (New York: Grove Press, 1988), pp. 229–54. For more detail on debt-environment connections, see John Cartwright, "Conserving Nature, Decreasing Debt," *Third World Quarterly,* vol. 11, no. 2 (April 1989); Oscar Arias Sanchez, "For the Globe's Sake, Debt Relief," *New York Times,* 7/14/89.

77. The authors of *Betraying the National Interest* advance the following arguments concerning economic manipulation via food aid: nonmilitary aid often becomes money for guns through elaborate procedures; the choice of which countries the United States supports with such aid is politically motivated. El Salvador receives four times more food per capita than drought-stricken Africa; 90 percent of food aid is sold by Third World governments to those who can afford it rather than being used for famine relief.

78. Quoted in *Reshaping the International Order: RIO, A Report to the Club of Rome,* Jan Tinbergen, coordinator (London: Hutchinson, 1977), p. 11.

79. Quoted in Ford et al., *Beyond the Freeze,* p. 32.

80. George Kennan has observed, "If there is any one lesson to be plainly derived from the experiences we have had with disarmament in the past half-century, it is that armaments are a function and not a cause of political tensions and that no limitation of armaments on a multilateral scale can be effected as long as the political problems are not tackled and regulated in some realistic way." Kennan, *Memoirs 1950–63,* p. 109.

81. Moreover a provision allows for signatories to withdraw with only three months' notice.

82. In addition, the United States stores nuclear weapons in Puerto Rico. See Judith Berkan et al., "Violating the Treaty of Tlatelolco," *Arms Control Today,* vol. 15, no. 1 (January 1985), pp. 4–5.

83. Johan Galtung, *There Are Alternatives!* (Nottingham, 1984), pp. 137–38.

84. Complete disarmament may not, in the end, result from deliberate policies. Richard Barnet writes: "The last nuclear weapon will disappear, if it ever does, long after it has come to be seen as useless for any purpose whatever, probably long after its very existence has been forgotten." Richard Barnet, "The Four Pillars," *The New Yorker* (Mar. 9, 1987), p. 4. On the relevance of minimum deterrence, see also Jane Sharp, "Arms Control: Alliance Cohesion and Extended Deterrence," *Prospects for Peace Making* (Boston: MIT Press, 1987), pp. 96–97.

85. Article 1, "Treaty Between the United States of America and the Union of Soviet Socialist Republics on the Limitation of Underground Nuclear Weapons Tests," *Arms Control and Disarmament Agreements* (Washington, DC: Arms Control and Disarmament Agency, 1980), p. 167.

86. The operative word here is "might." A test ban conference to be convened in 1990 not only may not yield such a treaty but, according to some, might jeopardize other accords. See Kevin Clements, "Will Test Ban Conference Self-Destruct?" *Bulletin of Atomic Scientists*, vol. 45, no. 6 (July–August 1989).

87. Paul Montgomery, "NATO Is Studying an Airborne Force," *New York Times*, 12/2/88.

88. Weapon-specific campaigns have had only temporary effect in the face of the continuing appeal of modernization. The anti-MX campaign, waged from 1979 until 1982, succeeded only in temporarily defeating particular basing modes. And by 1987, Defense Secretary Carlucci was again talking about the most expensive and destabilizing mode, rail-basing. The B-1 bomber, shelved by Carter in 1977, rebounded in 1982 and remains popular in the Pentagon despite exposés of enormous cost overruns and repeated crashes in test flights.

89. Barry Blechman, "Cost Reduction Dubious," *Bulletin of Atomic Scientists*, vol. 45, no. 6 (July–August 1989).

90. Stephen Alexis Cain, "One More for the Gipper," *Bulletin of Atomic Scientists*, vol. 45, no. 6 (July–August 1989).

91. Martin Olav Sabo, "The Accountant's Budget: Bush and Cheney Fail to Respond to a Changing Era," *Arms Control Today*, vol. 19, no. 5 (June–July 1989), p. 11. Sabo goes on to say: "The Bush administration and the Cheney Pentagon have done a good job of 'trimming around the edges,' but their budget fails to take even minimal notice of the far-reaching events under way in the Soviet Union and Eastern and Western Europe. We can only hope that future defense budgets will acknowledge the changed international situation facing the United States. Our national security policy needs to change as well."

92. The arms control community is not, of course, unaware of the limitations of the technique. See, e.g., Kosta Tsipis, "New Tasks for Arms Controllers," *Bulletin of Atomic Scientists*, vol. 45, no. 4 (May 1989).

4 : BEYOND DÉTENTE

1. See Paul Kennedy, *The Rise and Fall of the Great Powers: Economic Change and Military Conflict From 1500 to 2000* (New York: Random House, 1987). For a more elaborate description of U.S. global decline, see Walter Russell Mead, *Mortal Splendor: The American Empire in Transition* (Boston: Houghton Mifflin, 1987).

2. Quoted in Leon Wofsy, "Gorbachev's New Thinking and World Politics," *Monthly Review*, vol. 40, no. 5 (October 1988), p. 20.

3. For examples of this new "consensus-building," see Cyrus Vance and Henry Kissinger, "Bipartisan Objectives for Foreign Policy," *Foreign Affairs* (Summer 1988); James Chace, "A New Grand Strategy," *Foreign Policy* (Spring 1988); Richard Lugar, "A Republican Looks at Foreign Policy," *Foreign Affairs* (Winter 1987–88); Richard Burt, "U.S. Security in the 1990s," *Washington Quarterly* (Spring 1988); David Abshire, *Preventing World War III: A Realistic Grand Strategy* (New York: Harper & Row, 1988).

4. *Americans Talk Security, A Series of Surveys of American Voters: Attitudes Concerning National Security Issues*, Nos. 3, 6 (March and June, 1988).

5. According to the Defense Budget Project in Washington, DC, the military budget increased 55 percent (adjusted for inflation) between FY80 (Fiscal Year 1980) and FY85. The budget decreased 10 percent (adjusted for inflation) between FY85 and FY89. These figures refer to *appropriations*. Figures for military *spending* differ, but FY88 is the first year that military spending declined. As William Hyland points out: "It is probable that the decade from 1985 to 1995 will mark an end to the cycle of strategic armaments that began after the Second World War and has continued unabated for more than 40 years. The domestic and international pressures on both superpowers are likely to be strong enough to lead them in this direction. It may well be that, at long last, Soviet and American approaches to strategic weapons and national security are converging." Hyland, "East–West Relations," in *Gorbachev's Russia*, p. 459.

6. "The Global Vision Thing," *The New Republic*, vol. 199, no. 22 (Nov. 28, 1988).

7. Seymour Melman, "Conversion from Military to Civilian Economy" (Washington, DC: SANE/FREEZE, 1987), p. 1.

8. The Chinese government has already looked to economic conversion to solve some of its economic problems. In 1985, it demobilized 20 percent of its troops and dramatically increased the number of military industries switching over to civilian use. Goldman, *Gorbachev's Economic Challenge,* p. 194. At the same time, China has become one of the premier arms sellers in the world.

9. See, e.g., Melman, *The Permanent War Economy,* and Connell, *The New Maginot Line.*

10. See, e.g., Michael Dee Oden, *A Military Dollar Really Is Different* (Lansing: Employment Research Associates, 1988). Also "The Economic Burden of the Arms Race: An Interview with Michael Oden," *Bulletin of Municipal Foreign Policy,* vol. 2, no. 4 (Autumn 1988), pp. 10–16. On the effects of the Reagan administration's $2.13 trillion spending spree in particular, see Ann Markusen, "Cold War Economics," *Bulletin of Atomic Scientists,* vol. 45, no. 1 (January–February 1989), pp. 41–46. Other economists, however, have argued that the true effects of military spending are unclear. See, e.g., Gordon Adams and David Gold, *Defense Spending and the Economy: Does the Defense Dollar Make a Difference?* (Washington DC: Defense Budget Project, 1987).

11. The three Congressional bills are: Defense Economic Adjustment Act, HR10 (Weiss bill), the Defense Production Act, HR486 (Oakar bill), and the Draft Economic Diversification Act, HR2252 (Gejdenson bill). Some examples of municipal activism around conversion include: Baltimore (city charter change), Chicago (conversion commission), Philadelphia (Navy shipyard), San Jose (conversion ordinance), and Pittsfield (business incubator).

12. Melissa Healy, "Base-Closing List Due Out This Week," *Philadelphia Inquirer,* 12/26/88.

13. For Soviet perspectives on conversion, see, e.g., Alexei Kireyev, "Cost Accounting for Disarmament Economics," *New Times,* no. 4 (January 1989); Kirill Samsonov, "Beating Missiles into Prams," *New Times,* no. 11 (March 1989).

14. The 1928 Kellogg-Briand treaty outlawing war is an excellent example of good intentions and poor strategy. Sixty-four countries eventually signed this treaty, which, among other shortcomings, failed to prevent the outbreak of World War II.

15. Les Aspin, "The World After the INF" (transcript of a September 29, 1987, speech), p. 9.

16. The perversely titled "forward-based defense" is present NATO doctrine requiring air strikes deep into Warsaw Pact territory in the event of a Warsaw Pact attack. Such attacks involve follow-on-forces attacks (FOFAs), which target the second wave of Warsaw Pact forces that follow an initial Warsaw Pact attack.

17. An indispensable guide to alternative defense is the September 1988 issue of the *Bulletin of Atomic Scientists* (vol. 44, no. 7), which features articles by Anders Boserup, Horst Afheldt, Randall Forsberg, Stephen Flanagan, and others. In addition to these articles, the following articles have been consulted: Jonathan Dean, "Alternative Defense: Answer to NATO's Central Front Problems?" *International Affairs*, Winter 1987–88, pp. 61–82; Jonathan Dean, "Will Negotiated Force Reductions Build Down the NATO–Warsaw Pact Confrontation?" *Washington Quarterly*, vol. 11, no. 2 (Spring 1988), pp. 69–89; Albrecht von Muller, "Conventional Stability in Europe: Outlines of the Military Hardware for a Second Détente" (Starnberg: Max Planck Society, 1987); Gwyn Prins, " 'Non-Offensive Defence' and the Challenge of Europe," from the UNA-USA/UNIDIR symposium, Sept. 6–8, 1989.

18. Lutz Unterseher, "Defending Europe: Toward a Stable Conventional Deterrent" (University of Maryland: Center for Philosophy and Public Policy, 1987), p. 13.

19. Tatchell, *Democratic Defense*, p. 108.

20. The leading U.S. proponent of CBD is Gene Sharp and his Program on Nonviolent Sanctions in Conflict and Defense at Harvard University. Many international conflicts are being studied at the program, including the Palestinian uprising, the South African struggle against apartheid, and Solidarity in Poland. Sharp's most comprehensive work on Europe is his book *Making Europe Unconquerable: The Potential of Civilian-Based Deterrence and Defence* (London: Taylor and Francis, 1985).

21. Two well-established peace groups exploring the subject of alternative defense in depth are the Institute for Defense and Disarmament Studies and the Institute for Peace and International Security, both in the Boston area.

22. As Anders Boserup points out, alternative defense did not really gain any currency in the West until the Warsaw Pact began championing the issue: "Attractive as the concept of nonoffensive defense was in principle, it had a hard case to make when presented from [a] unilateralist perspective. There was no way to prove that more defensive postures in the West would ever be copied in the East. Many therefore saw it as an unsound gamble, with real military risks and only hypothetical political benefits." Anders Boserup, "A Way to Undermine Hostility," *Bulletin of Atomic Scientists*, vol. 44, no. 7 (September 1988), pp. 18–19.

23. Military analyst John Lough makes this point in "Structural Changes in the Soviet Army," *Soviet Analyst*, vol. 18, no. 9 (May 3, 1989). "Future stability," he writes, "may require NATO to grasp the nettle, and move towards the adoption of a new defensive posture *à la russe*" (p. 7).

24. Three such organizations are the American Friends Service Commit-

tee, the British-American Security Information Council, and the Institute for Defense and Disarmament Studies.

25. Dietrich Fischer, "Protective Defense," *Nuclear Times*, vol. 6, no. 3 (January–February 1988), p. 32.

26. In recent years, cultural exchanges between the two countries have blossomed, representing an extraordinary upsurge in citizen diplomacy. Scientists, artists, veterans, business people, and students have all exchanged visits. To the degree that such informal exchanges begin to develop beyond a U.S.–Soviet focus to include other countries and peoples of the world, citizen diplomacy becomes an ever more powerful force for change. *U.S.–Soviet Cooperation: A New Future*, ed. by Nish Jamgotch, Jr. (New York: Praeger, 1989), discusses at length some of the critical aspects of cooperation not touched upon in this chapter, for instance, academic and cultural exchanges, trade, environmental protection, joint space ventures, and health.

27. Lamperti, *What Are We Afraid Of?*, p. 51.

28. For a detailed analysis of U.S. manipulation of the human rights issue for political purposes, see Noam Chomsky and Edward Herman, *The Washington Connection and Third World Fascism* (Boston: South End Press, 1979).

29. See Edward Herman and Noam Chomsky, *Manufacturing Consent* (New York: Pantheon, 1988), pp. 37–86.

30. From "Giving Real Life to the Helsinki Accords," European Network for East–West Dialogue, April 1987, p. 4.

31. Stone, *The Hidden History*, pp. 12, 20. In both cases, the U.S. government undertook contrary policies, defending the Nationalist government in Taiwan and committing forces in the Korean War.

32. Gaddis, *Strategies of Containment*, p. 31.

33. Ibid., p. 132.

34. Donna Eberwine, "To End the Cold War," *Nuclear Times*, vol. 6, no. 6 (July–August 1988), pp. 29–30.

35. Randall Forsberg, "The Case for a Nonintervention Regime," *Defense and Disarmament News*, vol. 3, no. 1 (August–September 1987), p. 4.

36. Jane Perlez, "Ethiopia's President Looks Toward Better U.S. Relations," *New York Times*, 11/28/88.

37. See, e.g., "Learning to Deal With Cuba," *The Nation*, vol. 247, no. 11 (Oct. 24, 1988).

38. Williams, *Third World Political Organizations*, p. 61.

39. Mead, *Mortal Splendor*, pp. 311–17.

40. Korner et al., *The IMF and the Debt Crisis*, pp. 165–69.

41. For an interesting account of how international agreements can restrict military abuses, see Françoise Hampson, "Winning by the Rules: Law and Warfare in the 1990s," *Third World Quarterly*, vol. 11, no. 2 (April 1989).

42. Tom Farer, "International Law: The Critics Are Wrong," *Foreign Policy*, no. 71 (Summer 1988), pp. 22–45; Farer refers in his article to Thomas Hughes, "The Twilight of Internationalism," *Foreign Policy*, no. 61 (Winter 1985–86), pp. 25–48.

43. Paul Lewis, "U.S. Proposes that Soviet Let World Court Settle Disputes," *New York Times*, 10/6/88.

44. Michael Gordon, "Paris Conference Condemns the Use of Chemical Arms," *New York Times*, 1/12/89. The Soviet Union meanwhile announced several days previous that it was unilaterally cutting its chemical weapons arsenals. Michael Gordon, "Soviets to Start Trimming Arsenal of Chemical Weapons," *New York Times*, 1/9/89.

45. The Soviet Union is a newcomer to environmental questions, having built its industrial strength with little regard for ecology. But in the post-Chernobyl era, Soviet activists have succeeded in making the government more conscious of resource depletion and environmentally unsound projects. The move away from a policy of exporting only raw materials, the canceling of a plan to divert Siberian waters to Central Asia, concern over water pollution in Lake Baikal—these are positive signs. One wing of the Soviet ecology movement looks to the West German "Green" movement for inspiration; the other wing is more nationalist, allied with conservative political tendencies. Despite this division, the heightened attention given to the environment in the Soviet Union offers another point of possible cooperation. For more information on this topic, see the extremely useful *From Below: Independent Peace and Environmental Movements in Eastern Europe and the U.S.S.R.*, Helsinki Watch, 1987.

46. For a brief rundown of these problems, see Lester Brown and Edward Wolf, "A Sustainable Society," *Breakthrough*, vol. 9, no. 1–3 (Fall 1987–Spring 1988), pp. 4–9. For a more extensive treatment, see Lester Brown, *Building a Sustainable Society*.

47. See, e.g., Jonathan Schell, *Fate of the Earth* (New York: Knopf, 1982); Hal Harvey, "Natural Security," *Nuclear Times*, vol. 6, no. 4 (March–April, 1988), pp. 24–26; "Platform for Peace and Common Security and for a Healthy, Just and Sustainable Environment," Peace and Environment Project, May 1988; Jessica Tuchman, "Redefining Security," *Foreign Affairs*, vol. 68, no. 2 (Spring 1989); Norman Myers, "Environment and Security," *Foreign Affairs*, vol. 68, no. 3 (Summer 1989).

48. Rajiv Gandhi, "Action Plan for Ushering in a Nuclear Weapon-Free and Non-violent World Order," submitted to the 3rd United Nations Special Session on Disarmament, June 1988.

49. Mead, *Mortal Splendor,* pp. 87–100.

50. The Panshilah are: mutual respect for each other's territory; noninterference in other countries' internal affairs; equality and mutual benefit; peaceful coexistence; and nonaggression; Williams, *Third World Political Organizations,* p. 52.

51. Among the demands in the program are an end to colonialism, respect for self-determination, an end to apartheid, general and complete disarmament, removal of foreign bases, strengthening of the United Nations, and economic development; ibid., pp. 58–59.

52. See Alan Durning, "Mobilizing at the Grassroots," *State of the World 1989,* ed. by Linda Stark (New York: W. W. Norton & Co., 1989), pp. 154–73.

Appendix 1
Glossary

ABM treaty: Anti-Ballistic Missile treaty. U.S.–Soviet arms control measure signed in 1972 as part of the first Strategic Arms Limitation Treaty. The ABM treaty limits the number of antiballistic missile systems to one per side and specifies how such defensive systems should be built.

alternative defense: The structuring of a nation's defense to be primarily *defensive* rather than *offensive*. For instance, a shift from tanks and aircrafts to anti-aircraft, antitank weapons, and static defenses such as mines and sensors. Also "nonoffensive defense" and "nonprovocative defense."

arc of crisis: A term coined by President Carter's National Security Adviser Zbigniew Brzezinski in the late 1970s to refer to an area spanning Asia and Africa, bounded by Afghanistan in the northeast and Somalia in the southwest and with the Middle East falling roughly in the center. At the time the U.S. government considered this a region of Soviet military destabilization.

Baltic republics: The Soviet republics of Estonia, Latvia, and Lithuania. Incorporated into the U.S.S.R. in 1940 as part of the 1939 Soviet–German Non-Aggression Pact.

bean count: A purely quantitative measure of troops and military equipment. Used especially in comparing NATO and Warsaw Pact military forces in Europe.

Glossary

bipolarism: A belief that international relations rest essentially upon the confrontation between two irreconcilable blocs of power, for example Communism and capitalism. Contrast to *multilateralism.*

Bolshevik party: From *bolshinstvo,* or "majority." Grew out of the Russian Social Democratic Labor Party and, from 1903, was at the forefront of revolution in Russia. Seized power in October 1917. Later the Communist party.

Brest-Litovsk treaty: Agreement signed between U.S.S.R. and Germany in March 1918 that allowed the U.S.S.R. to withdraw from World War I in exchange for significant concessions.

Brezhnev doctrine: A government policy articulated by General Secretary Leonid Brezhnev in the 1960s pledging that the U.S.S.R. would interfere if necessary in the affairs of its bordering allies in order to prevent any retreat from socialism. Employed most visibly in Czechoslovakia (1968) and Afghanistan (1979).

burden sharing: A U.S. policy proposal that U.S. allies such as West Germany and Japan take on a greater share of their alliance commitment, primarily in the form of increased military outlays.

Carter doctrine: A government policy introduced by President Jimmy Carter in 1980 declaring the Persian Gulf to be within the scope of vital U.S. national security interests.

CDE: Conference on Confidence- and Security-Building Measures and Disarmament in Europe. Begun in 1984 and involving thirty-five nations, this set of negotiations took place within the framework of CSCE and addressed conventional forces in Europe. Yielded several important agreements on the notification and monitoring of military exercises.

CFE: Conventional Forces in Europe. Begun in 1989 to take over from CDE, these negotiations will address conventional weapons reductions in the region stretching from the Atlantic Ocean to the Ural Mountains.

Cold War: A war that does not involve a direct military confrontation. A conflict that features deflected hostilities, whether in the form of economic, political, social, or even oblique military campaigns. Characterizes the relationship between the United States and the Soviet Union in one form or another since 1917, but particularly since 1945.

collectivization: The consolidating of small peasant holdings into larger state or collectively held farms. In the early 1930s within the U.S.S.R., this involved the elimination of the *kulak,* or large landowner, class.

COMECON: Council for Mutual Economic Assistance. Founded in 1949 to ensure economic cooperation between socialist countries. Members are Bulgaria, Cuba, Czechoslovakia, the German Democratic Republic, Hungary, Mongolia, Poland, Rumania, U.S.S.R., Vietnam. Observers are Afghanistan, Angola, Ethiopia, Laos, Mexico, Nicaragua, the People's Democratic Republic of Yemen. Also CMEA or CEMA.

common security: National security based on international safeguards and economic and political interdependence with the ultimate goal of preventing war. A concept popularized by the 1982 United Nations commission headed by Sweden's former Prime Minister Olof Palme.

containment: A U.S. policy developed shortly after World War II of military and economic pressures designed to prevent a perceived expansion of Soviet interests in Europe and Asia. According to the original conception, the United States should prevent the U.S.S.R. from acquiring power in primarily four areas: the United States, Great Britain, Germany and Central Europe, and Japan. Under the Truman administration, however, the United States expanded the definition to prevent Soviet expansion into *any* area of the world.

CSCE: Conference on Security and Cooperation in Europe. Begun among thirty-five nations in 1973 to discuss military security, trade, and governing principles. Achieved in 1975 the ten principles known as the Helsinki Accords, which officially recognized European borders and produced several measures on human rights. In 1989, the CSCE produced another agreement following up on these principles.

CTBT: Comprehensive Test Ban Treaty. The expected successor to the Threshold Test Ban Treaty (yet to be ratified by Congress), which limits nuclear tests to a 150-kiloton limit. The CTBT would outlaw all nuclear tests. This arms control measure is designed to slow the development of new destabilizing nuclear weapons technology.

cult of personality: The mystique of infallibility and omnipotence that political leaders create around their own images. In the Soviet Union, Stalin, Khrushchev, and Brezhnev all have been accused by their political successors of having encouraged such beliefs among their subordinates and within the public. Leaders of other countries—Castro in Cuba, Mao in China, Chiang Kai-shek in Taiwan—have also developed this image.

debt crisis: An international situation of economic instability caused by the insolvency of many nations. Also the domestic instability caused by debt escalation: the securing of loans to pay the interest on previous loans. While many developing countries of the Third World are currently struggling with debts incurred from the costs of industrialization and rising oil prices, so-called developed countries are not immune. Eastern Europe, for instance, has a staggering debt problem.

demokratizatsia: A component of Gorbachev's political program that involves the greater decentralization of political and economic authority and the growing acceptance of pluralistic mechanisms.

détente: A lessening of tensions between two or more adversarial nations.

From a French verb meaning to slacken the string of a crossbow. The Russian term *razriadka* derives from a similar image: the removal of ammunition from a gun.

domino theory: A theory that Communism spreads from one country to another as revolution topples governments in succession (as one falling domino sets off an entire chain of falling dominos). Applied during the 1950s and 1960s to Southeast Asia, where the defense of South Vietnam from Communist North Vietnam was intended to prevent the spread of revolution throughout the area. In the 1980s, the Pentagon has applied the theory to Central America, arguing that Communism must be stopped in Nicaragua and El Salvador to prevent the rest of the region from turning toward the U.S.S.R.

Euromissiles: Intermediate-range Pershing II and Cruise missiles slotted for deployment in Europe in 1979 to counterbalance Soviet SS-20 missiles. U.S. deployment plans led to massive demonstrations throughout Europe, but deployments nevertheless began in late 1983. Dismantled as part of the INF treaty in 1988.

Five-Year Plan: A feature of the Soviet planned economy established in 1929. Entails the detailed projection of production quotas and the setting of prices for all Soviet goods and services across a five-year span of time.

GATT: General Agreement on Tariffs and Trade. Concluded by twenty-three nations in 1947 initially to regulate trade among industrialized countries. Later, GATT began administering to trade between developed and developing countries as well.

glasnost: Derived from the Russian word for "voice." Has been used in the U.S.S.R. to signify "openness," although it also carries a connotation of "publicity." The term first came into political usage in connection with Tsar Alexander II's emancipation of the serfs in 1861. Later, Lenin used *glasnost* to refer to political freedoms guaranteed under Communism.

gulag: Russian acronym for the system of corrective labor camps.

hammer and sickle: A symbol of the U.S.S.R. The hammer represents the worker, the sickle represents the peasant, and their superimposition represents worker-peasant unity.

hard currency: A currency that can be exchanged across national borders, such as the dollar, mark, or yen.

Helsinki Accords: See *CSCE.*

ICBM: Intercontinental ballistic missile. The first long-range device capable of delivering a nuclear warhead without human guidance.

IMF: International Monetary Fund. Established at the Bretton Woods Conference in 1944 to regulate currency exchange and international financial matters. By the 1950s, the IMF began to provide monetary assistance to countries with balance-of-payments problems (i.e., whose imports exceed their exports).

industrial democracy: The apportioning of greater responsibility for production decisions to the workers in factories.

INF treaty: The Intermediate Nuclear Force treaty. Concluded in 1987 and approved by Congress in 1988. Provides for the elimination of all intermediate-range nuclear missiles from Europe as well as 100 such missiles from Soviet Asia.

Jackson-Vanik amendment: Congressional legislation passed in 1974 linking trade benefits for the U.S.S.R. with improved human rights conditions within the U.S.S.R. Its principal sponsors were Henry "Scoop" Jackson (D-Wash.) and Charles Vanik (D-Ohio).

joint venture: A partnership of external capital and internal resources to establish an industrial concern. Profits are divided between the nations involved according to a pre-established agreement.

kombinat: An East German governmental organization that oversees industrial production.

Kremlinology: The study of the habits and behavior of Soviet leaders, and the rituals that determine hierarchy in the Soviet political system (e.g., the position of officials in relation to the general secretary at public functions).

LDC: Less-developed country. A designation that applies, according to the World Bank, to 94 out of the world's largest 126 countries.

LIC: Low-intensity conflict. War conducted in ways that fall beneath the threshold of conventional war: through proxies, espionage, economic manipulation, propaganda, and similar activities.

linkage: The linking of an international agreement such as an arms control measure with a domestic question such as treatment of human rights. More generally, the linking of two issues such that successful resolution of one is dependent upon the successful resolution of the other.

MBFR: Mutual and Balanced Force Reduction talks. Talks between NATO and the Warsaw Pact begun in 1973 to address conventional arms buildup in Europe. Disbanded in 1987 after achieving few tangible results. Superseded by the CDE and then CFE negotiations.

military-industrial complex: A web of relationships between government military organizations such as the Pentagon and the civilian weapons-producing industry. Coined by President Eisenhower.

minimum deterrence: The reliance on the threat of pre-emptive (first) strike provided by a small number of invulnerable nuclear weapons.

Glossary

MIRV: Multiple independently-targeted re-entry vehicles. A technological innovation of the late 1960s that enables a single missile to contain multiple warheads that, in the atmosphere, separate from the parent missile and strike separate targets.

Monroe doctrine: A government policy developed by President James Monroe in 1823 and expanded by President Theodore Roosevelt. Maintains that the United States reserves the right to protect its interests in its own backyard (Latin America), using force if necessary.

MPLA: Popular Movement for the Liberation of Angola. Guerrilla movement in Angola that participated in overthrowing Portuguese colonial rule in 1974 and established a nominally Marxist government in 1975.

multilateralism: A doctrine that encourages the dispersion of global political and economic power and looks to pluralistic international organizations such as the United Nations and the World Court to resolve regional and global conflicts. Contrast to *bipolarism.*

NATO: North Atlantic Treaty Organization. Established in 1947 to bind World War II allies in order to prevent Soviet expansion into Europe. Present members are Belgium, Canada, Denmark, Federal Republic of Germany, Greece, Iceland, Italy, Luxembourg, Netherlands, Norway, Portugal, Spain, Turkey, United Kingdom, United States.

NEM: New Economic Mechanism. Established by Hungarian party leader Janos Kadar in 1968 to align the Hungarian economy with Western capitalist models.

NEP: New Economic Policy. Adopted by Lenin in 1921 to liberalize the Soviet economy. Permitted free enterprise and private farming in association with cooperative and some state-managed ventures. Replaced by Stalin with collectivization and heavy industrialization.

new thinking: The new Soviet policy approach under the Gorbachev administration, especially on matters of foreign policy.

NIEO: The New International Economic Order. A document produced at the Nonaligned Movement's 1973 summit in Algiers calling for more favorable trade agreements between North and South and increased economic self-reliance among Third World countries.

nomenklatura: A powerful group of officials who have access to privileges (housing, food, travel) not available to the general public. The term is most frequently applied to privileged officials and managers in the Soviet Union and Eastern Europe.

Nonaligned Movement: An organization of over 100 nations formed in 1955 at the Bandung Conference in Indonesia to discuss economic and political issues affecting the Third World. Conducts summits every three years.

Glossary

OECD: Organization of Economic Cooperation and Development—twenty-two of the richest Western industrialized countries, as well as Japan, Greece, and Turkey.

OPEC: Organization of Oil Exporting Countries. A consortium established in 1960 to regulate oil production and pricing. In a display of unusual unity in 1973, OPEC scaled back on production and drove oil prices increasingly higher. In the early 1980s, dissension among members (particularly warring Iran and Iraq) greatly decreased the cartel's international power. The members are Algeria, Iraq, Kuwait, Libya, Qatar, Saudi Arabia, United Arab Emirates, Gabon, Nigeria, Indonesia, Iran, Ecuador, Venezuela.

Ostpolitik: German term for "Eastern Policy." A policy first proposed in West Germany in 1966 and given wider expression by West German Chancellor Willy Brandt in the 1970s. Promotes increased economic and political ties between West Germany and Eastern Europe, especially East Germany. Produced an agreement on reciprocal East and West German recognition in 1972.

Pamyat: From the Russian term for "memory." An organization of Russian chauvinists originally formed to preserve Russian historical memorials but which, under *glasnost,* has increasingly developed a political voice and a political program. The most conservative political group of any consequence now operating in the U.S.S.R.

PDPA: People's Democratic Party of Afghanistan. The Afghan Communist party that seized power in 1978.

peaceful coexistence: Doctrine of accommodation between the U.S.S.R. and the United States, first proposed by Lenin after the 1917 revolution and revived by Khrushchev in the 1950s. As used by Soviet politicians, the concept can mean anything from temporary reconciliation within a long-term struggle to permanent rapprochement.

perestroika: Russian term for "restructuring." The Gorbachev plan for remodeling the Soviet political and economic system. The program calls for varying degrees of political democratization, economic decentralization, and social liberalism.

permanent revolution: Policy, favored by Trotsky in the 1920s, of directing the Soviet government's efforts toward inspiring and funding Communist revolution worldwide. Contrasted to *socialism in one country.*

PLO: Palestine Liberation Organization. An organization of Palestinian peoples established in 1963 at the Arab Summit Conference.

Potsdam Conference: Allied conference held July 17–August 2, 1945, to determine the postwar future of Germany.

Realpolitik: German term for "realistic policy." A political ideology based on strategic rather than ethical considerations. Often associated with expansionist policies that advance national interest.

reasonable sufficiency: A Gorbachev military doctrine that emphasizes cost-effective military management and the desirability of decreased military size and power.

SALT I and SALT II: Strategic Arms Limitation Talks. Designed to set ceilings on the growth of strategic nuclear weapons. SALT I was ratified in 1972 and included the ABM treaty. SALT II did not pass Congress in 1979.

samizdat: Russian term for "self-published." Documents produced unofficially in the Soviet Union, often made on homemade presses and distributed by hand.

SDI: Strategic Defense Initiative. Introduced by Reagan in 1983. Conceived as a space shield of lasers and projectiles that intercept and destroy incoming nuclear missiles. Also known as "Star Wars."

self-financing: A form of industrial management under a system of central planning that allows a plant to retain a certain portion of its profits for worker bonuses and machine retooling.

self-management: A system that assigns more authority to workers' councils or to elected managers to determine prices, establish contracts, and generally control inputs and outputs.

Slavophiles: Those who follow the tradition of Russian chauvinism. Inherently conservative and suspicious of outside influences. Contrast to *Westernizers.*

socialism in one country: A policy favored by Stalin and others in the 1920s of concentrating the Soviet government's energies in building a socialist society within the Soviet Union. Contrasted with *permanent revolution.*

socialist orientation: A Soviet foreign policy term referring to those countries that the U.S.S.R. considers members of the socialist world. In Russian, often *sotsorientatsia.*

Southwest Asia: A geographic area roughly equivalent to the arc of crisis. A locus of increased U.S. military activity in the 1980s.

soviet: Russian term for "council." A local body of state government elected by popular vote.

Sovietology: The study of the Soviet Union. Can also include the study of pre-Revolutionary Russia.

Stalinism: Characteristic of the period of political authoritarianism under Stalin, 1929–1953, a time of political purges, economic centralization, and cultural censorship.

Glossary

START: Strategic Arms Reduction Talks. Begun in 1982 to follow up on SALT I and II. Latest proposal on the table would reduce long-range nuclear weapons in U.S. and Soviet arsenals by 50 percent.

strategic weapons: Weapons capable of directly striking an adversary's territory.

thaw: A détente or lessening of tension within the cycles of the Cold War. Also, the *Thaw*, a period of relaxed state controls on political dissent and artistic freedom following Stalin's death in 1953 and lasting until the mid-1960s.

theater weapons: Weapons of limited range designed to strike within a given area or "theater" of battle.

Third World: Originally a political idea from the late 1940s promoting an alternative to capitalism and Communism. Later, a group of countries, primarily developing nations of Asia, Africa, and Latin America. The First World is the capitalist industrialized countries; the Second World is the Communist industrialized countries.

Trilateral Commission: A commission formed in 1973 and composed of policy makers and experts from the United States, Western Europe, and Japan. Developed policies designed to link the three regions in taking advantage of a newly interdependent political and economic world.

Warsaw Pact: A military alliance formed in 1955 and today composed of Albania, Bulgaria, Czechoslovakia, German Democratic Republic, Hungary, Poland, Rumania, the U.S.S.R. Albania is no longer invited to meetings though formally is still a pact member. Also known as the Warsaw Treaty Organization (WTO).

Westernizers: Those who follow a Russian tradition of looking to the West for political, economic, or social inspiration. Contrast to *Slavophiles*.

White Army: The politically diverse and often uneasy alliance of forces fighting the Bolshevik Red Army during the Civil War period, 1918–1921.

Yalta Conference: Allied conference held February 1945 to discuss postwar status of Eastern Europe and the Far East.

zero option: A 1981 U.S. offer to forgo Euromissile deployment in exchange for the Soviet dismantling of SS-20, SS-4, and SS-5 missiles, leaving the European theater with "zero" INF weapons. When the U.S.S.R. offered to eliminate all short- as well as medium-range INF missiles, the standing proposal became a "double zero option." When the U.S.S.R. agreed to include its Asian INF missiles, the final proposal became a "global double zero option," a formulation which later served as the basis for the INF treaty. A third zero option—eliminating short-range or battlefield nuclear weapons—is a possible future arms control treaty.

Appendix 2
Chronology to 1985

9th c.	Formation of early Russian state
988–89	Adoption of Christianity
1219–21	Conquest of Central Asia by Mongol-Tartars
1325–40	Reign of Ivan Kalita and the rise of the Muscovy Province
1395	Defeat of the Mongol-Tartars
1533–84	Reign of Ivan the Terrible; expansion of Moscow's sovereignty
1682–1725	Reign of Peter the Great; opening of Russia to Western influences
1762–96	Reign of Catherine the Great
1812	Napoleonic invasion of Russia; Russia drives Napoleon back deep into Western Europe

1825	Decembrist rebellion; disgruntled army officers herald a new age of revolutionary sentiment
1861	Emancipation of serfs
1881	Assassination of Alexander II by revolutionaries
1898	First Congress of the Russian Social Democratic Labor Party (RSDLP), from which the Bolshevik faction eventually emerges
1904–5	Russo-Japanese War
1905	Tsarist government suppresses first large-scale worker and peasant revolution; creation of first state legislature (*duma*)
1906	Beginning of Stolypin agrarian reforms
1914	Russia enters World War I on the side of Great Britain and France
1917	*Feb.:* Abdication of the tsar and the transfer of power into the hands of a provisional government
	Oct.: Bolshevik Revolution
1918–21	Civil War begins; period of War Communism; several nations, including the United States, invade the Soviet Union
1921	Creation of the New Economic Policy
1924	Death of Lenin; a struggle for power ensues, pitting Politburo members Stalin, Trotsky, Bukharin, Kamenev, and Zinoviev against one another
1926	Trotsky and Kamenev expelled from Politburo
1927	Chiang Kai-shek suppresses Communist movement in China
1928	Shakhty trials: first public trials of so-called saboteurs, in this case non-Communist technicians
1929	*Feb.:* Trotsky exiled from the U.S.S.R. as Stalin successfully consolidates power and initiates first significant party purges

Chronology

Apr.: First Five-Year Plan approved

Oct.: Forced collectivization accelerates

1930   Stalin's "dizzy with success" speech which signals a moderation of forced collectivization

1933   Diplomatic relations established between the United States and the Soviet Union

1934   Assassination of moderate Politburo member Kirov triggers a new wave of violent party purges

1935   Moscow show trials of Zinoviev, Kamenev, and other Old Bolsheviks accused of "moral" complicity in Kirov's assassination

1936   New constitution adopted

1937   Red Army purges begin

1938   Trial and execution of Bukharin

1939   *Aug.:* Nonaggression Pact between U.S.S.R. and Nazi Germany

Sept.: Germany invades western Poland, initiating World War II; U.S.S.R. invades eastern Poland

Nov.: U.S.S.R. invades Finland

1940   U.S.S.R. annexes Baltic countries and Bessarabia

1941   *May:* Japanese-Soviet Neutrality Pact

June: Germany invades U.S.S.R.

1942   Battle of Stalingrad begins

1943   *Jan.:* Siege of Leningrad broken

Nov.: Teheran Conference

1944   *June:* D-Day

1945   *Feb.:* Yalta Conference

May: Germany surrenders

June: United Nations charter signed

Chronology

1946

1947

1948

1949

1950

1953

1954

July: Potsdam Conference

Aug.: United States drops atom bomb on Hiroshima

Sept.: Japan surrenders

Feb.: Kennan's "long telegram"

Mar.: Churchill's "Iron Curtain" speech

May: Soviet troop withdrawals from China and Iran

June: Marshall Plan proposed

July: National Security Act establishes National Security Council and Central Intelligence Agency

Sept.: Zdanov speech promoting the division of world into two camps

Feb.: Communist coup in Czechoslovakia

Apr.: European Common Market established

June: U.S.S.R. establishes Berlin blockade

Yugoslavia expelled from Soviet sphere of influence

Jan.: Chinese revolution

Council for Mutual Economic Aid (COMECON) established

Apr.: NATO formed

Aug.: U.S.S.R. explodes its first atom bomb

Apr.: NSC-68 institutionalizes U.S. policy of containment

June: Korean War breaks out

Mar.: Stalin dies

June: East German uprising suppressed by Soviet troops

Geneva Conference negotiations spell the end of Korean and Indo-Chinese wars

Chronology

1955	*May:* Warsaw Pact treaty
	Austrian neutrality treaty
	Sept.: Soviet withdrawal from postwar bases in Finland
1956	*Feb.:* 20th Party Congress featuring Khrushchev's denunciations of Stalin
	Oct.: U.S.S.R. and U.S. intercede in Suez Canal crisis
	Nov.: Soviet invasion of Hungary
1957	U.S.S.R. develops first orbiting satellite (Sputnik) and tests world's first ICBM
1959	Cuban revolution
1960	*Apr.:* Soviets withdraw advisers and cancel contracts with China as Sino-Soviet split emerges
	May: U-2 reconnaissance plane shot down over Soviet territory, causing U.S.–Soviet rift
1961	*Apr.:* U.S. directs invasion of Cuba at Bay of Pigs
	Aug.: Berlin Wall erected
1962	Cuban missile crisis
1963	*June:* "Hot line" established between U.S.S.R. and United States
	Oct.: Limited Test Ban Treaty
1964	Khrushchev deposed; Brezhnev and Kosygin take over collective political leadership
1966	Trial of Soviet writers Sinyavsky and Daniel (for publishing their work overseas) unofficially brings cultural "thaw" to an end
1968	*July:* Non-Proliferation Treaty signed
	Aug.: Soviet invasion of Czechoslovakia

1972   U.S.–Soviet relations improve with the signing of SALT I and a treaty of friendship, the extension of substantial trade privileges to the U.S.S.R., and the Soviet agreement to pay World War II debts

1973   Yom Kippur war

1974   Angolan civil war escalates as Portugal withdraws; Jackson-Vanik and Stevenson amendments passed by Congress

1975   Helsinki Accords

1977   War breaks out between Ethiopia and Somalia

1979   *Jan.:* Vietnam invades Cambodia

            June: SALT II signed

            Dec.: Soviet invasion of Afghanistan prompts U.S. boycott of 1980 Summer Olympics in Moscow and declaration of a grain embargo of U.S.S.R.

1980   Rise of independent trade union, Solidarity, in Poland

1981   Martial law declared in Poland

1982   Brezhnev dies

1983   *Sept.:* Civilian jetliner, KAL 007, shot down over U.S.S.R.

            Oct.: U.S. invasion of Grenada

1984   *Feb.:* Andropov dies

            July: U.S.S.R. boycotts 1984 Summer Olympics in Los Angeles

1985   Chernenko dies

Appendix 3
Chronology 1985 to 1989

3/85   Mikhail Gorbachev becomes general secretary of the Communist party

4/85   In his first major East–West policy speech, Gorbachev calls for a U.S.–Soviet summit and announces a moratorium on deployment of Soviet medium-range missiles in Europe

7/85   Eduard Shevardnadze, former Georgian Republic Communist party leader, is appointed new foreign minister, replacing Andrei Gromyko

Gorbachev announces unilateral test-ban treaty, which eventually lasts for nearly eighteen months

11/85   Geneva summit; SDI emerges as chief stumbling block

1/86   Gorbachev announces Disarmament 2000 plan

4/86	Chernobyl nuclear power plant disaster
7/86	At Vladivostok, Soviet Asia, Gorbachev announces several initiatives for the Asia/Pacific region
9/86	U.S. journalist Nicholas Daniloff is arrested on espionage charges and eventually swapped for an accused Soviet spy
10/86	Iceland summit; Reagan and Gorbachev agree to disarmament plan but SDI again proves problematic
12/86	Kazakhs protest removal of local party leader
	Andrei Sakharov released from internal exile
1/87	Test-ban moratorium ends, but Gorbachev says that Soviets won't test until United States does
	Publication of Boris Pasternak's long-banned *Dr. Zhivago* in the U.S.S.R. announced
2/87	United States conducts first nuclear test since the end of the Soviet test-ban moratorium
	Soviet government releases 140 political dissidents
	Publication of Anna Akhmatova's *Requiem* cycle of poems
	Gorbachev's latest arms proposal for intermediate-range missile cuts independent of SDI
	U.S.S.R. conducts first post-moratorium nuclear weapons test
4/87	Reagan orders inquiry into U.S. embassy in Moscow, charging that the $100 million complex has been compromised by Soviet surveillance devices
	Gorbachev proposes "second zero option": a plan to eliminate short-range as well as long-range intermediate nuclear missiles

Multicandidate party and government elections announced for June

5/87   New laws on private and cooperative enterprises go into effect

Defense minister Sokolov is dismissed in the wake of the West German Mathias Rust's surprise airplane landing in Red Square

6/87   *Glasnost*, a dissident journal, appears for the first time in the U.S.S.R.

7/87   An official Soviet delegation visits Israel for the first time in twenty years

Merdeka interview in which Gorbachev agrees to a global double zero option

9/87   U.S. delegation visits Krasnoyarsk radar facility

In an *Izvestia* article, Gorbachev calls for greater powers for the United Nations

INF agreement reached in principle

10/87   Soviets pay U.N. debt

11/87   Boris Yeltsin, head of Moscow party organization and outspoken Gorbachev supporter, is removed from the Politburo

12/87   Washington summit; INF treaty signed

2/88   Bolshevik economist and Stalin victim Nikolai Bukharin is rehabilitated by Communist party

Riots break out in the Nagorno-Karabakh region of Azerbaijan as Armenian nationalists call for the region to become part of neighboring Armenia

5/88   Central Committee approves dramatic political restructuring plan that would establish new state organs, limit political terms of office, and dilute the power of the Communist party

Soviet troops begin to withdraw from Afghanistan, a process scheduled to take nine months

Moscow summit; little headway made on START treaty

6/88   Alliance of independent political clubs meet in an unprecedented conference to develop political platform

Popular Front organization emerges in Estonia

At first Party Conference since 1941, reformers battle for political changes proposed 5/27/88; changes approved with several concessions to party interests

8/88   In Prague, 10,000 Czechs mark the 1968 invasion

9/88   In a speech on Asia/Pacific issues, Gorbachev offers: to turn controversial Krasnoyarsk radar over to international control; to remove Soviet forces from Cam Ranh Bay, Vietnam, in exchange for the removal of U.S. bases from the Philippines; to establish economic links with South Korea

Major Politburo reshuffling as Andrei Gromyko retires, Yegor Ligachev is transferred to the agricultural post, and Vadim Medvedev becomes new party ideologist; Gorbachev assumes presidency, the titular head of state

10/88   Medvedev rejects notion of irrevocable struggle with the West

Gorbachev pushes for limited decollectivization

12/88   U.S.S.R. and China announce first summit in thirty years set for 1989, signaling thaw in relations

In a speech to the United Nations, Gorbachev pledges a unilateral reduction of 500,000 troops and 10,000 tanks

Earthquake kills tens of thousands in Armenia

Agreement concluded among Cuba, Angola, and South Africa on withdrawal of foreign forces from Angola and the subsequent independence of Namibia

221

2/89   Roundtable negotiations begin in Poland between out-
lawed Solidarity trade union and the government

Soviet Union completes troop withdrawal from Afghanistan

Shevardnadze undertakes eleven-day Mideast tour,
including a meeting with Palestinian leader Yasser
Arafat and Israeli Foreign Minister Moshe Arens

3/89   Two days before the Conventional Forces in Europe
(CFE) talks begin, Soviets present a three-stage plan
for conventional weapons reductions; NATO offers
counterproposal

Gorbachev announces new farm policy providing
funds and legal guarantees for private farmers; agricultural superministry, Gosagroprom, dismantled

Soviet elections to Congress of People's Deputies;
Yeltsin wins; key party leaders lose

4/89   Gorbachev visits Cuba

Vietnam promises troop withdrawals from Cambodia
in fall, 1989

Khrushchev's 1956 Party Congress speech denouncing
Stalin and Stalinism officially published in Soviet
Union

Gorbachev announces U.S.S.R. will unilaterally stop
producing uranium for arms

Soviet special forces kill at least twenty Georgian demonstrators

Independent Soviet legislators form bloc

Soviet tanks begin leaving Hungary as part of unilateral reductions promised in December 1988

5/89   Soviet government permits right to strike

Gorbachev, calling again for talks on short-range nuclear weapons, promises unilateral cut of 500 of Moscow's 10,000

Moscow offers to destroy Krasnoyarsk if United States
holds to strict ABM interpretation

During Gorbachev's trip to China, the two countries resume ties after thirty years

Congress of People's Deputies opens; Gorbachev elected president; Supreme Soviet selected; Yeltsin eventually elected to this body as well

6/89   Riots in Uzbekistan leave over 100 dead

Prime Minister Ryzhkov announces that military spending will be cut 33 percent

Solidarity wins all but one of the contested seats in Polish elections

7/89   Over 300,000 coal miners strike in Ukraine and Siberia; eventually go back to work after various commodities are delivered

Congress of People's Deputies supports economic and political autonomy for Baltic republics

8/89   United States and U.S.S.R. agree to allow World Court to arbitrate seven treaties

20,000 Russians strike in Estonia

Hundreds of thousands of Estonians, Latvians, and Lithuanians join hands across the entire length of the Baltic republics on the anniversary of the 1939 Soviet–German nonaggression pact

9/89   Solidarity activist Tadeusz Mazowiecki forms first non-Communist coalition government in Poland in forty years

Soviets remove demand for an agreement on space-based missile system prior to a strategic arms reduction treaty

Hungary opens border with Austria; East Germans flood through

10/89   Protests break out in East Germany; Egon Krenz replaces Erich Honecker

Hungarian Communist Party renames itself Socialist Party

Playwright Vaclav Havel arrested in Czechoslovakia; draws mass protest

11/89 Protests intensify in East Germany as Krenz shuffles Politburo; Politburo eventually resigns; Berlin Wall opened; opposition group New Forum emerges

Petar Mladenov replaces Todor Zhivkov in Bulgaria; promises free elections

Mass protests in Czechoslovakia eventually yield unified opposition group, Civic Forum, with Havel as leader; after some Politburo changes, Party agrees to give up its monopoly of power

Free referendum held in Hungary in which voters repudiate Party call for presidential election before parliamentary elections

12/89 Soviet parliament suspends debate over whether to end Communist Party monopoly of power

Andrei Sakharov dies

Lithuanian Communist Party declares independence from Moscow

United States invades Panama

Rumanian leader Nicolae Ceausescu deposed; after bloody battle with security forces, opposition forms new interim government, Council of National Salvation

Alexander Dubcek, deposed Czech leader from 1968, becomes new chairman of national parliament; parliament subsequently elects Vaclav Havel as President

Polish parliament votes in new economic program, privatizing state-owned companies and eliminating government subsidies

Appendix 4
Politburo Members
(as of October 1989)

Full members:

M. Gorbachev (1931)
>Communist party leader and Soviet president

Ye. Ligachev (1920)
>Head of agriculture policy commission

N. Ryzhkov (1929)
>Prime minister

L. Zaikov (1923)
>Head of Moscow party

V. Kryuchkov (1924)
>Chairman of KGB

Yu. Maslyukov (1937)
>Chairman of state planning agency Gosplan

A. Yakovlev (1923)
>Head of commission on international policies

N. Slyunkov (1929)
>Chairman of commission on socioeconomic policies

V. Medvedev (1929)
>Head of ideology commission

Politburo Members

E. Shevardnadze (1928)
  Foreign minister
V. Vorotnikov (1926)
  President of the Russian Republic

Candidate members:

G. Razumovski (1936)
  Head of party personnel commission
D. Yazov (1923)
  Defense minister
A. Vlasov (1932)
  Prime minister of Russian Republic
A. Lukyanov (1930)
  Soviet vice president
A. Biryukova (1929)
  Deputy Prime Minister
B. Pugo (1937)
  Chairman of Central Committee's party control committee
Ye. Primakov (1930)
  Chairman of the Council of the Union

From Francis Clines, "Gorbachev Ousts Five More Hard-Liners From the Politburo," *New York Times,* 9/21/89

Appendix 5

Structure of New Soviet Government

Congress of People's Deputies

Supreme government body; convenes annually; 2,250 members, 1,500 elected territorially, 750 appointed from various official organizations

President

Elected by secret ballot by Congress; broad legislative powers; limited to two five-year terms of office

Supreme Soviet

Elected by Congress; 542 members; considers all legislation; spring and autumn session that last three to four months apiece

Council of Ministers

Actual government; headed by prime minister

Presidium of the Supreme Soviet

Guided by president; a coordinating body composed of a senior vice president and vice presidents from each of the fifteen republics

Appendix 6
Suggested Reading

For readers interested in pursuing any of the topics explored in *Beyond Détente*, the following list provides one or two books in each of the major subject areas. Books have been chosen primarily for their readability. The list is by no means exhaustive.

Alternative defense
Anders Boserup et al. Special section on alternative defense. *Bulletin of Atomic Scientists*, vol. 44, no. 7 (September 1988).

Peter Tatchell. *Democratic Defence*. London: GMP, 1985.

Arms control
Jonathan Dean. *Watershed in Europe: Dismantling the East–West Military Confrontation*. Lexington, MA: Lexington Books, 1987.

Alan Sherr. *The Other Side of Arms Control: Soviet Objectives in the Gorbachev Era*. Boston: Unwin Hyman, 1988.

Eastern Europe
Karen Dawisha. *Eastern Europe: Gorbachev and Reform*. Cambridge: Cambridge University Press, 1988.

Suggested Reading

Economic conversion

Seymour Melman. *The Permanent War Economy.* New York: Simon and Schuster, 1985.

Gorbachev era—overviews

Padma Desai. *Perestroika in Perspective.* Princeton: Princeton University Press, 1989.

Thomas Naylor. *The Gorbachev Strategy: Opening the Closed Society.* Lexington, MA: Lexington Books, 1988.

Multilateralism

Common Security. New York: Simon and Schuster, 1982.

North–South

Susan George. *A Fate Worse Than Debt.* New York: Grove Press, 1988.

North–South: A Programme for Survival. Independent Commission on International Development Issues. Cambridge, MA: MIT Press, 1980.

Opposition movements in the East

From Below: Independent Peace and Environmental Movements in Eastern Europe & the USSR. Helsinki Watch, 1987.

George Konrad. *Antipolitics.* New York: Harcourt Brace Jovanovich, 1984.

Russian and Soviet history

Lionel Kochan and Richard Abrams. *The Making of Modern Russia.* Second edition. New York: Penguin, 1983.

James Billington. *The Icon and the Axe: An Interpretative History of Russian Culture.* New York: Vintage Books, 1970.

Soviet economy

Abel Aganbegyan. *The Challenge: Economics of Perestroika.* London: Hutchinson, 1988.

Anders Aslund. *Gorbachev's Struggle for Economic Reform.* Ithaca, NY: Cornell University Press, 1989.

Soviet military

Andrew Cockburn. *The Threat: Inside the Soviet Military Machine.* New York: Vintage Books, 1984.

Suggested Reading

Michael MccGwire. *Military Objectives in Soviet Foreign Policy.* Washington, DC: Brookings Institution, 1987.

Sovietology

Stephen F. Cohen. *Rethinking the Soviet Experience.* New York: Oxford University Press, 1985.

Soviet policy in the Third World

Jerry Hough. *The Struggle for the Third World.* Washington, DC: Brookings Institution, 1986.

Rajan Menon. *Soviet Power in the Third World.* New Haven, CT: Yale University Press, 1986.

Soviet politics

Leon Baradat. *Soviet Political Society.* Englewood Cliffs, NJ: Prentice-Hall, 1986.

Jerry Hough. *Russia and the West: Gorbachev and the Politics of Reform.* New York: Simon and Schuster, 1988.

U.S. foreign policy

Jonathan Kwitny. *Endless Enemies.* New York: Penguin Books, 1986.

Walter Russell Mead. *Mortal Splendor: The American Empire in Transition.* Boston: Houghton Mifflin, 1987.

U.S.–Soviet relations

Raymond Garthoff. *Détente and Confrontation.* Washington, DC: Brookings Institution, 1985.

Fred Halliday. *The Making of the Second Cold War.* London: Verso, 1983.

Index

Index

INF (Intermediate Nuclear Force)
Treaty, 55, 56–62, 65, 102, 108, 138, 146
internationalism, 154–57, 158–60;
Soviet economic, 34–37, 47; Soviet
political, 106–8; *see also*
multilateralism
Inter-Regional Group, 17
investment capital, 34–36, 69, 105;
Soviet need for, 3, 19, 20, 23, 35, 69
Iran, 94, 96, 98, 99, 113, 119, 134, 153
Iran-contra scandal, 115
Iran-Iraq War, 100, 155
Iraq, 98, 99–100, 116
Israel, 98–99, 100, 106, 117, 122, 153

Jackson-Vanik amendment, 37, 124, 150
Japan, 51, 72, 103, 104–5, 116, 132,
142, 158; burden sharing by, 139; as
capital exporter, 36, 69, 104–5;
economic strength, 19, 25, 49, 105
Jaruzelski, Wojciech, 76, 77
Jewish emigration, 37, 124
joint economic ventures, 36, 67, 69, 94

Kadar, Janos, 27, 78
Kagarlitsky, Boris, 44
Kamenev, Lev, 12
Kazakhstan, 41–42
Kennan, George, 72, 112, 118, 152
Kennedy, John, 119, 121, 131, 133, 137
Khrushchev, Nikita, 8, 11, 12, 15, 17,
18, 20, 22–23, 29; foreign policy, 54,
73–74, 76, 83, 85, 87, 94, 103, 123,
137
Kirkpatrick, Jeane, 142–43
Kissinger, Henry, 130, 136
Kiszczak, Czeslaw, 77
Kolko, Joyce, 34
Konrad, George, 80
Korean Airlines 007 flight, 114
Korean War, 54, 113, 116
Krasnoyarsk radar, 102
Kurile Islands, 54, 104

labor productivity, Soviet, 25–26, 29
Latin America, 134–35, 150; Central
American parliament, 142; map of,
86; Soviet policies toward, 82, 83,

85–89, 117; U.S. interventionism,
117, 119, 131–32, 134–35
Latin American Nuclear-Free Zone
Treaty, 137, 138
Latvia, 17, 42
Lebanon, 94, 98, 99, 122
Lenin, Vladimir Ilich, 7, 13, 21, 35, 38,
52; NEP, 21, 27, 28, 48, 53
Leninism, 7, 12, 14, 18
Levin, Carl, 123
Libya, 92, 117, 119, 132, 153
Limited Test Ban Treaty (1963), 113,
137, 138
Lithuania, 17, 42, 51
low-intensity conflict (LIC), 131–32,
152

Machel, Samora, 89, 91
Malenkov, Georgi, 124
market socialism, 33, 34–35; in China,
34–35; Hungarian, 24, 27–28, 33; in
U.S.S.R., 28–32, 35, 47
Marshall Plan, 72, 112, 134
Marxism-Leninism, 14, 27; African, 89
Mazowiecki, Tadeusz, 77
MBFR (Mutual Balanced Force
Reduction), 55, 64, 66, 67
Medvedev, Vadim, 6, 85
Mexico, debt crisis, 133
Middle East, 94, 130; map of, 95; Soviet
policies in, 83, 97–100, 116, 153
military, the, Soviet, 108, 122;
Gorbachev and, 13, 61–62, 64, 65,
105, 126; *see also* defense budget,
Soviet military-industrial complex,
144–46
MIRV (multiple independently
targetable re-entry vehicles), 120–21,
138
"missile gap" myth, 119
Mitterand, François, 33, 47
Mozambique, 89, 91–92, 117
Mugabe, Robert, 92
multilateralism, 55, 107, 114–15, 142,
154–57, 158–59
multipolarism, 106–7, 158

Nagorno-Karabakh, 42, 43
Namibia, 92, 93, 153, 155
Nasser, Gamal Abdel, 98

Index